D1359698

THE PIONEER HISTORIES

EDITED BY V. T. HARLOW, M.A., AND J. A. WILLIAMSON, D.LIT.

# ENGLAND'S QUEST OF EASTERN TRADE

*THE PIONEER HISTORIES*

*Edited by V. T. Harlow, M.A., & J. A. Williamson, D.Lit.*

*First Titles*

THE EUROPEAN NATIONS
IN THE WEST INDIES

ARTHUR PERCIVAL NEWTON, D.LIT.
*Rhodes Professor of Imperial History, University of London*

ENGLAND'S QUEST OF EASTERN TRADE

SIR WILLIAM FOSTER, C.I.E.
*Formerly Historiographer to the India Office*

*In Preparation*

THE PORTUGUESE PIONEERS

EDGAR PRESTAGE, D.LITT.
*Camoens Professor of Portuguese Language and History in the University of London*

THE EXPLORATION OF NORTH AMERICA

J. B. BREBNER, M.A., PH.D.
*Assistant Professor, Department of History, Columbia University*

THE GREAT TREK

ERIC A. WALKER, M.A.
*Professor of History, University of Cape Town*

THE SPANISH CONQUISTADORES

F. A. KIRKPATRICK, M.A.
*Reader in Spanish in the University of Cambridge*

THE REVELATION OF THE PACIFIC

J. C. BEAGLEHOLE, PH.D.

# ENGLAND'S QUEST OF EASTERN TRADE

BY

SIR WILLIAM FOSTER, C.I.E.

FORMERLY HISTORIOGRAPHER TO
THE INDIA OFFICE

'To speake a word of that just commendation
which our nation doe indeed deserve . . . they
have bene men full of activity, stirrers
abroad, and searchers of the remote
parts of the world.'

RICHARD HAKLUYT
Principall Navigations, 1589
(Dedication)

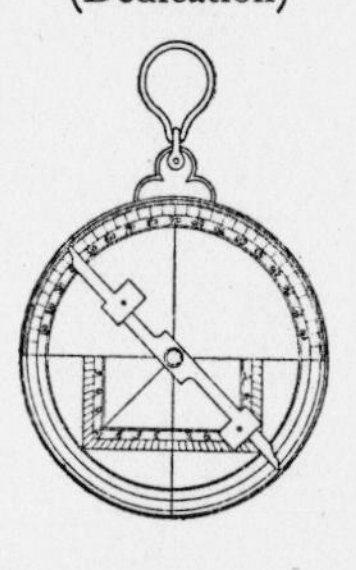

A & C BLACK LTD
4, 5 & 6 SOHO SQUARE LONDON W.1
1933

*New York*
THE MACMILLAN COMPANY
*Melbourne*
THE OXFORD UNIVERSITY PRESS
*Cape Town*
THE OXFORD UNIVERSITY PRESS
*Toronto*
THE MACMILLAN COMPANY OF CANADA
*Bombay Calcutta Madras*
MACMILLAN AND COMPANY LTD

PRINTED IN GREAT BRITAIN
BY R. & R. CLARK LTD. EDINBURGH

# EDITORS' PREFACE TO THE SERIES

THE Pioneer Histories are intended to provide broad surveys of the great migrations of European peoples—for purposes of trade, conquest and settlement—into the non-European continents. They aim at describing a racial expansion which has created the complex world of to-day, so nationalistic in its instincts, so internationalised in its relationships.

International affairs now claim the attention of every intelligent citizen, and problems of world-wide extent affect the security and livelihood of us all. He who would grasp their meaning and form sound judgements must look into the past for the foundations of the present, and, abandoning a local for a universal perspective, must take for his study the history of a world invaded by European ideas. It was less so in the days before the Great War. Then the emphasis was upon Europe itself: upon such questions as that of France's eastern frontier inherited from Richelieu and Louis XIV, the militarism of Germany derived from Frederick the Great, and the Balkan entanglement which originated with the medieval migrations of Slavonic peoples and with the Turkish conquests of the fourteenth century. Now the prospect is wider, for these ancient domestic difficulties in modern form cannot properly be estimated except by correlation with the problems of a Europeanised outer world.

The Orient is in ferment and Asiatic difficulties compel the attention of Geneva because long ago the Portuguese, followed by the Dutch and the English, rounded the Cape and came to India. For the same reason, Africa is no longer an unknown continent but a vast area in which civilised enterprise demands direction and control. Knowledge of the process by which North America was discovered and gradually filled with Europeans is the necessary basis for an understanding of the modern reactions upon each other of the new continent and the old. In South America the same process is to be seen at work, though incomplete while Nature is yet unsubdued. Similarly, it may be appreciated how the search for an unknown but credited continent lying about the South Pole has helped to shift the centre of gravity to the Pacific, and has created a white Australasia. The present series will show how the permanent factors in these great regions first presented themselves to European minds and how achievements were then effected which have governed all subsequent relationships.

But if the subject has this interest for students of affairs, it has also its appeal to those who dwell most on individual character, courage and ingenuity. Movements are made by men, and in these stories of European expansion are to be met men worth knowing, whose deeds carry inspiration for this generation as for all others.

Each volume takes for its subject the history of an important movement and, while related to others in the series, is thus complete in itself. The authors whose co-operation we have been fortunate to secure have all had experience of research in the original evidence pertaining to their subjects, and in their contributions to this series they give the results of that research in narratives which should appeal to the general reader. Each book is designed to embody the most recent information available, and some will be found to deal with subjects of which no full treatment has hitherto been accessible in English.

V. T. HARLOW
J. A WILLIAMSON

# CONTENTS

CONTENTS

# MAPS

# PREFACE

IT would be difficult to make dull any narrative of early ventures to the East—so picturesque were the surroundings, so great the hazards, so marvellous the bravery and endurance of those pioneers of commerce. But the story gains in depth and value when it is told, not as a jumble of disconnected experiments, but as a drama of sustained effort, extending over more than a century, to establish trade between our own small island and the vast and populous empires of the Orient, at that time supposed to be filled with riches. England was vigorously bestirring herself and seeking new outlets for her fast-growing manufactures. The markets of the East seemed to offer endless possibilities for that purpose, and to reach those markets became the aim alike of statesman, merchant and mariner. The ventures that resulted called forth all the energy and courage of our race; and those who can see the oak in the acorn will discern in them the germs, not only of Britain's sea-power, but also, in great measure, of her overseas empire. It is a story of epic grandeur, to which no pen can hope to do justice; yet so interesting in its details, so full of colour, that even a passable account must arrest attention.

To some readers the names of many of the actors in this drama will be unfamiliar, for they have never attracted so much attention as the Westward adventurers, Drake, Ralegh and their contemporaries. Even those who have read widely on the present subject will find some new items of information; for example, fresh facts are given concerning the later life of that notable adventurer, Ralph Fitch. Perhaps it may likewise be claimed that justice has at last been done to other pioneers, such as Newbery and Courthope, whose achievements, partly because they lacked the crown of success, have not hitherto received the recognition which they so richly deserved.

W. F.

# ENGLAND'S QUEST OF EASTERN TRADE

# CHAPTER I

## WILLOUGHBY AND CHANCELLOR SEEK CATHAY

THE daring of English seamen and the enterprise of English merchants bulk so largely in our national tradition that it is surprising to find how slow was the development of our overseas trade. It is true that an English ship was actually the first to reach the American mainland (1497); but the leader of the expedition, John Cabot, was a Venetian subject, and the voyage itself was largely stimulated by royal support. And for half a century after that venture what do we find? A few attempts were made to discover a way round the northern part of the new continent; a few trading voyages were undertaken to the West Indies and the countries adjacent. Meanwhile our neighbours were boldly exploring the New World the portals of which had been opened by the genius of Columbus. Spain was discovering and settling huge tracts in Central and Southern America; and under her flag Magellan had pushed still farther afield. In 1519–20 he succeeded in crossing the Pacific and reaching the mysterious Spice Islands; and after his death his vessel returned by way of the Cape of Good Hope and thus completed the first circumnavigation of the globe. The Portuguese, who had already explored the western side of Africa, rounded the Cape and, under the leadership of Vasco da Gama, reached the Indian coast in 1498.

Thereafter they traversed the Asiatic seas in all directions and established the beginnings of an overseas empire in those regions, besides discovering and taking possession of a large tract in Brazil. French seamen explored the coastline of North America from Florida to Labrador, followed the Portuguese into the Indian Ocean, and reached the island of Sumatra (1529). England alone, of the European countries bordering on the Atlantic, seemed backward in the race of discovery.

The reasons for this state of things were partly political, but still more economic. The overseas enterprises of the continental powers were subsidised by the state and formed part of the national policy. In England on the other hand, though Henry VII had patronised Cabot's venture and Henry VIII took a personal interest in subsequent schemes for the discovery of Cathay, little or no support was forthcoming from national funds. Moreover, policy forbade encroachment upon the regions covered by Spanish and Portuguese claims to exclusive possession. So trade and discovery were virtually left to private enterprise, and this was necessarily of slow growth. It must be remembered that, in comparison with its continental neighbours, England was a poor and backward country. Situated on the edge of Christendom, she had, throughout the Middle Ages, reflected but faintly the civilisation that radiated from Italy—the centre of European culture and commerce. With semi-barbaric elements to assimilate, hindered by many wars, both external and internal, she moved forward slowly, with many hesitations and setbacks. For long she was a nation to be traded with, rather than a nation enjoying an overseas trade of her own. Galleys from Venice brought her the wares of the Mediterranean and the spices of the East; the Hanseatic League sent its ships to London with the produce of the Baltic; and even the wine trade with Gascony was largely in French hands. In fact it was not until the Wars of the Roses were over, and a peaceful régime of strong government was inaugurated under the first of the Tudor monarchs, that English merchants began to feel their feet and to endeavour to come into line with their continental competitors. Even then, capital had to be accumulated, manufactures developed, and shipping improved, before they were ready to embark upon large schemes of foreign trade.

Powerful impulses intensified this process. The spread of education awakened curiosity and made the narratives of early travellers more widely known. The religious controversies of the day, resulting in a repudiation of Papal control, gave a certain unity to the nation as against the rest of Europe. There was a marked growth of patriotic feeling in consequence; and this became more fervent as the sixteenth century progressed. Not less cogent were tendencies of a more materialistic nature. The influx of precious metals into Europe from the Spanish mines of the New World was producing a steady rise in the cost of living. The population of the country was increasing. The manufacture of woollen cloth was outstripping the demands of the home market; and the continental markets, though ready enough to take the raw material, had little or no need for the manufactured equivalent.

Thus, by the middle of the sixteenth century, the need of finding new outlets for English products had become insistent. The most hopeful project seemed to be that of discovering markets in the Far East.[1] But

[1] It is commonly asserted that English endeavours to open up trade with the East were mainly prompted by a desire to obtain pepper and spices for

how to reach these, in face of the monopolistic claims of Spain and Portugal, was the problem. Even if suitable vessels had been available, the idea of trying the Portuguese route round the Cape of Good Hope or of following the track of Magellan into the Pacific, seemed to be out of the question. There remained the possibility of discovering a new approach, either round the northern parts of the American continent (the so-called North-West Passage) or along the northern shores of Europe and Asia (the North-East Passage). Could either be found, the discovery would not only give England a claim to its exclusive enjoyment, but would provide an actually shorter route to Cathay (Northern China) than either the Spanish or Portuguese routes. The advocates of this scheme asserted with confidence that in Cathay, with its cool climate, its teeming and (it was believed) wealthy population, a lucrative market for English woollens would certainly be found; [1] while, once the dangers of the northern ice had been passed, it would be a comparatively easy matter to proceed from Cathay to the Moluccas, and there lade for the return voyage the spices so much in demand in the European markets.

Many years before (1527), Robert Thorne, an English merchant resident at Seville, had submitted to Henry VIII a scheme for sailing right across the North

home consumption; and it is further explained that the demand for these condiments was constant and urgent, owing to the fact that only preserved meat was available during the winter season. It may be conceded that the prospect of procuring a valuable return cargo added materially to the attraction of the venture; but that the principal object was to find fresh markets for English manufactures, especially for woollen goods, will, it is hoped, be made abundantly clear in the pages which follow.

[1] 'Because our chiefe desire is to find out ample vent of our wollen cloth (the naturall commoditie of this our realme), the fittest places . . . are the manifold islands of Japan and the northern parts of China and the regions of the Tartars next adjoyning' (Hakluyt, in the dedication of vol. ii of the second edition of *The Principall Navigations*).

Pole to the straits separating Asia from America, and had pointed out the supposed advantages of this bold course. It was hoped to find that the polar area was occupied by open sea, little encumbered by ice. Progress, it was argued, would be rapid, thanks to the fact that daylight was practically continuous in those regions for half the year. Once lower latitudes were reached on the other side, the vessel employed had three courses open to her. She might turn towards the Asiatic shore for Cathay; she might follow down the American coastline and return by way of Magellan's Straits; as a third possibility, she might sail on through the middle of the Pacific, in the hope of finding new islands rich in spices, gold and precious stones. Thorne's death, five years later, prevented him from backing his dream in a practical manner. In 1541, however, his former associate, Roger Barlow, approached King Henry upon the subject; but the project came to nought, apparently for want of a suitable leader.[1]

Hesitation may well have been felt in adopting so venturesome a course; but it was widely agreed that any attempt to discover a sea-way to the East could most profitably be made in a northerly direction. Of the two possible routes we have indicated, the North-Western had been tried without success. True, inlets leading westward had been found, which might or might not provide the desired passage into the Pacific; yet the land in general seemed to continue indefinitely in a northerly direction. The route round Europe and Asia, on the other hand, seemed far more hopeful. No doubt was felt that the coastline ran fairly straight from west to east, and the Siberian coast was believed to slope

[1] Full particulars of the Thorne-Barlow scheme have been given by Professor Taylor in the introduction to her recent edition of Barlow's *Briefe Summe of Geographie* (Hakluyt Society, Series II, vol. lix, 1932).

rapidly down in a south-easterly direction to China. This gave rise to hopes that, once the northern ice had been penetrated, a passage would be found practicable.

It was apparently with the idea of aiding in some such scheme that Sebastian Cabot (the son of John), who had been in the service of Spain since 1512, was induced to settle in London in 1548 and was given a pension from the royal exchequer. He had a high reputation for cartographical knowledge, and had himself led voyages of exploration both towards the North-West and to the river Plate in South America. For thirty years he had held the important post of pilot-major in the Spanish service, and he might well be supposed to know all that there was to be known regarding the countries of the Far East and possible routes thither. It was a time when geographical information was kept secret; and probably Cabot designedly gave the impression that he had special knowledge of the utmost importance for the purpose in view. Indeed, if we may credit Richard Eden, Cabot 'long before had this secret [*i.e.* the North-Eastern route] in his minde'. In any case, such was the general confidence in the scheme that, in the spring of 1553, an association of about two hundred persons was formed in London to open up trade with Cathay by that route. The capital consisted of 240 shares of £25 each, making a total of £6000, which was then a large sum to risk; and Cabot was appointed Governor of the new body, to which a charter of incorporation was granted by Edward VI.[1]

The expedition 'for the discoverie of Cathay and divers other regions . . . unknowen' consisted of three

[1] This is deduced from the 20th article of the instructions for the first voyage, as given by Hakluyt, though the grant itself has not been traced. Possibly it was drafted, but not actually completed, before the death of the King. Hence its absence from the Patent Rolls.

ships (the largest being only of 160 tons) under the command of Sir Hugh Willoughby as captain-general, with Richard Chancellor as pilot-general; and its departure from Ratcliff took place on 10 May 1553. Gay with flags and streamers, its mariners 'all apparelled in watchet or skie-coloured cloth', the little fleet paused off Greenwich to salute the royal palace; but the young King, already stricken with mortal sickness, was unable to respond to its greeting. Joyous anticipation soon gave way to uncertainty and gloom. Early in August, after passing the Lofoden Islands, a storm separated Chancellor's ship, the *Edward Bonaventure*, from her consorts, who thereupon made for Vardö, the rendezvous appointed in such a case. That port, however, Willoughby failed to reach. His two vessels wandered through ice and mist, now eastwards, now westwards, sighting (it is believed) the coast of Novaia Zemlia, until in September they took refuge in the bay of Arzina (Nokujeff), on the coast of Lapland. There they resolved to pass the winter. That the commander and most of his men were still alive in January 1554 was shewn by a will afterwards found on the spot. The ships had been provisioned for eighteen months, and so the crews cannot have been short of food; but the intense cold of the northern winter, possibly aggravated by scurvy, proved too great for their endurance and they perished to a man. In the following spring some Russian fishermen found the two ships and their frozen occupants. The English merchants then in the country were notified of the discovery, with the result that the vessels were recovered; and later, manned by fresh crews, they were despatched to England as part of the return fleet. It has been asserted that Willoughby's corpse was sent home for interment; but of this no confirmation has been found. Possibly the report arose from the tradition that his clothes were forwarded to England and were used in painting the reputed portrait of Willoughby still preserved at Wollaton House.[1] This has often been reproduced as an authentic likeness of Sir Hugh, and the only one known; but recently Mr. C. R. Beard, writing in the *Connoisseur* (June 1931), has declared that it cannot be correct, as the costume, he says, belongs to the early part of the seventeenth century.

Chancellor, after his separation from Willoughby, rounded the North Cape and reached Vardö, where he waited a week for the rest of the fleet. Then, sailing again, he entered the White Sea (hitherto unknown to the Western nations) and anchored at the little port of Nenoksa, near the mouth of the Dwina. From the natives he learned that the country in which he found himself formed part of Russia. With commendable enterprise Chancellor made the long and difficult journey to Moscow and interviewed the Tsar, Ivan IV. That monarch received him cordially, and gave him a letter to Edward VI, which invited the latter to establish commerce between their two countries and assured him that 'your countrey marchants . . . shall have their free marte with all free liberties through my whole dominions'. Rejoicing over his success, the Englishman retraced his footsteps to the White Sea, and in 1554 sailed back home.

Though two of the three vessels had come to grief and little progress had been made towards discovering a practicable way to the Indies, Chancellor's achievement had been considerable. He had found an all-sea route to Russia, a country which at that time had no outlet upon either the Baltic or the Black Sea. It yielded

[1] A copy may be seen in the Painted Hall at Greenwich.

furs, hides, tallow, wax, flax and hemp; while, to say nothing of other commodities, its climate afforded good hopes of a steady demand for English woollens. Moreover, Moscow (which is in fact farther east than Aleppo) might well prove a convenient half-way house for the exploration by land of the Orient. Thus encouraged, the promoters of the enterprise sought and obtained a fresh charter (6 February 1555) from Queen Mary, the new occupant of the throne, and her Spanish husband. This established the petitioners as a corporation, by the name of 'The Marchants Adventurers of England for the Discovery of Lands, Territories, Iles, Dominions, and Seigniories unknowen and not before that late adventure or enterprise by sea or navigation commonly frequented'.[1] The grant covered the full benefits of the commerce which the new body had been formed to develop, and forbade all other English subjects to visit those parts without the express permission of the Company. The latter's future operations were limited to voyages made northwards, north-eastwards or north-westwards (thus providing for the exploration of all permissible routes to the East), and no region already frequented by the subjects of other Christian monarchs was to be intruded upon (a very natural stipulation, seeing that a Spanish sovereign was sharing the English throne). Sebastian Cabot was made Governor of the Company for life, and was to have the co-operation of four consuls and twenty-four assistants, all to be elected annually.

No time was lost in following up the new commerce. In the summer of 1555 the *Edward Bonaventure* sailed again, accompanied by a second vessel. Chancellor was in command, and several merchants were sent to remain

[1] This cumbrous title was soon ousted in common parlance by the more convenient term 'Russia' or 'Muscovy' Company.

in the country as factors and carry on a regular trade. Their instructions, be it noted, included an injunction to 'use all wayes and meanes possible to learne howe men may passe from Russia, either by land or by sea, to Cathaia'. A royal reply to the Tsar's letter was entrusted to Chancellor for delivery; and he carried also a suitable array of presents for that monarch, provided by the new company.

On reaching Moscow (October 1555) Chancellor experienced no difficulty in obtaining from the Tsar a formal grant of trading facilities, including exemption from customs dues. The importance attached by Ivan to the relations thus opened up with England was shewn by his resolve to send thither a special envoy with a further missive. Accordingly, when Chancellor, in July 1556, embarked upon his return voyage, he was accompanied by a Russian ambassador, named Ossip Grigorjevitsch Nepeja. The sequel was disastrous. Of the four ships of the fleet, two were lost on the Norwegian coast. A third was obliged to winter at Drontheim, and did not arrive in the Thames until the following year. The *Edward Bonaventure*, carrying Chancellor and Nepeja, managed after four months to reach the Scottish coast, only to be wrecked (Nov. 1556) in Pitsligo Bay in Aberdeenshire. Chancellor and the Russian envoy attempted to reach land in the ship's boat; but this was quickly overset and, although Nepeja and a few others succeeded in struggling ashore, Chancellor was never seen again. Thus perished the man to whom was chiefly due the opening up of commerce between England and Russia, at the very moment when those relations appeared to be most promising.

The search for the hoped-for passage to Cathay had not been forgotten in the stir made by the new trade. In the spring of 1556 Stephen Borough, who had been master of Chancellor's ship in the first voyage, was despatched in a pinnace called the *Searchthrift*, to examine the Russian coast to the eastward of the White Sea. From the account given in Hakluyt we learn that, while the tiny vessel lay off Gravesend, ready for departure, she was visited by Cabot, 'accompanied with divers gentlemen and gentlewomen'. After inspecting the pinnace, the company dined 'at the signe of the Christopher'; and after dinner, old as he was, Cabot, 'for very joy that he had to see the towardnes of our intended discovery, entred into the dance himselfe, amongst the rest of the young and lusty company; which being ended, hee and his friends departed most gently, commending us to the governance of Almighty God'. This is almost the last glimpse we get of Cabot, who seems to have died towards the close of the following year.

Borough's gallant attempt met with scant success. Accompanying the *Edward Bonaventure* (which was making its third and last voyage to the White Sea) as far as Vardö, the *Searchthrift* then departed upon its mission. The coast was followed as far as the mouth of the Pechora river, and next Borough stretched over to the coast of Novaia Zemlia. He reached Vaigats Island; and then, battered by storms and threatened by gigantic icebergs, the vessel's prow was turned westwards again. With much difficulty she managed to get to Kholmogori, at the mouth of the Dwina, where some of the Company's factors were stationed. There Borough remained through the winter, intending to resume his explorations in the spring. When the time came, however, his pinnace was requisitioned for other duties; and so the search for the North-East Passage had perforce to be deferred until a more favourable opportunity should present itself.

## CHAPTER II

# JENKINSON'S JOURNEYS INTO CENTRAL ASIA AND PERSIA

INTO the breach made by the death of Chancellor there quickly stepped a yet more remarkable man, Anthony Jenkinson. Of his previous life we know little. Leaving England in 1546, he spent several years in travelling in the principal countries round the Mediterranean, including Algeria, Tunis, Palestine, Syria and Turkey. In 1553 he had an interview at Aleppo with the Turkish sultan, Suleiman the Magnificent, who was preparing for a campaign against the Persians; and from that monarch he procured a grant of free trade throughout the Turkish dominions. This was evidently sought in pursuance of some scheme for developing a trade between England and the Levant and thus securing a regular supply of spices and other Eastern produce. Such goods still came to the Mediterranean by the ancient channels, either by way of the Persian Gulf and across the desert to Aleppo, or else by the Red Sea route to Cairo and Alexandria. This commerce, which had enriched Venice, Genoa and Marseilles, had been seriously weakened by the discovery of the Cape route; for, long and dangerous as was the ocean voyage, it was far cheaper than the older routes, which involved both sea and land journeys, with risks of robbery in the one case by pirates, in the other by marauding Arabs. Moreover, the charges for land carriage were high; the customs rates at the various ports were heavy; while most burdensome of all were the arbitrary exactions of the Turkish governors, who lost no opportunity of fleecing a foreign trader. However, the profits to be made, if fortune favoured, were sufficiently alluring to keep the trade alive; and even to tempt English merchants to endeavour to secure a footing therein, if only as a supplement to their commerce with Italy. Hakluyt tells us that from 1511 onwards ships from London, Southampton and Bristol made voyages to Sicily, Crete and Scio, and occasionally visited the Syrian ports of Tripoli and Beyrout. The goods which they carried out were chiefly kerseys and other woollens; while the return cargoes consisted of silks and camlets, rhubarb, wines, oil, galls (for use in dyeing), raw cotton, drugs, pepper, cinnamon and other spices. No attempt, however, had been made to establish 'factories', that is to say, 'regular settlements of merchants'; and without such settlements the commerce must necessarily have been of a desultory character.

Whether Jenkinson took steps to follow up the concession he had obtained does not appear. Judging from his energetic character, we may assume that he endeavoured to do so; and that either he failed to secure the necessary capital or else found that the obstructions and exactions were obstacles too formidable to be overcome. Whatever his reasons, it is evident that he soon abandoned all hope of tapping by this method the trade in Eastern produce, and turned his attention instead to the schemes for direct intercourse, of which Chancellor's establishment of trade with Moscow seemed so promising a beginning.[1] Under the influence of this diversion,

[1] By a strange coincidence Chancellor, like Jenkinson, had tried the Levant trade before taking up the project of a north-eastern voyage; for in 1550 he

English trade with the Levant, according to Hakluyt, 'was utterly discontinued and in maner quite forgotten, as if it had never bene, for the space of twenty yeares and more'; and the field was thus left open to the French and the Italians. All this while the London merchants concentrated their efforts upon the trade with Russia and Persia, and its hoped-for extension in an easterly direction.

We must now return to the Russian ambassador, Nepeja, who, as the earliest envoy to England from that distant and barbarous country, was the object of the liveliest curiosity as he slowly made his way from the north of Scotland to the metropolis. Drawing near London, he was met at Tottenham by the representatives of the Russia Company, 'riding in velvet coates and chaines of gold'; at Islington by the Viscount Montague, Master of the Horse, with an escort of the royal guards; and at Smithfield by the Lord Mayor and Aldermen, who led him to his temporary abode in Fenchurch Street. The burden of entertaining him fell upon the merchants concerned in the trade, not upon the royal purse; but King Philip and Queen Mary received him with much cordiality when, on 25 March 1557, he delivered the Tsar's letters and presents; and he certainly had no reason to complain of the consideration with which he was treated during the whole period of his stay in England.

The loss sustained by the shipwreck of three out of the four vessels of the return fleet had been heavy, and on top of this had come the expense of entertaining the ambassador for several months and providing him with all necessaries, since he had lost practically everything.

is mentioned by Hakluyt as participating in a venture to Sicily, Scio and Crete in a vessel commanded by Roger Bodenham.

Nevertheless, such was the confidence felt in the value of the new trade that by April 1557 the Russia Company had fitted out a fresh fleet of four vessels, with cargoes of broadcloth, kerseys and pewter. Nepeja, having received from the King and Queen their replies to the Tsar's letters, accompanied by an imposing array of presents, embarked at Gravesend in the flagship on 3 May; and nine days later the fleet sailed. 'Anthonie Jenkinson, gentleman' was in command, and in a letter he carried from the Company to their agents already settled in Russia he was referred to as 'a man well travelled, whom we mind to use in further travelling'. This is a clear intimation that he had been sent, not so much to supervise the trade in Russia itself, as to undertake further exploration. There is no record of the negotiations preceding his appointment or of the specific instructions given to him by the Company; but evidently he was engaged for the express purpose of pushing eastwards from Moscow, in order to ascertain whether it were possible to get into touch with Cathay by land. Doubtless the knowledge which he had acquired in the Levant of the trade in Eastern products was judged to be an important qualification for the task.

The White Sea was reached in safety, and on 12 July 1557 the fleet anchored 'at the roade of St. Nicholas', where later arose the city of Archangel. Jenkinson proceeded by land to Kholmogori, thence to Vologhda (another of the Company's stations), and so to Moscow, which he reached on 6 December. On Christmas Day the English envoy was feasted by the Tsar, who made no difficulty about giving him letters of recommendation for the journey he was contemplating. Accompanied by two other Englishmen, Richard and Robert Johnson, and a Tartar interpreter, Jenkinson set out on

23 April 1558, seven months before the accession of Elizabeth to the throne of England. Passing down the Volga, the party reached Astrakhan, the farthest outpost of Russia towards the Caspian Sea. There a boat was purchased; and on 10 August Jenkinson and his two colleagues found themselves on the waters of the Caspian. They were, we may note, the first Englishmen to navigate that inland sea and display thereon 'the redde crosse of S. George'. Coasting round its northern shores, they landed on the Mangishlak peninsula, and were 'gently intertained' by the Turkoman governor. The English party, it would seem, had no great amount of merchandise with them; but their Tartar and Persian associates must have had a great deal, for, when the caravan left the coast, it consisted of a thousand camels. Moving slowly through desert country, and submitting of necessity to the exactions of various Turkoman chiefs, on 16 October it reached Urgenj, on the old bed of the Oxus, where a halt of six weeks was made. Resuming the march and repelling a determined attack by a party of marauders, the caravan crossed the Oxus and on 23 December arrived safely in the city of Bokhara. Three days later Jenkinson presented to the Khan the letters he had brought from the Tsar, and was well received. The Khan was much interested by the arquebuses carried by the Englishmen, 'and did himselfe practise the use thereof'; and he plied his visitors with many questions concerning Russia, Turkey and their own country. He bought also some of the travellers' goods; though after his departure upon a raid into Persian territory his servants could not be persuaded to discharge the debt fully, and Jenkinson was forced to take what he could get, and that in goods, not money.

In Bokhara the trio of Englishmen remained for two

JENKINSON'S TRAVELS

months and a half. As a meeting-place of caravans the city enjoyed a certain amount of trade. Indian merchants brought thither their cotton goods; Persians their silks and linens; Russians their sheepskins, hides and various manufactured articles. Bokhara had also been a resort of merchants from China laden with musk, rhubarb, satins, etc. But at the time of Jenkinson's visit the whole of the country to the eastwards had for some time been in a state of turmoil, and all intercourse with Cathay had ceased. Even in times of peace, he was told, the journey from Bokhara to Peking would occupy nine months; and since he had taken eight months to reach the former city from Moscow, it was obvious that, even under the most favourable conditions, there was no hope of establishing a profitable commerce with Cathay by this route. So Jenkinson turned his attention to other possibilities. The Indian merchants brought to Bokhara neither spices nor precious stones, and they had no use for the woollen cloths tendered by the Englishmen. The Persians declined these likewise, declaring that they could purchase all they wanted in their own country, to which such goods came in abundance by way of Syria or Turkey. Bokhara itself had no industries of importance, and its inhabitants were too poor to buy European products in any quantity; while the wares they had to offer were chiefly horses and slaves, and neither of these commodities attracted the English merchants.

Disillusioned as to the prospects of trade in those parts, Jenkinson and his companions quitted Bokhara on 8 March 1559, with a caravan bound for the Caspian. They departed opportunely, for ten days later an army arrived from Samarkand and laid siege to the city—a development which confirmed Jenkinson in the view that commerce was out of the question in such unquiet regions. He had entertained the idea of returning to Russia by way of Persia, in order to investigate the chances of trade in that direction. But the raid into Persian territory on which the Khan had just started had rendered all the roads unsafe, and for these and other reasons the project was abandoned.

It is unnecessary to relate the adventures of the three travellers on their return journey to Moscow, which occupied nearly six months. In the middle of February 1560 Jenkinson started from the Russian capital for England by way of the White Sea, and, after waiting some time for a ship, reached London safely, apparently in the summer or autumn of that year. He and his companions had made a memorable journey, which he himself described as 'so miserable, dangerous, and chargeable . . . as my penne is not able to expresse the same'. They had penetrated into parts practically unknown to Europeans; and material success had not been wanting, for, despite robberies and exactions, they had secured a profitable return upon the goods which they carried with them. The really important result, however, was that they had thoroughly explored the prospects of trade in that direction and were able to satisfy their employers that a further venture to Central Asia would be quite useless. This verdict was accepted as final, and centuries passed before Bokhara saw another English visitor.

While in Russia Jenkinson had formed the opinion that attempts to open up trade with Persia by way of the Caspian were hopeless, because the country was difficult of access and its inhabitants poor, while such demand as existed for European goods was easily satisfied by imports from Turkey. Further reflection, however, seems to have suggested that there were possibilities in this direction not to be neglected. The Persians, who had developed the Shiah form of Muhammadanism, bore a fanatical hatred for the Turks, who adhered to the Sunni tenets of that religion. In consequence there were frequent wars between the two countries, with the result that for long periods all trade between them came to a standstill. Obviously this might afford an opening for the introduction of English goods from the north. Still more promising was the prospect of tapping the stream of Oriental produce which flowed up the Persian Gulf on its way to Syria and thence to Europe.[1] Either the merchants of Asia might be induced to bring these goods to Persian marts, there to exchange them for English produce; or, better still, the Russia Company's factors might pass through Persian territory to seek the goods for themselves.

The undaunted Jenkinson was quite ready to venture in this direction, and he easily persuaded his employers to sanction the experiment. As the result, in the May of 1561 he sailed once more for Russia, carrying letters of recommendation from Queen Elizabeth to the Russian emperor and to 'the Great Sophie', *i.e.* the Persian shah. His instructions from the Company were, to obtain, in the first place, permission from the Tsar to carry on a commerce with Persia through his dominions, subject to the payment of a reasonable *entrepôt* tariff on that transit trade. Then, accompanied by such of the

[1] The idea was not entirely original, for some thirty-five years earlier an Italian named Paulo Centurione had formed a scheme for bringing the products of Asia into Europe by way of Persia and Russia. With this end in view he made two or three journeys to Moscow from Italy, which, however, produced no further result than an interchange of embassies between the Tsar and the Pope. Centurione then proceeded to England, where he managed to interest Henry VIII in his schemes and was promised shipping for the furtherance thereof; but before anything was effected the sanguine adventurer died in London, and the whole project came to nought.

Company's servants as he might choose for the purpose, he was to proceed into Persian territory, seek out the Shah, present the royal letters, and ask for a grant of privileges. This was to include, not only liberty to trade freely in Persia itself, but 'free passage also for us at all times to passe, as often as we will, with our goods and merchandize into any part of India, or other countryes thereunto adjoyning, and in like manner to returne through his dominions into Russia or elsewhere'. If, by the summer of 1562, Jenkinson had not succeeded in making his way into Persia, he was to dispose of the wares reserved for that purpose, and then either return to England or make an endeavour 'for the search of the passage by Nova Zembla'. It was, however, left to his discretion to keep his goods a year longer, if there appeared to be a reasonable chance of penetrating into Persia in 1563. In the event of the prospect being deemed hopeless, and of there being no opportunity to sell his goods in Russia itself, he might try to carry them to Constantinople or elsewhere for sale. A suggestion was made that Richard Johnson should be sent from Kholmogori eastwards, to investigate a report that the northern ocean could be reached in that direction in thirty or forty days, as this might prove 'a great helpe for us to finde out the straight and passage that way, if any be there to be had'.

Jenkinson arrived at Moscow on 20 August 1561, and after some delay was admitted to the presence of the Tsar, to whom he delivered the letters from the Queen. His application for leave to proceed to Persia was at first refused, on the pretext that the Tsar was contemplating an invasion of Circassia, which would render the journey too hazardous. Thereupon he demanded and obtained permission to return to England; but when he was about to start, the late ambassador, Nepeja, intervened with such success that not only was Jenkinson licensed to go to Persia, but he was given a recommendation from the Tsar and commissioned to purchase silk and gems for that monarch. Accordingly, on 27 April 1562 he set out from Moscow, accompanied by a

THE CASPIAN PORTS AND N.W. PERSIA

Persian envoy who was returning to his own country. Astrakhan was reached on 10 June, and after a month's delay Jenkinson (the ambassador having already departed 'in a barke of his owne') sailed down the Volga delta and out into the Caspian. What Englishmen were with him is uncertain, for he names only Edward Clarke. After riding out a violent storm, on 4 August their vessel arrived at Derbend, which was then in

Persian hands. Having taken in water, they resumed the voyage, and two days later anchored off Shabran, in the Persian province of Shirvan, which was under the government of Abdullah Khan. The vessel was unloaded, and Jenkinson journeyed up to (Old) Shemakha, the capital of the province. There he interviewed Abdullah Khan, who was so autocratic in his methods that the visitors formed the impression that he was the absolute king of the country. He received them with much favour, and indeed was so much pleased with their behaviour that he remained a steadfast friend to the English until his death a few years later.

Early in October Jenkinson started for the Persian court, escorted by a guard of soldiers furnished by Abdullah Khan. The reigning monarch, Shah Tahmasp, was then at his capital, Kazvin; and in that city our travellers arrived at the beginning of November. On the 20th Jenkinson had an audience with the Shah, to whom he delivered 'the Queenes Majesties letters, with my present'. The letters were written in Latin, Italian and Hebrew; and on learning this fact the monarch remarked that he had nobody in his dominions who understood those languages. He proceeded to question his visitor regarding the political state of Europe, and then demanded to know what his religion was. Jenkinson replied that he was a Christian. 'What is that? said he unto the King of the Georgians sonne (who, being a Christian, was fled unto the said Sophie); and he answered that a Christian was he that beleeveth in Jesus Christus, affirming him to be the sonne of God and the greatest prophet. Doest thou beleeve so? said the Sophie unto me. Yea, that I do, said I. Oh thou unbeleever, said he, we have no neede to have friendship with the unbeleevers; and so willed me to depart. I being glad therof, did reverence and went my way; being accompanied with many of his gentlemen and others, and after me followed a man with a basanet [*i.e.* basin] of sand, sifting all the way that I had gone within the said pallace, even from the said Sophies sight unto the court gate'.

Though thus dismissed with contumely—even the ground which he had trod was treated as defiled—the Englishman and his errand were the subject of much curiosity at court, and the Shah sent several members of his entourage to discuss matters with Jenkinson. Insinuations were not wanting that he was really a spy in the pay of Portugal and that, in asking leave to pass through Persia to other countries, his object was to reach Hormuz, the Portuguese stronghold at the entrance to the Persian Gulf, and so escape by sea to Europe. Jenkinson, however, knowing the hostility with which the Portuguese were regarded at the Persian court, took pains to make it clear that, though both nations were Christian, Portugal and England were by no means on friendly terms, and that he dared not trust himself in the territories of the former. This adroit explanation seems to have been accepted; but a yet greater danger threatened the intrepid Englishman. Four days before his own arrival, an ambassador had come from the Turkish sultan to negotiate means for putting an end to the war subsisting between the two countries; and an agreement was quickly reached, to the great satisfaction of the Shah, who stood in no little awe of his powerful neighbour. The merchants interested in the trade between Persia and Turkey fully realised that any diversion of that traffic in the direction of Russia would be a serious blow to them. Accordingly, before the departure of the ambassador, they persuaded him to remonstrate with the Shah on the subject and to hint that any favour shewn to the infidel envoy would endanger the friendship so newly established between the two Muhammadan powers. When, therefore, the Shah conferred with his courtiers respecting the answer to be given to the demands of the Englishman, he was advised to return an uncompromising refusal, and further 'to send me, with my letters, unto the said Great Turke for a present'. This course Tahmasp decided to take; but Jenkinson was saved by the interposition of his good friend Abdullah Khan, who, hearing of his danger, wrote a strong letter to the Shah, pointing out that to treat a foreign envoy in this fashion would not only be dishonourable but would infallibly discourage other strangers from resorting to Persia. Thereupon, says Jenkinson, 'the saide Sophie . . . changed his determined purpose, and the twentieth of March 1562 [*i.e.* 1563] he sent to me a rich garment of cloth of golde, and so dismissed me without any harme'.

During his stay in Kazvin Jenkinson got into touch with some Indian merchants there, for the purpose of learning whether, in the event of his succeeding in establishing a settled trade in Persia, they could undertake to furnish a regular supply of spices. They told him that, if they were certain of a market, they would bring him any quantity he might desire, an assurance which filled him with high hopes for the future.

Immediately after the receipt of the Shah's present Jenkinson departed on his homeward way. At Javat he encountered Abdullah Khan, who soothed him with assurances that the Shah was really well disposed towards him and that the only reason for the rejection of his overtures was the league concluded with the Turks. For his own part the Khan readily sealed a grant, drawn up by Jenkinson, giving the servants of the Russia Company permission to buy and sell freely in the province of Shirvan, with exemption from all customs duties. This was a valuable concession, for not only did it afford the English merchants a useful base from which to make further efforts to open up trade in other parts of Persia, but it provided opportunities for the acquisition of large quantities of raw silk, for which the province was famous, in exchange for English woollens. Thus encouraged, and accompanied by an ambassador whom Abdullah Khan was sending to the Tsar, Jenkinson bade farewell to his noble friend and journeyed on to Shemakha, and so to Shabran. Refitting the vessel in which he had come, in May he set sail for Astrakhan.

While at Shemakha Jenkinson received a message from the King of Georgia, who, sorely harassed by both Turks and Persians, was desirous of seeking aid from the Tsar and begged his intervention to that end. Our traveller encouraged the Georgian monarch to send an envoy to Moscow to prefer his request; and in addition despatched his colleague, Edward Clarke, to Arrash, the centre of the silk industry, with instructions to endeavour to penetrate into Georgia and obtain from the King permission to trade in his country. Clarke, however, found, on reaching Arrash, that he could not proceed farther 'without great suspition'. It was clearly unwise to hazard the good relations established with Abdullah Khan by treating openly with a hostile power; and so, pretending that he had come merely to buy silk, Clarke made his way back to Shemakha and rejoined his chief.

On reaching Moscow in August 1563, Jenkinson duly delivered to the Tsar the jewels and silk goods he had been commissioned to buy for him, and related the outcome of certain secret matters—possibly negotiations with Abdullah Khan—which had been entrusted to him. Ivan was much pleased with the results; and Jenkinson took the opportunity to urge the grant to his employers of 'a newe priviledge more ample then the first'. This was readily conceded; and then the wearied travellers proceeded to the White Sea and there embarked for England. The voyage was long and dangerous, and Jenkinson did not arrive in London until the close of September 1564, after an absence of three and a quarter years. In that period he had made a journey no less remarkable than his venture into Central Asia, and had for the first time opened up commercial relations between England and Persia.

## CHAPTER III

# ATTEMPTS TO TRADE WITH PERSIA THROUGH RUSSIA

BEFORE leaving Moscow for England, Jenkinson arranged that a second expedition to Persia should be made in the summer of 1564.[1] The two factors employed, Thomas Alcock and Richard Cheney, reached Shemakha in August of that year, and were warmly welcomed by Abdullah Khan. In October Alcock proceeded to Kazvin to buy merchandise, leaving Cheney to collect the money owing at Shemakha for the goods already sold. How Alcock fared at the Persian capital is not recorded; but we learn that on his way back he was joined by Cheney at Javat, where Abdullah Khan then was. The murder of a Moslem by an agent of the Tsar angered the Governor and excited fears lest the Shah should order reprisals against the party, and Alcock therefore deemed it prudent to despatch his colleague with their stock of goods to Shemakha, so as to be within easy reach of the port. He himself followed a few days later, only to be murdered on the way. Thereupon Cheney embarked all his goods for Russia, where they arrived in safety under the charge of two servants, while he himself lingered for six weeks at Shemakha, collecting debts. In the report which he made to the Company after his return to Moscow, he expressed a favourable view of the prospects of trade in Persia. He

[1] Hakluyt says 1563, but this appears to be a mistake.

had heard encouraging accounts of the silk-producing province of Ghilan, on the southern shores of the Caspian, and was sanguine enough to believe that, if the English could establish themselves there, merchants might be induced to bring them spices from Hormuz, which was, he declared, only a six weeks' journey.

A third expedition was made in 1565 by Richard Johnson (who, as we have seen, had accompanied Jenkinson to Bokhara), Alexander Kitchin and Arthur Edwards, together with some English sailors. Embarking at Jaroslav in a vessel which had been specially built for the purpose, the party reached Shemakha in September and found Abdullah Khan as friendly as ever. His death, which occurred a few weeks after their arrival, was a great blow; for many months elapsed before his successor was appointed, and meanwhile all was in confusion. There was, however, a fair demand for English kerseys, and with the proceeds the factors laid in a good stock of raw silk and alum. Johnson had intended to despatch Kitchin to Kazvin to negotiate with the Shah; but the death of that merchant upset the plan, and it was not until April 1566 that Edwards started for the capital in his place. The reception accorded to him by Shah Tahmasp ('Shaw Thomas', as the English always called him) was far different from that experienced by Jenkinson. Fresh disputes had arisen between Turkey and Persia, and the Shah was faced with threats of closing his western frontier. This would not only debar European cloth and other goods from entering Persia by that route, but would also prevent the Persian silk, which was an important source of revenue to the Shah, from enjoying its usual outlet to the Mediterranean. Consequently Tahmasp offered a flattering welcome to his English visitor, professed great eagerness for the importation of woollens in large quantities, and gave him a letter granting ample privileges, including exemption from customs duties and unrestricted access to all parts of the Shah's dominions.

Much encouraged by this change of attitude, Edwards hastened back to Shemakha, and was mortified to discover that Johnson (with whom he was not on the best of terms) had returned to Russia without waiting for him. After spending some months in recovering debts due for goods delivered, Edwards quitted Shemakha, and by June 1567 was back in Astrakhan, whence he proceeded to Moscow. He was evidently filled with hopes of an abundant and profitable trade in Persia. Like Cheney, Edwards had heard good reports of Ghilan, which he inclined to think might prove a better base for English trade than Shemakha, especially now that their friend Abdullah Khan was dead. He was particularly encouraged by the overtures of some Armenian merchants to provide a regular supply of spices, which they undertook to deliver at stated prices. It should be added that, while lingering by himself in Shemakha, Edwards had conceived the idea of going in disguise to Hormuz and then home by way of Aleppo; but, no Englishman being available to take his goods back to Russia in his place, he reluctantly gave up the project. This is interesting as shewing how constantly the factors kept before their eyes the desirability of finding means to tap the spice trade before it entered Turkish territory.

It is now time to turn back to Jenkinson. His experience of the cost and danger of land journeys had evidently convinced him that a profitable trade with the East Indies was most likely to be obtained by an all-sea route, and he was of opinion that the most promising direction for this was the north-eastern one. At the end of May 1565 he addressed a memorial to Queen Elizabeth on the subject. In this he urged her to despatch an expedition to find out the way to 'the famous region of Cathaye and infynyte ilondes neare thereunto, all wiche are replenished with infynyt treazures, as golde, sylver, precious stones, bawmes, spices, drogges, and gumes'. He pointed out that woollen goods would be in much demand 'in those colde countryes betwene the imagyned straighte (of no dowghte to be fownde) and the said lannd of Cathaye'; and he averred that, even if it were necessary to prolong the voyage as far as the Moluccas, the distance to be covered in all was 2000 leagues shorter than the route to those islands by way of the Cape of Good Hope. Finally, he humbly begged the Queen to put him in charge of the expedition, and pledged himself to do his utmost to carry it to a successful conclusion. Elizabeth, however, was not disposed to spend money for such a purpose, and nothing came of the proposal. However, in the autumn of the same year she gave Jenkinson the command of a small war vessel and sent him to the Scottish coast to seize pirates and to prevent the Earl of Bothwell and other nobles from effecting a landing.

On his return from that service Jenkinson again took up the project of a voyage of discovery to the north-eastwards. In this he found for a time an enthusiastic coadjutor in the person of Humphrey Gilbert. Early in 1566 he wrote to Sir William Cecil, begging his help in procuring from the Queen a grant of privileges, in which case he and Gilbert, with the assistance of other adventurers, would undertake the voyage at their own expense. No progress had been made in the matter at the time of the despatch of Jenkinson to Russia on the errand next to be described; and before long Gilbert had become convinced that a venture to the north-west was more likely to be successful than one to the north-east. By November 1566 he was busy soliciting the Queen for a grant to himself and his two brothers of the exclusive use of the North-West Passage, should they effect its discovery. But the Russia Company represented that any such grant would be an infringement of its chartered rights, and so Gilbert's application was refused.

The formulation of schemes of exploration in what it regarded as its own exclusive sphere seems to have stirred the Russia Company to energetic action. Already in November 1564 it had complained to the Privy Council that a merchant named William Bond was seeking to open up relations with Russia by way of the Baltic, and that this competition was discouraging its members from subscribing the further money required for carrying on the Company's trade. As a result, in 1566 an act of parliament was passed, confirming the right of the Company to the exclusive use of trade routes 'lying from the city of London northwards, north-westwards, or north-eastwards', and forbidding all other Englishmen to trade with the dominions of the Tsar. As a further encouragement, the Queen agreed to the despatch of Jenkinson once more to Russia, in the character of an envoy from herself, to counteract the schemes of an Italian named Barberini, who, availing himself of an introduction obtained from Elizabeth, had secured from the Tsar a concession of trading privileges for himself and his countrymen. On this mission Jenkinson sailed in May 1566, and reached Moscow towards the end of August. He was successful in procuring a fresh grant to the English Company, extending its privileges and giving it a monopoly of the White Sea traffic. Thereupon, it would seem, Jenkinson journeyed to London overland in the winter of 1566, returning to Russia in the following spring. Towards the end of 1567 he again went home, carrying a message from the Tsar, proposing an alliance between the two countries, and asking for a supply of artillery and other munitions of war, together with the loan of skilled shipwrights and navigators.[1]

A letter of 18 April 1567[2] from the Company to its agents in Russia urged the continuance of the commerce with Persia, adding: 'our chef desire is to have a greate trade for the said spices and drugges to serve this reallme, for that we have undertaken (at this late parliament tyme) to perfourme the same to the Quenes Majestie and the nobillitie of this realme' (a reference to the recent act). In another clause allusion was made to information received from Arthur Edwards that there were to be found at a Caspian port certain slaves 'which have ben at Oromes [Hormuz] (the staple of spices) and speake the Portugal and Persia tounge'. Should this prove to be correct, the factors were to buy some of the

[1] Since at this point Jenkinson disappears from our narrative, the reader may be interested to hear something of the rest of his career. In 1571–72 he was employed by the Queen on a further mission to Russia, and succeeded in conciliating the Tsar, who had been irritated by Elizabeth's refusal to conclude an offensive and defensive alliance and had consequently withdrawn the privileges he had granted to her subjects. Jenkinson is next found taking an active interest in Frobisher's expeditions to the North-West, to the funds for which he was a subscriber. In 1577 he and another person were sent to Emden, to negotiate with the King of Denmark's commissioners regarding that monarch's claims to control the navigation of the seas round Norway and to levy dues upon English ships passing into the Baltic. This was his final public service, and he subsided into private life, residing mostly in Northamptonshire, first at Sywell and then at Ashton. His death occurred at Teigh, in Rutlandshire, where he was buried on 26 February 1611.

[2] Brit. Mus. *Cotton MSS., Nero B* xi, f. 321.

slaves and send them, 'with some one or two of our men, to Oromes or hard by, ther to practise for the trade of spice and drugges to be brought to the Casbin from Oromes or Callecut'. The result of these injunctions was the despatch, in the summer of 1568, of Edwards, accompanied by four other merchants, upon a fourth expedition into Persia. The party arrived at Bilbil (a port near Shabran) in August, and proceeded as usual to Shemakha, where a new governor was found installed. The markets at that place were already glutted with goods similar to those the Englishmen had brought; and Edwards, leaving two of his companions behind to sell part of the stock, set out for Kazvin with the remainder, accompanied by John Spark and Lawrence Chapman. At Ardebil some kerseys were bartered for a parcel of cinnamon, and at his own suggestion Chapman was sent to Tabriz. There he managed to secure a further quantity of spices in exchange for his goods. His enquiries, however, shewed that the city could not be relied upon as a regular source of supply for such commodities, as the quantity brought from Hormuz was merely sufficient to meet local demands.

The three merchants met again at Kazvin, where Edwards was accorded an interview with the Shah. Tahmasp had evidently forgotten the Englishman's previous visit, and Edwards had some difficulty in making the monarch understand his nationality, until 'one of the noblemen said Londro, meaning thereby London, which name is better knowen in farre countries out of Christendome then is the name of England'. Many questions followed concerning Queen Elizabeth, King Philip of Spain, and the hostilities betwixt the latter and the Turks. Edwards was then permitted to set out the object of his visit. He explained that he desired to establish a trade through Russia, by means of which English goods could be delivered in Persia much cheaper and with greater expedition than those brought by the Venetians by way of Turkey. The Shah appeared to be impressed by his arguments and gave him a fresh grant of privileges, including specific permission to visit Ghilan; but he shewed no willingness to purchase the cloth which the Englishman had brought. Chapman was sent to investigate the prospects of trade in the province of Ghilan. After a trying and dangerous journey, that enterprising merchant returned and reported that he had visited Lahijan and two neighbouring ports, only to find that the latter were quite unsuitable as harbours and that the people in general were too poor to buy English cloth. Of the further experiences of the party we have no information, but it is clear that they got safely back to Moscow in due course.

In June 1568 Queen Elizabeth despatched Thomas Randolph to Russia to carry on the negotiations with the Tsar. In his train went two merchants, Thomas Banister and Geoffrey Ducket, who were specially commissioned to make another attempt to settle a trade with Persia. Randolph's proceedings do not here concern us, save to note that in the grant he procured from the Tsar there was a clause that 'no nation stranger shall travell through his dominions into Media and Persia, but only the Company'. We must also record that (acting doubtless upon instructions received in England) Randolph and his merchant associates planned to send three Englishmen in a Russian pinnace from the White Sea to search 'the coast from the river Pechora to the eastwardes'. Whether the attempt was ever made is not known; but certainly nothing of importance resulted.

The expedition of Banister and Ducket into Persia

proved at once the longest and the most adventurous of the whole series. A vessel of seventy tons having been specially built for the voyage, in July 1569 the two merchants embarked at Yaroslav, on the Volga, accompanied by two other factors, Lawrence Chapman and Lionel Plumptre, about a dozen English sailors, and forty Russian servants. Whilst going down the Volga they had a stiff fight with a band of marauding Tartars, in which Banister received a couple of wounds. At Astrakhan they were detained six weeks by the unsuccessful siege of that city by a large force of Turks and Tartars; and as the result of this delay it was late in October when their vessel anchored on the Persian coast. The party spent the winter at Shemakha, and in April 1570 set out for Ardebil. A sojourn of five or six months in that city produced little in the way of sales, though it gave opportunities for the purchase of galls and other products of the country. From Ardebil, at the invitation of Shah Tahmasp, Banister repaired to Kazvin. There the monarch bought most of his cloth and, despite the protests of the Turkish ambassador, granted all his requests, save one 'to transport and carie through his dominions certaine horses into India'. This seems to hint at some project to send one or more of the factors down to Hormuz, there to endeavour to get to India. One curious incident of Banister's visit was the following. Tahmasp, having determined 'to send a great summe of money to Mecca in Arabia, for an offering to Mahomet their Prophet, hee would not send any money or coine of his owne, but sent to the English merchants to exchange his coyne for theirs, according to the value of it; yeelding this reason for the same, that the money of the merchants was gotten by good meanes and with good consciences, and was therefore woorthie to bee made an oblation to their holy Prophet, but his owne money was rather gotten by fraud, oppression, and unhonest meanes, and therefore was not fit to serve for so holie a use'.

After spending six months in Kazvin, Banister returned *via* Tabriz to Shemakha, in order to arrange for the shipment of his goods to Astrakhan. A visit to Arrash for the purchase of silk proved fatal to seven of the Englishmen, including Banister himself (July 1571), and the leadership of the party now devolved upon Ducket. He found himself obliged to make a fresh journey to Kazvin, in order to obtain from the Shah an order for the release of their merchandise, which had been seized by the Governor of Shemakha upon the news of Banister's death.[1] This secured and the goods regained, Ducket made an enterprising venture south-eastwards to Kashan, where he spent about ten weeks, buying silk goods, spices and turquoises. The account given in Hakluyt declares that in travelling from Shemakha to Kashan Ducket passed through the ruins of Persepolis; but the statement is clearly erroneous. An interesting episode that occurred during his absence from Shemakha was an attempt made by Plumptre to proceed from that place in the direction of Cathay with a caravan bound for Bokhara. In this he was foiled by the Governor of Shemakha, who, hearing of his departure, sent a band of horsemen in pursuit. They overtook him and brought him back, when he had been six days on his way.[2] The incident is instructive as shewing how

[1] Vincentio d'Alessandri, who was in Persia at the time as envoy from Venice, alludes to the death of Banister (whom he calls 'Mr. Thomas') and the resultant trouble over his goods, the release of which cost, he says, 'a great deal of money' (*Italian Travels in Persia*, Hakluyt Society, 1873, p. 225).

[2] The narrative in Hakluyt (1589) says that the Governor acted 'by the

eager the factors were to seize any opportunity of exploring to the eastwards.

On his return from Kashan to Shemakha Ducket spent some time in buying merchandise, and then proceeded with his remaining companions to Shabran, where in May 1573 they embarked for Astrakhan. The voyage proved disastrous. After experiencing much trouble from the weather they were attacked, while at anchor, by a band of Cossack pirates. A desperate fight ensued, in which the Englishmen were all wounded, and were obliged to surrender their ship and goods, which they estimated to be worth from £30,000 to £40,000—a large sum when we remember the difference in the value of money then and now. Ducket and his associates were turned adrift in a boat, and managed to reach Astrakhan. Upon their complaint to the Governor an expedition was sent in search of the pirates; but the latter succeeded in making good their escape, though later some of their number were captured and part of their booty was recovered. From Astrakhan the Englishmen proceeded to Yaroslav, though not without losing on their way some more of their goods, owing to their boats being caught in the ice of the Volga. Ducket got back to England in October 1574.

There was then a pause of five years, due perhaps partly to the discouragement produced by the experiences of Banister and Ducket, and partly to the diver-

procurement of Humfrey Greensell [Greenfell?], who afterwards, beyng at Ormuz in the East Indias, was there cruelly burnt in the Inquisition by the Portingals'. No other reference to this individual has been found; but the particulars given suggest that he was a subordinate member of the party who had decided to desert and was trying to curry favour with the Governor. Possibly he became a Muhammadan for the same purpose, and then, having drifted down to Hormuz, was there seized and put to death as a renegade. The date may have been any time between 1571 and 1589, and so he may have been the first Englishman to reach Hormuz.

sion of attention to the possibility of discovering the North-West Passage and the voyages of Martin Frobisher to that end. When these failed, the Russia Company once more took up the attempt to develop trade with Persia.[1] Under the leadership of Arthur Edwards a strong party set out from Yaroslav in September 1579, and reached Astrakhan in the middle of the following month. There they learnt with consternation that the Turks, aided by the Krim Tartars, had conquered the province of Shirvan from the Persians. Unwilling to turn back, the factors decided to remain where they were for the winter months and await developments. Better news arrived in the following spring, when intelligence came that the Shah's forces were getting the upper hand; and thereupon it was resolved that, while Edwards remained at Astrakhan with half the stock, the other three merchants should venture to the southwards. Towards the end of May 1580 the party reached the port of Bilginski, near Baku; but there they received information which caused them to abandon all idea of proceeding farther. The earlier reports of Persian victories had been too optimistic; Shemakha, they were now told, was destroyed and the neighbourhood desolate; while Baku itself and the surrounding districts were in the hands of the Turks, who had also a strong garrison in Derbend. There being evidently no prospect of getting into Persian territory with any safety, the factors came to the conclusion that their best course was to endeavour to sell their goods to

[1] For this purpose a dyer, named Morgan Hubblethorne, was sent out, with instructions drafted by the elder Hakluyt. These enjoined him to endeavour to ascertain the methods used by the Persians in dyeing their carpets and silks and in staining linens; also to try to procure slips or seeds of the plant that produced indigo, with a view to its cultivation in England. Whether Hubblethorne ever reached Persia does not appear.

the victorious Turks. The Governor of Baku shewed himself disposed to help them in this, and with his assistance some of their number journeyed to Derbend. There Osman Pasha, the Turkish leader, encouraged them to bring their vessel round to that port, promising them facilities for the sale of their wares. This was accordingly done, but little trade resulted. Part of their stock was then despatched by sea to Baku, under the charge of three of the Englishmen; and from thence one of the factors ventured towards Shemakha, but was set upon by robbers and had a narrow escape of being murdered. When the party reassembled at Derbend, preparations were made for departure northwards. Osman Pasha sold them a quantity of raw silk (doubtless part of his loot) and bought the best of their goods, though upon his own terms. He then dismissed them abruptly. The return voyage proved difficult and dangerous; their vessel became imprisoned in the ice, and its occupants were almost starved when help arrived from Astrakhan. Reaching at length that city (where they found that Edwards had died during their absence), they spent the winter there, and in the spring of 1581 proceeded up the Volga to Yaroslav. A few months later the factors departed for England.

Their report seems to have convinced the governing body of the Russia Company that any immediate effort to continue the trade was inadvisable. It was true that the profits made had been encouraging, and as a matter of fact a dividend of 106 per cent. was declared in October 1581.[1] But the state of Persia had been growing steadily worse. Tahmasp, who died in 1576, was succeeded by two weak monarchs, whose reigns were marked by internal disturbances and by a long war with

[1] W. R. Scott, *The History of Joint Stock Companies*, vol. iii, p. 46.

the Turks. This involved especially the north-western districts; and until peace returned it would have been folly to risk valuable merchandise. Further, on taking a wide survey, the prospects of establishing a permanent commerce between the two countries were far from encouraging. For one thing, intercourse was entirely dependent on the whims of the Tsar, who some years before had stopped all trading and seized the Company's property to mark his displeasure with the way his envoy had been received in England. In the second place, even in the most favourable circumstances, goods carried by so roundabout a route—from London to the White Sea, thence by land and river down to the Caspian and so by sea to a Persian port, and thence again by land to the inland markets—were obviously at a great disadvantage compared with similar articles transported *via* the Mediterranean to Scanderoon and so overland into Persia; and the same applied to the reverse traffic. Moreover, it is significant that the very year (1581) of the return of the last expedition by way of the Caspian saw the establishment by charter of the first association of London merchants for the purpose of trading into the Levant, in accordance with privileges obtained at Constantinople in the preceding year; and the Russia Company may well have deemed it wise to wait and see what success attended this new effort. Further, there were political complications. Considerable importance was attached to the relations opened up with the Turkish sultan, which seemed to promise much advantage to English trade. His ministers were fully alive to the desirability of maintaining the flow of Persian goods through Turkish territory and of the reverse current of European manufactures; and any movement which aimed at diverting this traffic would be sure to arouse their hostility. On the other hand, it had been found by experience that the Persian shah, who stood in much awe of his powerful neighbour, would only lend countenance to schemes for such a diversion when hostilities supervened. To these considerations we may add that evidently English goods were in small demand in Persia, and stood little chance in competition with similar articles imported by way of Turkey; while raw silk, the chief product of Persia itself, could not be absorbed to any great extent in England, where there was as yet no manufacture of silk goods on a large scale. Nor could it be exported on favourable terms to France or Italy, as those countries were already furnished by the more direct route. In these circumstances, we may judge that the attempts to develop a regular trade between Persia and England *via* Russia were foredoomed to failure. The gallantry with which such efforts were persisted in can only be ascribed to the national unwillingness to admit defeat, and to the hope that a footing in Persia might lead to the establishment of traffic with India and the countries beyond. To this hope a shrewd blow had been dealt by Drake's success in reaching the Moluccas by sea; while the preparations that were at once set on foot for following up his venture must have been an additional discouragement to those who had pinned their faith to the possibilities of obtaining regular supplies of spices through Persia.

Before leaving the subject, we may note that in 1580 the Russia Company made one more attempt to find the longed-for North-East Passage. Two tiny vessels, of forty and twenty tons respectively, were despatched in that direction under Arthur Pet and Charles Jackman. Hakluyt fills several pages with the instructions given by the Company itself, by William Borough, by the elder Hakluyt and by Dr. John Dee, including advice to the explorers how to comport themselves should they arrive in China or Japan. Needless to say, the venture was unsuccessful. The two pinnaces sighted Vaigats Island in the middle of July, and for ten days longer struggled on, hindered by fog and ice and baffled by contrary winds. At last they gave up the attempt, and with much difficulty made their way back to the Norwegian coast. There Jackman wintered, only to perish with his vessel on resuming the voyage in the spring. Pet, however, held on his course and reached England towards the end of 1580, bringing news of the failure of the enterprise.

And here we must leave the story of the North-East Passage, merely recording that further attempts to discover it were made by the Dutch in 1594–96, under Willem Barentszoon, and by the English in 1607 and 1608, under Henry Hudson, whose voyages are dealt with later; but all without success. In Milton's day it was still 'the imagined way, beyond Petsora eastward, to the rich Cathaian coast' (*Paradise Lost*, x, 291-3); and it was not until the latter part of the nineteenth century that, with the aid of steam, the passage was at last accomplished. Part of the credit for this must be given to Captain Joseph Wiggins, of Sunderland, who in 1874–76 made two voyages, the second of which took him as far as the river Yenisei. His object was the severely practical one of opening up trade with Northern Siberia; but his success led to a series of scientific expeditions from Sweden, under the leadership of Professor (afterwards Baron) Nordenskiöld. In the third of these the Professor, in a steam-whaler called the *Vega*, explored during 1878 the coastline to within 100 nautical miles of Behring's Strait. Then his vessel was frozen in for the winter; but resuming her voyage in the spring, she passed triumphantly through the strait on 20 July 1879, and reached Japan early in September.

CHAPTER IV

## THE EXPLORATIONS OF FROBISHER TOWARDS THE NORTH-WEST

WHEN the Russia Company, in January 1567, made representations which resulted in quashing Gilbert's scheme for a voyage to the North-West (see p. 35), that body asserted its determination to renew its efforts for 'the discovery of Cathay . . . either by the north-east or by the north-west'. When, however, years passed without any sign that the Company intended to redeem this promise, the advocates of further exploration grew increasingly restive, and opinion hardened in favour of an attempt to find a passage round the northern coast of America. It was currently supposed that, just as the new continent tapered at the south towards a point, so its northern extremity narrowed in like manner; and it was believed that, if one pushed sufficiently to the north through the straits separating Greenland from North America, the coast of the latter would be found to slope rapidly to the south-west, with the north-eastern extremity of Asia on the other side of the passage. To reach the shores of Cathay would then be a comparatively easy matter.

A prominent advocate of an attempt in this direction was Michael Locke, whose father, Alderman Sir William Locke, had been engaged in early ventures to the Levant; while he himself had made several voyages to the same parts. At the time of which we are writing, he appears to have been an agent in London of the Russia Company, and we may suppose that he had done his best to interest his employers in his schemes before seeking outside help. These efforts failing, he boldly allied himself with others of the same way of thinking, notably Humphrey Gilbert, Stephen Borough, the geographer John Dee,[1] and especially his old acquaintance Martin Frobisher, a skilled navigator who had had much experience of the Guinea trade. Frobisher took the lead, and in December 1574 presented himself to the directors of the Russia Company with a letter from the Queen, exhorting them either to make a fresh attempt to discover a passage to Cathay or else to grant a licence to others who were ready to do so. The Company returned an unfavourable answer; but this only resulted in a second and more peremptory letter from Elizabeth, reiterating her demand. The upshot was that in February 1575 the Company granted a licence to Locke, Frobisher and any others willing to adventure, for a voyage to the north-west. It may have been with the object of stimulating interest in the project that Gilbert's *Discourse for a Discovery for a New Passage to Cathaia* (written ten years earlier) was published in 1576. In this were embodied all the current arguments for the practicability of such a scheme.

In spite of its being countenanced by Ambrose Dudley, Earl of Warwick, and viewed with favour by the Queen herself, the project languished for want of funds; and in the end these had to be furnished largely by Locke himself. Consequently it was not until June 1576 that Frobisher was able to start. His fleet con-

[1] For the important part played by Dr. Dee in the promotion of both Frobisher's and Drake's voyages the reader should consult Prof. Taylor's *Tudor Geography*, 1485–1583.

sisted of two small barques, the *Gabriel* and the *Michael*, of twenty-five tons each, and a pinnace of ten tons; the crews of all three numbering only thirty-four persons in all. In passing Greenwich Palace they were cheered by a glimpse of Her Majesty, 'shaking her hand at us out of the window'. About a month after their departure they sighted Greenland, and here their tiny pinnace foundered in a storm; while shortly afterwards the *Michael* gave up the attempt and stole away homewards, leaving Frobisher in the *Gabriel* to his own devices. Running up the coast of Labrador, he passed, without noticing it, what is now known as Hudson Strait, and entered the extensive inlet which is still called Frobisher Bay, although at the time its discoverer (who never found out that it was land-locked) gave it the name of Frobisher's Straits. This inlet he navigated for some distance, making no doubt that the coast to the northwards (part of Baffin Land) was the shore of Asia, and that he had succeeded in finding the desired passage into the Pacific.

Going on shore, Frobisher found certain Eskimos, who appeared disposed to be friendly and readily bartered fish and furs for looking-glasses and similar trifles. Such was the confidence engendered that five of the crew one day took the *Gabriel's* only boat, against the captain's orders, and landed for the purpose of continuing the trade. They were never heard of again, and of course it was concluded that they had been treacherously killed by the natives. This unlucky incident brought the expedition to a premature end; for Frobisher, having but thirteen men left on board to work the ship, and no boat, judged it prudent to return at once to England. Before doing so, he kidnapped one of the Eskimos, in retaliation for the supposed murder

THE NORTH-WEST PASSAGE

or detention of his five sailors. The bait of a bell enticed the poor wretch to the side of the ship, when suddenly Frobisher himself leant over the rail, 'cought the man fast, and plucked him with maine force, boate and al, into his bark out of the sea'. With this 'strange infidell' on board, the *Gabriel* arrived at Harwich at the beginning of October 1576. The Eskimo, who did not long survive his transportation, was held to be a striking proof that the shores of Asia had actually been reached, as his features were thought to be undoubtedly of a Tartar cast.

The news of the discoveries that had been made naturally created a sensation, and Frobisher 'was highly commended of all men for his great and notable attempt, but specially famous for the great hope he brought of the passage to Cataya'. Preparations were at once commenced for a fresh voyage. With (presumably) the consent of the Russia Company, a new association was formed, known as the Company of Cathay or the Company of the Adventurers of the North-West Voyages,[1] to exploit the field thus opened. The subscribers to the late expedition formed the nucleus, with power to admit other members; Locke was to be governor for six years, Frobisher admiral of all voyages, and each was to have one per cent. on the goods imported by the new route. Towards the second voyage the Queen contributed £1000 and Locke £300; while the list contained also the names of several of the nobility, and of prominent merchants such as Sir Thomas Gresham. No doubt the rush to subscribe was partly due to rumours that were

[1] In the article on Frobisher in the *Dictionary of National Biography* it is stated that a charter was granted to the Company on 17 March 1577; but after search, both at the Public Record Office and at the British Museum, I have failed to discover any confirmation of the statement.

circulating to the effect that during the recent expedition a deposit of precious metals had been found. As a matter of fact, Frobisher had brought home a piece of ore picked up on Hall's Island, and had given this to Locke without thinking it to be of any special importance. Several assayers failed to find in it anything more valuable than a minute trace of silver; but one (an Italian) declared that he had recovered gold from the portion submitted to him. The promoters were easily persuaded that the mineral was really auriferous, and it was resolved to send out in the new fleet a number of miners and refiners, with instructions to bring back large quantities of ore. Three vessels, viz. the two previously employed and the *Aid* (200 tons) lent by the Queen, were fitted out. Frobisher, as chief commander, took charge of the *Aid*; Edward Fenton was made captain of the *Gabriel*, and Gilbert York of the *Michael*.

Frobisher Bay was reached in the middle of July 1577. Both the land to the southward, known as Meta Incognita, and the northern shore of the bay were explored to some extent; but the minds of all concerned were chiefly bent upon the discovery of gold and every other consideration was subordinated to this. Having laden his ships with nearly 200 tons of minerals selected by the experts, after about five weeks' stay Frobisher turned homewards, arriving in England in September. The ore was assayed, with varying results. Some of it, however, was declared to contain a little silver and traces of gold; and the report in general was favourable enough to induce the Queen to sanction a third attempt with a much larger fleet, comprising no less than fifteen vessels. Fenton was again Frobisher's second in command, and it was determined to leave 100 men 'to inhabite Meta Incognita all the yeere', of whom thirty were to be miners, to dig large quantities of ore ready for a subsequent fleet.

The third expedition sailed in May 1578. Most of the ships reached the southern point of Frobisher Bay early in July, only to be scattered by a great storm. Making towards the shore again, Frobisher, with such vessels as he still had with him, entered by mistake the strait now known as Hudson's, and up this he sailed for fifty or sixty leagues. Its width and the strength of the current seemed to indicate that this, rather than Frobisher Bay, was 'the passage which we seeke to find to the rich countrey of Cataya'; but Frobisher recognised that the object of the expedition was to fetch ore rather than to make fresh discoveries, and so he turned back to Meta Incognita, and with much difficulty got at last into Frobisher Bay. All hands then set to work, and nearly 1300 tons of ore were got on board. The question of leaving men behind for the winter was next considered. It was found that few were willing to face the hardships involved, and in the end the proposal was abandoned. The return voyage was commenced at the close of August, and a month later the ships were back in English waters.[1]

The employment of so many vessels had made this last venture an exceptionally costly one; while a considerable proportion of the £20,000 which had been subscribed for the three voyages remained unpaid. The Privy Council brought pressure to bear upon the backward members, but with only partial success. Repeated efforts to extract gold from the ore brought home yielded no satisfactory results, and this entirely dis-

[1] In 1860–62 many relics of Frobisher's expeditions were discovered on the spot by Mr. Charles F. Hall, and these are now to be seen in the museum of the Royal Geographical Society.

heartened the unfortunate shareholders, with the consequence that no attempt was made to follow up Frobisher's discoveries and the Company of Cathay faded out of existence. Locke himself, who had ventured his all in the enterprise, spent months in the Fleet prison at the suit of some of the Company's creditors. After a time he managed to rehabilitate his fortunes, and from 1592 to 1594 he was consul at Aleppo for the Levant Company.

## CHAPTER V

# DRAKE REACHES THE MOLUCCAS, 1579. FENTON MAKES A SIMILAR ATTEMPT

BY the time of Frobisher's return from his third expedition, a quarter of a century had passed since Willoughby and Chancellor had sailed from the Thames on their voyage for Cathay and the Spice Islands; yet the goal seemed as distant as ever. Now, however, events moved more rapidly, and in the autumn of 1580 England was thrilled by the news that Francis Drake had actually reached the Moluccas by way of the Pacific and had returned round the Cape of Good Hope, thus effecting the first circumnavigation of the globe by an English ship.

How this had come about needs some preliminary explanation. Although hostility between Spain and England had been steadily growing, Elizabeth throughout the earlier part of her reign had prudently refrained from coming to an open quarrel with her royal brother-in-law, and she had therefore consistently refused to countenance any schemes for intruding upon the Spanish dominions in the New World. Even the revolt of the Dutch Netherlands against Philip in 1572 did not move her from this policy, in spite of the sympathy felt by most Englishmen for their fellow-Protestants in that quarter. Her hand was, however, gradually forced by the development of events on the Continent and by the enterprise of her own subjects. A profitable trade had grown up in the West Indies between the Spanish colonists there and certain English adventurers, notably John Hawkins, who kidnapped or purchased negroes on the Guinea coast and took them across the Atlantic for sale. Such traffic was of course strictly forbidden by the Madrid authorities, though the Spanish settlers welcomed it as supplying an urgent need. At length official wheels were set in motion to crush the English 'pirates', and in September 1568 Hawkins, while anchored off San Juan de Ulua with several vessels, was attacked by a Spanish squadron, and only the *Minion*, in which Hawkins himself had taken refuge, and the *Judith*, commanded by Francis Drake, managed to put to sea and escape. These hostilities naturally provoked retaliation, and during the next few years Drake made a series of raids on the Spanish possessions in the West Indies. In one of these (1572–73) he attacked Nombre de Dios, on the Atlantic side of the Isthmus, and then boldly marched his men across to Panama, being (according to a picturesque story) the first Englishman to sight the Pacific. At that period there was no direct communication between Spain and her settlements on the Pacific coast, and it was consequently the practice to concentrate at Panama the silver annually produced by the mines, and transport it thence to Nombre de Dios for shipment to Europe. The result was that Drake's unexpected raids brought him much booty. What is more, the information he had obtained gave him the idea of penetrating into the Pacific by way of Magellan's Strait, and there plundering the defenceless treasure-ships on their way to Panama.

The genesis of Drake's famous voyage is still obscure; but Professor Taylor has shewn that the original proposal was to explore the Pacific sector of the supposed vast southern continent (Terra Australis). There was also a suggestion that an attempt should be made to find the Pacific outlet of the North-West Passage; while later a visit to the Moluccas was included in the plan, since it was imagined that the coast of Terra Australis ran up in a north-westerly direction to a point just south of those islands. It can hardly be doubted, however, that Drake himself intended to make treasure raids a principal feature of the expedition. How far the Queen was aware of this intention is not known; but, acting on the advice of Walsingham, she not only permitted Drake to set out, but herself provided part of the funds; while the list of subscribers included also the Earls of Lincoln and Leicester, Sir Francis Walsingham, Christopher Hatton, Sir William Winter and John Hawkins.

Drake sailed from Plymouth in December 1577 in the *Pelican* (of only 100 tons), accompanied by four other vessels. Magellan's Strait, where the name of the flagship was changed to the *Golden Hind*, was successfully passed in August 1578. By this time the squadron had been reduced to three ships; and of these one was lost in a storm after entering the Pacific, while a second parted company and made her way home. Drake himself, nothing daunted, held on his course up the coasts of Chile and Peru, sacked Valparaiso, rifled a number of vessels at Lima, and off Cape Francisco took and plundered a rich treasure-ship. The whole coast was by this time thoroughly alarmed, and Drake, having as much booty as he could well carry, began to think of returning. Magellan's Strait was out of the question, for it was almost certain that the Spaniards would be waiting there to intercept him; while the route round Cape Horn had not yet been discovered. There were two alternatives left. The first was to imitate Magellan himself by crossing the Pacific and returning by way of the Moluccas and the Cape; the second, to endeavour to find the western outlet of the North-West Passage, which was supposed to debouch into the Pacific in a comparatively low latitude. Drake resolved to try the second alternative first; and so for several weeks the *Golden Hind* ploughed its way 'towards the pole Arctike', until the crew grew discontented with the increasing cold. The ship's head was then turned south-east towards the American coast, which was reached at some point near the present city of San Francisco. Landing, Drake took formal possession of the country, which he named Nova Albion; and then the vessel started upon her long and lonely voyage across the Pacific.

Her first landfall, more than two months later, was what is now known as the Pelew group. Then, in November 1579, Drake anchored off Ternate, in the Moluccas, and got into touch with the king. That monarch, who claimed dominion over all the Spice Islands, was anxiously endeavouring to maintain his independence against the encroachments of the Portuguese; and, according to the chronicler of the voyage, he 'sent to our Generall with speciall message that hee should have what things he needed and would require with peace and friendship, and moreover that hee would yeeld himselfe and the right of his island to bee at the pleasure and commandement of so famous a prince as we served; in token whereof he sent to our Generall a signet'. This declaration is noteworthy, because later on the English appealed to it as conferring upon them special rights in the Moluccas. Some time was spent at Ternate, lading cloves, and then the voyage was resumed. Early in January 1580 the *Golden Hind* ran

THE EAST INDIAN ARCHIPELAGO

upon a rock, and it seemed likely that the great adventure would come to a disastrous end; but by taking out some guns and part of the cargo, and with the aid of a fortunate gust of wind, she was got off again without harm. After calling on the coast of Java, a course was set for the Cape of Good Hope. Passing this on 18 June, Drake continued his voyage to Sierra Leone, where a fresh stock of provisions was obtained; and England was safely reached in the autumn, after an absence of nearly three years. The voyage was an astounding feat of seamanship, far transcending anything that had yet been accomplished by an English vessel, and Drake became at once the national hero.

The year of Drake's return was noteworthy also for the death of Dom Henrique, King of Portugal. He left no direct heirs, and the succession was promptly claimed by Philip II of Spain, whose mother had been the daughter of a former occupant of the throne. There were of course other claimants; but a Spanish army quickly reduced all opposition, and Philip became sovereign of both countries, under pledges to keep the administration of Portugal and its dependencies entirely distinct from that of Spain. To England the union of the two crowns was a matter of deep concern, for it meant that the East as well as the West Indies were now under the sway of her bitter and powerful enemy. Drake had trespassed upon both spheres, and this ominous fact lent vigour to the remonstrances of Philip's ambassador in London, who demanded the condign punishment of the offender and the surrender of the booty he had brought home. Elizabeth returned an equally vigorous reply. She said that Drake should be punished, if and when he was proved to have deserved punishment, but that the Spaniards had really brought all the evils on themselves by ill-treating her subjects and prohibiting commerce. She absolutely refused to admit the pretensions of Spain to monopolise the whole of America, by the donation of the 'Bishop of Rome', and to prevent other nations from trading or colonising in parts where the Spaniards had not already settled. Still less would she admit that Philip had the right to prevent Englishmen from freely navigating the ocean. 'The use of the sea and air', she asserted, 'is common to all', 'as neither nature nor public use and custom permitteth any possession thereof' (Camden's *History*, ed. 1675, p. 255). After this declaration, in which the high-spirited Queen fairly threw down the gage, on 4 April 1581 she visited the *Golden Hind* at Deptford and bestowed a knighthood on Francis Drake.

While to the popular imagination Drake's seizure of Spanish treasure made vivid appeal and gave immense encouragement to the appetite for adventure, more sober opinion regarded his opening up of trade in the Moluccas as a still more solid achievement. The welcome he had received, both there and elsewhere in the East Indies, and the ease with which the voyage round the Cape had been accomplished, seemed to hold out every encouragement for an attempt to build upon the foundation he had thus laid; especially now that the question of trespassing upon the domains of England's ancient ally no longer presented an obstacle, seeing that those domains had fallen under the authority of that national enemy, the King of Spain. The Queen's attitude to such ventures was not now in doubt, and so the scheme for a fresh voyage was taken up with enthusiasm. From a letter written in September 1581 by the Earl of Shrewsbury to Robert Dudley, Earl of

Leicester (Elizabeth's favourite), we learn that the latter was actively promoting the preparations which were being made to despatch a fleet to the East Indies, of which Martin Frobisher was to be the leader. Drake readily promised to give every assistance in his power and put down his name for £700 in the subscription list, which soon amounted to about £11,600. Upon one point the promoters were emphatic—the object of the voyage was to be trade, not discovery; and possibly it was this proviso that caused Frobisher to relinquish his intention of taking part. Thereupon Edward Fenton, who, as we have seen, had been Frobisher's lieutenant in the recent voyages to the North-West, was chosen for the post of 'Captain-General'. By this time the scheme had been widened to include China in the possible scope of the voyage; and in April 1582 Lord Leicester and Secretary Walsingham instructed Fenton, should he succeed in reaching that country, to leave there some fit persons, with a stock of goods for trading purposes. Fenton's formal instructions, however, as given by Hakluyt, make no mention of China, but direct him to proceed by the Cape route 'to the iles of the Malucos'; adding, rather mysteriously, 'for the better discovery of the North-West Passage, if without hinderance of your trade . . . you can get any knowledge touching that passage, whereof you shall do wel to be inquisitive'. Since he was not to pass latitude 40° N., and the Strait of Magellan was not to be used, either in going or returning (for fear of being attacked there), it would seem that he was expected to return by the Cape; but no specific instructions were given on the point, perhaps for fear lest the document should fall into wrong hands.

The ships employed were the *Leicester* of 400 tons,

the *Edward Bonaventure* of 250 (or 300), and two smaller vessels of 50 and 40 tons respectively. Quitting Southampton far too late (May 1582), the fleet made its way slowly down the African coast, until in August it reached Sierra Leone. At that season such a course left little hope of reaching the Cape; and after wasting several weeks it was decided to stretch over to Brazil and thence to go to the Rio de la Plata. Apparently Fenton, finding the Cape route hopeless, was contemplating, despite his instructions (which, however, did leave him a certain discretion in the matter), a venture through Magellan's Strait, as the only alternative left to him. However, from a prize taken on the way it was learnt that the strait was guarded by a Spanish squadron; so, after much hesitation, it was determined to repair to 'St. Vincent', on the coast of Brazil, there to provision the fleet and endeavour to trade. That port was safely reached; but its governor refused to have anything to do with the English, declaring that he and his compatriots were now the subjects of the King of Spain, who had prohibited all intercourse. After a while, however, he relented, and not only allowed them to buy victuals but also sold them some sugar. Suddenly three Spanish warships appeared, and at once attacked the English squadron, which was by this time reduced to the *Leicester* and the *Edward Bonaventure*. A stiff fight ensued, in which one of the assailants was sunk; whereupon the other two drew off. Nevertheless, Fenton, thoroughly disheartened by his persistent ill-success, made up his mind to abandon the voyage. The two vessels soon lost company; but they both got safely home, the one at the end of May 1583, the other a month later. The ill-success of the venture appears to have been largely the fault of the leader, who had none of the necessary qualifications for command, and was on bad terms throughout with William Hawkins, his chief assistant. Naturally the failure of the expedition caused great disappointment and effectually discouraged any further attempt in the same direction for some years.

CHAPTER VI

# THE ESTABLISHMENT OF THE LEVANT COMPANY

THE ventures described in the two preceding chapters were largely due to the encouragement and active participation of the Queen and prominent members of her court. There was always in the City a feeling of distrust of such association, at least on the financial side; and all this time a group of London merchants, headed by Edward Osborne and Richard Staper, had been quietly endeavouring to organise trade in the Near East, where, in addition to indigenous products, the spices and drugs of the Orient were still obtainable in considerable quantities, in exchange, it was hoped, for such wares as England could offer. As we have seen (p. 15), a profitable trade had been carried on in the Levant by English ships earlier in the century, though for many years it had been virtually discontinued. It was now decided to make a fresh attempt on a more solid basis, by procuring permission to settle factories in the dominions of the 'Grand Signor', as the Turkish sultan was generally termed. The French and Italians had long enjoyed such privileges, and there was every reason to suppose that they would not be denied to Englishmen.

For this purpose Osborne and Staper, about the year 1575, sent a couple of representatives overland to Constantinople, where, after a stay of eighteen months, they obtained a safe-conduct for William Harborne, whom it was intended to despatch thither as the actual negotiator. Harborne reached the Turkish capital in October 1578 and, after the usual delays, procured, not only a grant of privileges for himself and his employers, but also a letter from the Sultan, Murad III, to Queen Elizabeth, promising that the merchants for whom facilities had been sought should enjoy the same advantages as those of any other nation. With this letter Harborne returned to London in 1579; and in October of the same year the Queen sent an acknowledgement, assuring the Sultan of her goodwill and gratitude, and requesting him to extend his favour, not to 'two or three men onely', but 'to all our subjects in generall'. Harborne was the bearer of this letter, and such was the impression it produced that in June 1580 he obtained without difficulty the grant of the first of the 'capitulations' that for so long governed the trading relations of the two countries. By this document the safety of the English merchants was guaranteed, trade was freely allowed them throughout the Sultan's dominions, on payment of the usual customs duties, and liberty was granted to establish consuls for their protection in any city or port.

Steps were at once taken in London to organise the new commerce, and on 11 September 1581 the Queen issued letters patent, granting a monopoly for seven years to Osborne, Staper, Thomas Smythe[1] and William Garret, with power to admit not more than twelve other merchants. There were also two government nominees. The grant was contingent upon the syndicate driving such a trade, after the first year, that

[1] Father of the better known Sir Thomas Smythe, afterwards Governor of the East India, Levant and other companies.

the customs thereon should amount to not less than £500 a year. It might be determined by the Crown at any time upon giving a year's notice; and hopes were held out that it would be renewed at the expiration of the term. Osborne was to be governor for the whole period, should he live so long, and in the event of his death Staper was to succeed.

It was requisite that the new body should maintain an agent at Constantinople, and the choice naturally fell upon Harborne, who, to give him the necessary status, was at the same time appointed by the Queen as her resident ambassador. He sailed accordingly in January 1583, and landed at the Turkish capital towards the end of March. About a month later he was received by the Sultan with much oriental splendour, when he exhibited his letters of appointment and delivered the presents he had brought. These, which had of course been provided by the new Company, included thirteen dogs, a quantity of silver plate, and a silver clock studded with jewels and valued at £500. This clock appears to have been a wonderful piece of work, for it had over it 'a forrest with trees of silver, among the which were deere chased with dogs, and men on horsebacke following, men drawing of water, others carrying mine oare on barrowes; on the toppe of the clocke stood a castle, and on the castle a mill. All these were of silver, and the clocke was round beset with jewels.'

Harborne had arrived none too soon, for during his absence the French ambassador, taking alarm at the prospect of English competition, had persuaded the Sultan to cancel the grant. However, Harborne's representations, and the presents he had brought, created a revulsion of feeling at court, with the result that the former concession was renewed, despite the efforts of both the French and the Venetians. English consuls were appointed for Egypt and Syria, including Palestine; factories were started at Constantinople, Aleppo, Scanderoon, Tripoli (in Syria), Cairo and Alexandria; and soon English commerce was active at all these places. For sales the factors relied upon broadcloth, kerseys, rabbit skins (fur trimmings were much in demand), tin, quicksilver and amber; while the return cargoes consisted of spices, pepper, drugs, galls, indigo, silk, cotton, linens, etc. Some indication of the value of the trade in its early days is afforded by the fact that in 1587 the *Hercules* returned to London with a cargo which realised considerably more than £70,000, a figure we must multiply by at least ten to obtain its present-day value.[1] It is also significant that in the same year the Venetians, who had for so long regularly brought Mediterranean and oriental produce by sea to Southampton, gave up that practice.

Harborne remained at Constantinople as ambassador until August 1588. He had obtained a strong position at the Turkish court, and his influence had contributed powerfully to the establishment and maintenance of English trade throughout the Sultan's dominions. He claimed later to have rendered a special service by his efforts to induce the Turks to attack the Spaniards, as the common enemy of the two countries; and if little actually resulted, he at least succeeded in embarrassing the Madrid authorities by the dread of such an attack

[1] For purposes of comparison with later figures it is worth noting that in the previous June the prices per pound in London of oriental produce were: pepper, 3s.; cloves, 5s.; mace, from 5s. to 6s. 8d.; nutmegs, 5s.; cinnamon, 4s. to 6s.; ginger, 10d.; indigo, 6s. 6d.; raw silk, 20s.; cotton yarn, 1s. 4d.; raw cotton, 1s. 2d. (Sanderson, p. 131 *n*.).

at the very moment when the great armada for the invasion of Britain was under preparation.[1]

The difficulties of trade during these early years are well exemplified by two letters written from Cairo by John Sanderson and a colleague in October and December 1586.[2] It would seem that customs duties might be taken in kind instead of in money; and on one occasion when this course had been adopted in the case of some pepper and cassia, the Pasha found himself with a large stock of each on his hands. Thereupon he placed an embargo upon the sale of such goods by private merchants, declaring that the official stocks must be sold first, of course at his own prices. Since no remonstrances could move him from this decision, an appeal was made to Constantinople in the case of the cassia; and meanwhile all dealings in that article were held up. As regards the pepper, an offer was made to buy the stock at the current price, but the Pasha would not hear of it. At last, as the caravan for Mecca, which carried much merchandise, was about to depart, a Venetian merchant purchased the stock at a higher figure, at the same time stipulating that none but Venetians were to be allowed to buy pepper in the open market until the caravan had departed. Only then was freedom of trade restored. In another instance, on the arrival of a parcel of raw silk for the English factors, the customs officials demanded a payment of ten per cent., though the regular duty was only about a third of that rate. An appeal to the law resulted in a declaration that the lower figure was correct; yet the Pasha

[1] After his return Harborne retired to Norfolk, his native county. He died at Mundham in November 1617, and was buried in the parish church. An interesting account, by Professor H. G. Rawlinson, of him and his mission to Turkey will be found in the *Transactions of the Royal Historical Society*, Fourth Series, vol. v, pp. 1-27.

[2] Sanderson, pp. 131-9.

insisted upon the ten per cent., until he was bribed to accept the usual rate. In such cases the only remedy was either bribery or an appeal to Constantinople—a lengthy proceeding, which crippled all trade for the time being. Hence the advantage of having on the spot a consul to make representations officially to the local authorities, and behind him an ambassador known to possess considerable influence at court; for the mere threat of complaining to him would often bring the Pasha to his senses.

Harborne's successor as ambassador was Edward Barton, who had been his secretary and was left in charge at his departure. Some time elapsed, however, before he was confirmed in the post, owing to the uncertainty caused by the expiration in 1588 of the privileges granted to Osborne and his associates. The expenses of the ambassador and his establishment fell, not upon the Queen, but upon the merchants engaged in the trade; and until a new charter could be obtained, all was uncertainty. The negotiations between the Privy Council and those concerned were prolonged by disputes with the merchants trading to Venice, who claimed a monopoly of the commerce in Crete; while there were other merchants who petitioned for freedom to participate in the Levant trade. A further complication was added by the war with Spain, which made the voyage hazardous for merchant vessels. An apt illustration of this danger is supplied by Hakluyt's account of the 'worthy fight performed in the voyage from Turkie by five ships of London against eleven gallies and two frigats of the King of Spaines . . . anno 1586'. The unequal combat continued for five hours. Then the Spaniards withdrew, with three of their vessels in a sinking condition and great loss among their crews from the accurate gunfire of the English; while the latter, 'contented, in respect of their deepe lading, rather to continue their voyage then to follow the chase, ceased from further blowes, with the losse onely of two men slaine'.

In London the various disputants came at last to an agreement, and on 7 January 1592 a charter was granted to a new body which was virtually an amalgamation of the former Turkey and Venice Companies. Its title was 'The Governor and Company of Merchants of the Levant', and Osborne (now Sir Edward) was its first governor. Fifty-three members were named in the charter, together with twenty others who were to be admitted upon application; while the Crown (as before) reserved the right to nominate two members. The monopoly was to last for twelve years, and the sphere of operations included not only the Turkish dominions but also those of the Venetian republic. It cannot be doubted that a powerful stimulus to the conclusion of the negotiations had been given by the return of Ralph Fitch in April 1591 from his epoch-making journey to India (described later); for the grant included the right to trade 'by lande, through the countries of the sayde Grand Signor, into and from the East Indies, lately discovered' by that enterprising traveller.

Barton retained his post as ambassador at the Porte until his death at the close of 1597. His period of office was troubled by continual controversies with the French, who were very jealous of English competition; but his influence with the Sultan and his chief ministers was such that his position remained unshaken throughout. Indeed, so marked was his interference in Turkish affairs[1] that it caused some concern to his employers,

[1] Sanderson notes (p. 61) 'the extraordinary esteme [that] was had of the

who afterwards warned his successor (Lello) to confine himself to his proper duties.

The death of Sultan Murad in January 1595, and the accession of his son Mehmet III, made it necessary to commence negotiations for the renewal of the privileges of the English traders, since these expired with the sovereign who had granted them. Custom prescribed that a fresh grant should be preceded by the arrival of a special envoy to congratulate the Sultan upon his succession, and that he should bring with him a suitable array of presents. Barton succeeded in persuading the ministers of the new sovereign to waive the point as to the special embassy; but they would not agree to forgo the presents, in which they hoped to share. The outlay involved was considerable, and the Levant Company, which was growing anxious regarding the prospects of the trade, was in no hurry to provide the wherewithal. The success of the Dutch in reaching Sumatra by the Cape route, and English schemes for establishing a direct commerce with the East by that route, threatened the future of the trade with Turkey; while the Company had other troubles to face. In May 1600 a dispute with the Privy Council, over the payment of a special levy upon its imports, led to a peremptory order closing down the Company's operations until the controversy was settled; while at the same time a rival group of merchants made an offer to undertake the trade upon the government's own terms. At last, however, an agreement was reached, by which the existing company was to receive a fresh charter (sealed on 31 December 1600), renewing its

ambassiatour . . . with them all in generall, both Christians, Turks, and Jewes. . . . He made and displaced both princes and patriarks, befrended viseroys, and preferred the sutes of cadies [*kazis*], who ar thier chefe preests and spirituall justisies.'

monopoly for a period of fifteen years, contingent upon the payment of £2000 each half-year. Smythe (afterwards Sir Thomas) was appointed the first governor.

Meanwhile Henry Lello, Barton's secretary, was carrying on the current duties of the post at Constantinople; and in October 1599 he received his letters of appointment as ambassador, together with the long-expected present. He now pressed the Turkish ministers for the grant of fresh capitulations, which should not only renew the old privileges, but add new ones, particularly a reduction of the customs payable and an agreement that Dutch merchants (who were now frequenting the Levant in increasing numbers) should count as English, and pay consulage to Lello accordingly. The latter contention had long been a source of friction with the French, who argued that their treaty rights included the protection of all foreigners not separately represented at Constantinople. The struggle was long and bitter, and bribery was freely employed by both parties, to the great satisfaction of the Sultan's ministers; but in the end Lello triumphed, and in the spring of 1601 the desired grant was at length obtained.

At home the Company's troubles were by no means at an end. The yearly payment which it had undertaken to make to the government proved a heavy burden; and much uncertainty was felt as to the effects upon its profits of the success of the new East India Company. Soon after the accession of James I the Levant Company took advantage of the proclamation against monopolies to surrender its charter, and was thereupon excused the payment of the last £2000 due. This did not mean that the merchants engaged in the trade intended to abandon it; they knew that the government could not contemplate the loss of the revenue derived therefrom, and they had a shrewd idea that they had only to hold out to get their privileges renewed on a more favourable basis. This was what in effect happened; for on 14 December 1605 a fresh charter was granted to them, which, confirmed in 1661 by Charles II, remained in force until the Company came to an end in 1825. The new body started with a membership of 119, but admission was to be open to all English merchants upon payment of a reasonable entrance fee. Sir Thomas Lowe was nominated in the charter as the first governor, and was re-elected annually until his death in 1623.

Save for the period 1581–88, when the trade was conducted by a syndicate rather than by a company, the system pursued was that of 'regulation', not joint-stock trading. The governing body at home superintended merely. It arranged the despatch of ships, provided for the salaries and establishments of the ambassador at Constantinople and the payments for consular duties, made the necessary appointments to those posts, and prescribed the conditions under which the members or their factors in the Levant carried on the traffic. The members in England employed their own capital in buying and shipping goods. These were consigned, either to their own factors in the Levant or to members of the Company settled out there, who sold them and made the prescribed returns, being themselves remunerated on a commission basis. This system, which allowed full play to individual enterprise, proved satisfactory to all concerned, and eliminated the constant disputes which, in the case of joint-stock bodies like the East India Company, ensued between the central authority and the factors it employed, concerning the right of the latter to trade also on their own account, often to their masters' detriment.

Though somewhat overshadowed in later years by its own child, the East India Company, the importance of the Levant Company in the development of English trade with the East was greater than is generally recognised. To the end it ranked high among the great trading corporations. True, it was forced to abandon the traffic in the coarser goods from the East, such as calicoes and pepper; but it found ample scope for its activities in selling English commodities and buying local produce. One striking feature of the change was that, as early as 1614, the Company was actually sending out to Italy and Turkey pepper which had been brought from Java and Sumatra by the ships of the East India Company. The commerce that resulted from the Company's operations, and the friendship thus established with Turkey, made England into a Mediterranean power, with far-reaching consequences upon its naval and political history; while the good relations subsisting between the British sovereign and the head of one of the principal Muhammadan states had a powerful influence upon our position in Asia generally. Incidentally, and of more direct interest for our present purpose, the footing obtained in the Sultan's dominions provided a useful base for the expeditions to the eastward now about to be narrated.

## CHAPTER VII

# NEWBERY FINDS HIS WAY TO HORMUZ AND RETURNS THROUGH PERSIA

WHILST Harborne was still negotiating with Murad III on his first visit to Constantinople, and more than two years before the grant of the Levant Company's first charter, a certain John Newbery, 'citizen and merchant of London', being 'desirous to see the world', set out to visit those Eastern countries of which there was so much talk. Of his previous history we know nothing. It is tempting to suppose that he was related to Ralph Newbery, the well-known London publisher; yet the only basis—a slender one—for the suggestion is the fact that John wrote later to Richard Hakluyt as his 'assured good friend', and Ralph was the publisher of the *Principall Navigations*.[1] It might be suspected that the traveller was being employed or backed by the Osborne-Staper group of merchants, as was certainly the case with his third journey; but I find no reason to think that at this stage he represented anybody but himself. This is not to say that his venture was one of pure curiosity and that he was in fact no more than a tourist. Doubtless his main purpose at the outset was to visit

> Those holy fields,
> Over whose acres walk'd those blessed feet,
> Which, fourteen hundred years ago, were nail'd
> For our advantage on the bitter cross.

[1] A further possible clue to Newbery's previous career is mentioned on p. 94.

But apart from this pious aspiration, shared with many other Europeans of the period, he was probably moved by a desire to see what the conditions of trade were in the Levant, with a view to later on venturing farther afield. It is quite conceivable, too, that he carried with him a certain quantity of merchandise, to test the markets and contribute to the payment of his expenses.

Newbery's first journey, of which we have only a mere sketch, lasted but eight months. Leaving London in March 1579, he proceeded through France to Marseilles, and there embarked for Tripoli, in Syria. That port was reached in the middle of May, and Newbery then took another ship to Jaffa and so went to Jerusalem, where he spent some time 'visiting the monuments of those countries'. Returning to Jaffa and Tripoli, after a delay of a fortnight he embarked for Marseilles, and from thence went back to London by way of Paris.

Encouraged by his experiences in this preliminary journey, on 19 September 1580 Newbery set out on a longer and more ambitious expedition. This time he sailed in an English ship direct to Tripoli, where he arrived at the beginning of January 1581, and travelled leisurely up to Aleppo. Thus far he had been accompanied by a merchant named William Barret, who now took up his abode in Aleppo, where he afterwards became the English consul. Newbery, however, had his eyes fixed upon a more distant goal, viz. the famous city of Hormuz. The route thither, by way of the Euphrates valley and the Persian Gulf, was well known to Venetian merchants, who traded freely both at Hormuz itself and throughout the Persian dominions, to say nothing of countries farther afield;[1] and he

[1] Gasparo Balbi left Aleppo for Basra in 1579, on his adventurous journey

NEWBERY'S SECOND JOURNEY

would have no difficulty in obtaining at Aleppo full information on the subject.

Dressed as an ordinary Muhammadan trader, and accompanied by a Greek servant, Newbery left Aleppo on 19 March 1581, and on the following day reached Bir, on the Euphrates. There, in accordance with the usual practice, he hired a bark, in which he proceeded down the river to Falluja. Disembarking at that place, he struck across country to Baghdad, reaching that city on 15 April. After a stay of nine days, he embarked on the Tigris and at the beginning of May arrived in Basra. On the 13th of the same month he and his servant took passage in a vessel that was bound down the Persian Gulf. Apparently she was not to call at Hormuz itself, for at Nakhilu Newbery and a number of other merchants left her and proceeded overland to a point opposite Laft, on the island of Kishm. On the way the party fell into the hands of a robber chief and 'were in great danger of being taken slaves; but God kept us'. In this extremity, it is worth noting, the Englishman's companions—all Muhammadans, with the exception of a Nestorian—cheerfully deposed on oath that he was a Christian inhabitant of Aleppo, 'and had wife and children and an house there'. From Kishm Newbery had no difficulty in getting carried over to Hormuz, where he arrived in safety on 22 June 1581.

At this time the Portuguese freely allowed the merchants of other nations to trade at Hormuz, and the commerce of the port, so far as it was directed towards Turkey and Europe, seems to have been largely in the hands of the Venetians. Newbery had an interview with

to India and Pegu; while Cesare Federici, returning to Venice after eighteen years of wandering in those same countries, arrived in Aleppo in 1581, probably soon after Newbery's departure.

the Portuguese governor, who appears to have taken no alarm at the arrival of an Englishman. Then he hired a house and began to look about him. Apparently he had brought no merchandise with him, and was thus able to sustain the character of one who was travelling with no ulterior object in view. But the mere fact of his nationality excited the suspicions of one of the Venetian merchants, Michael Stropene by name, who was probably well informed about the English negotiations at Constantinople; and this man succeeded in enticing away Newbery's Greek servant, in order to 'understand my secret purposes'. Nothing daunted, our traveller remained six weeks in the city, noting with a vigilant eye 'the trade and customes of the place', and then prepared to make his way home again. Probably no shipping was available at that season for Basra, and so he decided to return by land through Persia, the southern portion of which had not as yet been visited by any Englishman. He had picked up enough Arabic to make himself understood, and the fact that he had no European companion does not seem to have troubled him in the least. Before starting, he appears to have turned part of his stock of money into merchandise, for we find that later, at Tabriz, he sold a quantity of cloves.

Leaving Hormuz on 1 August 1581, Newbery crossed to Gombroon (Bandar Abbas), and from thence proceeded to Lar, the chief town of the Persian province of Laristan. There he engaged a Jew as his servant and interpreter, and the pair took the road for Shiraz. That city was reached without incident on 6 September, and the Englishman duly admired its beautiful buildings and busy bazaars. After a stay of sixteen days, the journey was resumed, and on 4 October he arrived at

Isfahan. So far as is known, he was the first of his race to visit that royal city; he remained, however, only three days, and his brief account of the place is confined almost entirely to commercial details. If he had at first meant to make across Western Persia to Basra or Baghdad, he had by this time abandoned that intention in favour of a more northerly route through Tabriz and Asia Minor to Constantinople. Proceeding therefore northwards, on 12 October he found himself at Kashan, an important commercial centre, where he remained until 4 November. The sacred city of Kum was the next stage of importance; but it was scarcely a safe place for a Christian, however inconspicuous, and Newbery made no stay. His direction was now north-westerly, through Sultanieh, and he did not pause until on 23 November he reached the 'great citie' of Tabriz. There he made friends with some Armenians, who remembered the visit of Thomas Banister in 1570–71, and whose recommendations seem to have been of much service to the traveller in the subsequent stages of his journey.

Departing on 1 December 1581, Newbery continued his journey to Julfa, on the Aras river, and thence to Nakhichevan. On the 8th he was 'under the arke', that is to say, near Mount Ararat, on the summit of which the ruins of Noah's ark were supposed to be still resting. Erivan was reached the next day, and here the traveller halted until 12 December. Nine days later he entered Erzerum, where he remained over Christmas. On 3 January 1582 he was at Erzingan, and made another halt of ten days. Tokat was his next objective, and after that Brusa, which was reached on 23 February. After resting until 5 March, Newbery and his servant made the short final stage to Constantinople, where they arrived four days later.

The easiest way back to England from the Turkish capital was to take ship for Venice, and from thence proceed overland. But Newbery's thirst for fresh experiences was not yet slaked, and he decided to go northwards to the Baltic coast and so home by sea. Accordingly, on 4 April 1582 he embarked in a Greek vessel bound for one of the Danube ports. After being sore buffeted in the Black Sea by a storm, the vessel succeeded in getting into the St. George's mouth of the Danube and, passing Tultcha, anchored on 25 April at Reni, at the mouth of the Pruth. There Newbery was much interested in watching the process of making caviare. The vessel in which he had come had now reached her destination; and 1 May our traveller started for Jassy, which he entered ten days later. From Jassy he proceeded to Chotin and Kaminietz, then a 'strong frontier towne of Poland', near the Russian boundary. Of his subsequent march through Poland to Dantzig we have only the briefest account; but we learn that from that port he took ship for Hull, and so reached London on 31 August 1582, after an absence of close upon two years.

In that period he had made, accompanied by no other European, a most remarkable journey, covering ground that was to a great extent unfamiliar to his fellow-countrymen. He was the first Englishman to pass down the Euphrates valley; the first (with the possible exception of the renegade mentioned on p. 41) to reach the world-renowned emporium of Hormuz; the first to traverse Southern Persia and visit Shiraz and Isfahan; the first to journey from the Persian frontier to Constantinople by way of Asia Minor; and the first to sail upon the Black Sea and travel through the Danubian countries to Poland and the Baltic. Yet small credit has been given to him for these amazing achievements, and he has not even been thought worthy of inclusion in the *Dictionary of National Biography*.[1]

It is much to be lamented that the only account we possess of this interesting journey is unsatisfactory in many respects. It first appeared, about forty years after Newbery's death, in *Purchas His Pilgrimes*, prefaced by a brief summary of the traveller's preliminary expedition to Palestine. One question in connection with the narrative is the period at which it was written. The fact that it contains a reference to Newbery's betrayal by Michael Stropene at Hormuz during his third expedition—to say nothing about two references to the wearing by children of thread or wire earrings 'after the order of India'—has given rise to the opinion that it must have been written during his third journey, either while he was a prisoner in the hands of the Portuguese or at some later date prior to his departure from Agra on his homeward way. Since he died on that journey and nothing was subsequently gleaned concerning the time and place of his death, it is clear that the document could not have been taken with him and afterwards recovered. Nor is it likely that, as has been suggested, it was entrusted either to Father Stevens at Goa, for transmission to England, or to Ralph Fitch at Agra. In the first place, if it did reach England by either channel, why was it not handed to Newbery's friend Hakluyt for publication? In the second, we cannot regard it as probable that Newbery, either as a prisoner or when travelling through India, would sit down to write or copy out an account of his Persian journey, and

[1] The *Dictionary* is very defective on the minor and even the major personalities of the period of the Elizabethan expansion, owing to its having been planned at a date when the importance of this subject was not fully recognised.

not give—what would be much more to the purpose—details of the one in which he was then engaged.

My own theory, derived from a study of the narrative itself, is as follows. In the busy five and a half months that elapsed between Newbery's return from his second journey and his departure upon the third, he did not find time to write any account of his past experiences, nor did he do so at any subsequent date. During that second expedition he had of course kept rough notes, chiefly of travel dates, prices, etc., and these he left behind when starting on his last and fatal journey. They may later have been shewn to Hakluyt (who would certainly have enquired for any information available), and he may have judged them to be too scanty for publication. Years after, however, by some unexplained means, they came into the hands of Purchas, who, recognising the great importance of the journey they described, himself wove them into a narrative, using the first person in order to keep the story in line with his other materials. In doing so, he was betrayed into employing his own knowledge of subsequent events by inserting the references to Stropene, etc., which have so completely puzzled later writers. This theory accounts for other difficulties which will occur to a careful reader of the narrative itself. Had Newbery been writing for publication, or even for the information of friends at home, he would surely have inserted from memory fuller descriptions of the important cities he had visited, and would at the same time have omitted trivial details of the prices of commodities. We can scarcely believe that he was responsible for various slips that occur, such as the confusion between certain coins and weights, or the situation of Basra in regard to the river; nor that he would have left in his text unexplained numerous Arabic or Persian terms, such as 'casder' (*qasdir*) for tin, 'non' (*nan*) for bread, 'meckhickan' (*mikhak*) for cloves, 'darchen' (*darchini*) for cinnamon, and so forth. These considerations lead me to believe that we have before us, not (as has been taken for granted) Newbery's own considered account of his journey, but a version compiled by Purchas, to the best of his ability, from the roughest materials. We are, however, none the less grateful to the reverend geographer, for, poor as the account is, it is infinitely better to have it in this state than to have no record at all.

## CHAPTER VIII

# NEWBERY REACHES INDIA

ON his return to England Newbery found that during his absence a Turkey Company had been established by royal charter and had been granted a monopoly of English trade in the Sultan's dominions. Since he was determined to follow up the results he had already achieved, he put himself into communication with the two principal members of the new Company—Osborne and Staper[1]—and it was arranged that he should head an expedition on behalf of that body in the new year. He was to be the leader of a party of six, who were to journey together as far as Baghdad. There two of them were to remain, with part of the stock of goods, while the other four went on to Basra. There again the party was to split, two merchants being deputed to trade in that city, while Newbery, accompanied by a merchant named Ralph Fitch, was to take £300 or £400 worth of stock and 'so to goe for the Indies'. Thus, in association with the new factory at Aleppo, would be established a chain of posts for mutual support. Since the services of an expert in precious stones were likely to be useful in the East,

[1] On Staper's monument—now in the church of St. Helen, Bishopsgate—he is described with some exaggeration as 'the greatest merchant in his tyme' and 'the chiefest actor in discovere [*sic*] of the trades of Turkey and East India'. There seems to be no doubt that he was more active than Osborne in promoting commerce with the East, though the latter's wealth and position gave him a certain pre-eminence.

the Company added to the party William Leeds, a gem-polisher; and a painter of the name of James Story, who was desirous 'to see the countries and to seeke his fortune', was permitted to accompany the merchants at his own expense.

Whilst preparations were being made for this momentous expedition, Newbery sought the counsel of Dr. John Dee, the geographical expert who was so prominent in most of the explorations of the period. Dee notes the visit in his diary (now in the Bodleian) under date of 9 November 1582; but apparently he did not pay much attention to what Newbery told him, for he states that the traveller 'had been in Cambaia in India', whereas we must assume that what his visitor really said was that he hoped to reach that place in his intended journey. Newbery also consulted Richard Hakluyt the younger, who lent him an extract from the writings of a Portuguese named Fernandez, and also an original letter from an English Jesuit at Goa, Thomas Stevens,[1] describing his voyage to India round the Cape of Good Hope. How useful this indirect introduction to the Jesuit himself proved will be learnt in the course of our story. Hakluyt also charged Newbery to endeavour to procure for him a copy of the

[1] Both these documents, which had been given him to copy, Newbery inadvertently carried off with him, and afterwards sent back to Hakluyt from Aleppo. Stevens, the first Englishman known to have set foot on Indian soil, had been born in Wiltshire and educated at Winchester and Oxford. Making his way to Rome, he there entered the Jesuit order. Having volunteered for service in India, he took ship at Lisbon in the spring of 1579 and reached Goa in the following October. For forty years he laboured there, dying in 1619 at the age of seventy. He was the first European to make a study of the Konkani language, and wrote two religious works, one of which, a long epic in Marathi, is still popular in Portuguese India. Though in a sense a pioneer, we cannot here treat him as such, seeing that his sole concern was with the duties of his calling, and he does not seem to have stirred outside the territory of Goa.

cosmography of Abulfeda, the Arabian geographer—a commission which the traveller did his best to fulfil, but without success.

How wide-reaching were Newbery's plans is shewn by the fact that he provided himself with letters of introduction from Queen Elizabeth, not only to the Mughal emperor of India—the great Akbar, who was addressed as 'King of Cambaia'[1]—but also to the 'King of China'. Both of these epistles recommended him to the favour of the monarch concerned, and requested the latter to recompense the pains the traveller had taken in this 'hard journey' by granting him trading privileges which would facilitate intercourse between the two nations. The second letter of course was never used; but that Newbery presented the first to Akbar at Fatehpur Sikri in August or September 1584 seems very probable. He may even have obtained from that monarch a reply and a safe-conduct throughout his dominions; but if so, these documents perished with him.

The party sailed from London in the *Tiger*[2] on 13 February 1583; but contrary winds forced the vessel into Falmouth, and it was not until 11 March that she got fairly to sea. After a preliminary storm the voyage proved prosperous, and at the end of April Newbery and his companions disembarked at Tripoli, in Syria.

[1] The kingdom of Gujarat, in Western India, was generally known as Cambaya, from the name of its principal port. It had been conquered in 1572–73 by Akbar, who had thus provided his dominions with an outlet to the western ocean. Evidently the fact that it was now possible to get into touch with that monarch's empire without infringing Portuguese rights—save their inadmissible claim to control the sea-way thither—was fully appreciated in England.

[2] 'Her husband's to Aleppo gone, master of the *Tiger*', says the First Witch in *Macbeth*—a proof that Shakespeare had read and recollected Hakluyt's great work.

After a fortnight's rest they proceeded to Aleppo, and there began their preparations for the venture to the eastward. Starting at the end of May, they followed the usual route by Bir down the Euphrates to Falluja, and reached Baghdad in safety about a month later, having suffered on the way various exactions at 'the hands of many bribeing dogs'. At Baghdad they left, as arranged, two of their number, while the rest took boat for Basra, arriving on 6 August. There John Eldred and William Shales remained, with the rest of the stock, save £400 in goods and money, which Newbery and Fitch were to take with them in their further journey.

Their first destination was Hormuz. In a letter[1] written from Baghdad, Newbery explained that 'my goinge to Ormus is more for necessitie then for any goodwill I have to the place; for I waunt [*i.e.* lack] a man to goe with me that hath the Indian tounge, the which is the only cause of my goinge thether, for to take on[e] ther. I was mynded to have gon from Balsara by sea to a place called Abowsher [Bushire], and from thence by land into the Indies; but the waunt of one to speake for me forceth me to leave that waie.' He had indeed hired at Aleppo two Nestorians, one of whom 'hath the Indian tounge and hath ben twise ther', but they were 'so lewdly geven' that they could not be trusted, and so he decided to leave one at Baghdad and the other at Basra. This scheme for making the long and unknown journey through Persia and Afghanistan into Northern India is characteristic of Newbery's cool and self-reliant daring.

The four travellers—Newbery, Fitch, Leeds and Story—embarked at Basra on their stirring adventure about the middle of August 1583, and on the 4th of

[1] Brit. Mus. *Lansdowne MS.* 241, f. 388*b*.

the following month they landed at Hormuz. A few days later, to their great astonishment and alarm, the Governor—a fresh one—had them arrested and put in prison. Newbery's old enemy, Michael Stropene, had been on the look-out for the English party, having been warned of their intentions by a letter from his brother at Aleppo. Going to the Governor, he denounced them as spies, sent to further the designs of Don Antonio, the pretender to the Portuguese throne, whose claims Queen Elizabeth for obvious reasons had shewn a disposition to uphold. It was added that the inclusion of an artist in the party was doubtless for the purpose of drawing plans of the Portuguese fortresses. In ordinary circumstances these accusations would probably have made little impression on the Governor; but Drake's visit to the Moluccas and his successful return to England round the Cape had profoundly disturbed Portuguese officialdom and disposed it to credit the English with far-reaching designs for the subversion of Portuguese supremacy in the East. The Governor therefore, while treating his prisoners with some indulgence, deemed it prudent to send them to Goa, to be dealt with by the Viceroy; and thither they were accordingly sent, arriving on 29 November 1583.

Since one of the accusations against the Englishmen was that they were heretics, the first care of the authorities was to examine them 'whether they were good Christians or no'; and as they spoke but little Portuguese, the examination was entrusted to a Dutch Jesuit.[1]

[1] Linschoten, who is our authority on this matter, says that two of the party 'spake good Dutch, as having bene certaine yeres in the Low Countreyes and there traffiked'. Which two are meant we cannot determine, but we may guess that one of them was the jeweller, Leeds, who may well have learnt his trade in Amsterdam. The other was probably Newbery himself, since Linschoten records that he had several conversations with him, and these were

The prisoners were wary, and perhaps the examiner was indulgent, for they came off with flying colours. Nor need we suspect them of insincerity in this; many Englishmen of that generation were lukewarm in their Protestantism, especially when they had lived in non-Christian countries.

Since no evidence could be found to convict the captives on the other charges preferred against them, the Viceroy, at the intercession of the Archbishop of Goa (Linschoten's employer), consented to release them on bail. Father Stevens, compassionating the distress of his fellow-countrymen, helped to find the necessary surety; and three days before Christmas Newbery, Fitch and Leeds were set at liberty, on condition that they did not quit Portuguese territory. Story had already obtained his release, for the Jesuits, who much needed the services of a painter to adorn their church, had persuaded him to enter their order as a probationer.

Newbery and his two companions, having had their stock returned to them, after depositing a sum of money with their surety as security for their observance of the conditions of their release, hired a house in the principal street of Goa and began to trade. They were in hopes that the storm had already blown over and that after a time they would be entirely freed from restraint and allowed to go home. At times, it is true, they were somewhat disturbed by warnings from their Jesuit friends that they would be deported to Lisbon at the first opportunity; but Linschoten declares that these warnings were prompted by a desire to frighten the Englishmen into following Story's example, and thus to secure their supposed wealth for the coffers of the

presumably in Dutch. If this identification is correct, we have here a new fact in our traveller's previous history.

order; and probably Newbery and his colleagues were very ready to take the same view. In any case, they seem to have been fairly confident as to the future. Newbery wrote: 'I have as great liberty as any other nation, except it be to go out of the countrey (which thing as yet I desire not); but I thinke hereafter (and before it be long), if I shall be desirous to go from hence, that they wil not deny me licence'; while Fitch, on his part, declared that 'if it please God that I come into England, by Gods helpe I will returne hither againe. It is a brave and pleasant countrey, and very fruitfull.'

Before long, however, the prospect darkened. After a few months the Englishmen were emboldened to demand that, since nothing had been proved against them, their bail should be cancelled and the money they had deposited with their surety should be returned to them. This application aroused suspicion. 'The Viceroy made us a very sharpe answere, and sayd we should be better sifted before it were long, and that they had further matter against us.' Thoroughly alarmed by these threats and by the Jesuits' warnings, the three determined to abscond. For this purpose they secretly turned most of their ready money into gems, which could be easily concealed and were readily saleable at any place of importance. Then, leaving their shop open, with its goods well displayed, they took advantage of a festival to make a seeming holiday excursion to a spot three miles out of Goa, and so easily slipped out of Portuguese territory (early in April 1584[1]) and took the road for Belgaum.

[1] Fitch, writing from memory long afterwards, put the year at 1585, and as a natural consequence dated Newbery's subsequent departure from Fatehpur Sikri as having taken place also in 1585. It is scarcely credible, however,

It was well for the fugitives that they had succeeded in escaping; for on learning of their arrival at Goa King Philip wrote to the Viceroy (February 1585), ordering him to punish them, if found guilty, and to take special care that neither they nor any of their compatriots should be allowed in Hormuz or other parts of Portuguese territory. He was informed in reply that the prisoners had escaped; whereupon he wrote again (both in 1587 and 1589), urging that efforts should be made to apprehend them and punish their abettors. In 1591 he ordered that Story, the painter—who had quitted the cloister, married, and settled down at Goa—should be sent to Lisbon. It is not known whether this order was carried out; but if so, the unlucky artist probably perished in one of the two homeward-bound vessels that were lost the following season.[1]

The three Englishmen were now in the South Indian kingdom of Bijapur, and from Belgaum they made their way to the city of Bijapur, the capital of the country.[2] Thence they made a detour to the city of Golconda, in the kingdom of the same name, famous for its diamond mines. Their object at this stage appears to have been to investigate the possibilities of the Indian markets as regards gold, silver and precious stones, using Leeds' expert knowledge as regards the last-named. From Golconda they turned north-west-

that they could have spent sixteen months in Goa, for it seems certain that the Viceroy intended to send them to Portugal by the first shipping available. Moreover, Newbery, when quitting Fitch in the following autumn, promised to meet him in Bengal in two years' time. Now, we find that Fitch actually deferred his departure from Bengal for Pegu until November 1586, no doubt in accordance with the arrangement made with Newbery. If we accept 1585 as the date of the flight from Goa, we must accuse Fitch of failing to carry out his agreement.

[1] See *The Travels of Pedro Teixeira*, pp. xxvii-xxx.

[2] Their route may be followed on the map accompanying the next chapter.

wards and, passing through Bidar and Balapur, reached Burhanpur, in the dominions of the Mughal emperor. From this city they followed the usual route to the capital by way of Mandu, Ujjain and Sironj, and thus reached Agra. Finding that the emperor Akbar was at Fatehpur Sikri, about twenty miles away, they proceeded thither, and probably, as already suggested, obtained an interview with the monarch for the purpose of presenting their sovereign's letter. Fitch's narrative, however, is provokingly meagre regarding their experiences at this period, and, although he describes the Emperor's dress and his court, he does not actually say that they had any personal communication with him.

Towards the end of September 1584 the three separated. Leeds accepted an offer of employment in the service of the Emperor, who was naturally eager to secure the services of a European expert. Newbery himself was anxious to return to England as speedily as possible, in order to report his experiences and arrange for a fresh venture. Now that the Portuguese were definitely hostile, it was evident that trade by way of the Persian Gulf was impossible, and that the only solution was to sail boldly round the Cape of Good Hope and make for Bengal, which was Mughal territory, or for Pegu, where the Portuguese had no political power. In the meantime he directed Fitch to proceed down the Ganges valley and explore the possibilities of trade in both countries, 'and did promise me,' says Fitch, 'if it pleased God, to meete me in Bengala within two yeeres with a shippe out of England'.

Accordingly, on 28 September 1584, Newbery said farewell to his two associates and set out cheerfully for Lahore on his long journey homewards. His plan was 'to goe for Persia, and then for Aleppo or Constantinople, whether hee could get soonest passage unto'. It was a reasonably safe undertaking, for there was a regular caravan route, by way of Kandahar, from India to Persia, and the latter country was already known to our traveller. But he was not destined to reach Christendom and reap the reward of his enterprise. On the way —'unknown how or where', as Purchas says—he met a lonely death. That he perished at the hands of robbers is unlikely, since merchants on that route moved only in large and well-guarded caravans; and so we may conclude that he probably fell sick of fever or dysentery, and expired at some caravanserai, with no Christian companion to cheer him. Whatever the circumstances of his death, we can but mourn the sad fate of as intrepid an adventurer as ever England bred. A pioneer, as already noted, in the exploration of Mesopotamia and Southern Persia, his crowning achievement had been to lead the first English commercial expedition to reach India; and had he survived, his enthusiasm and energy might have antedated the establishment of regular communication with that country by twenty years. It is a cruel irony that his due meed of praise has been so long withheld from him, while Fitch, his subordinate, who had the luck to survive and return to his own country, has been hailed as 'England's pioneer to India'.

## CHAPTER IX

## FITCH'S TRAVELS IN INDIA AND PEGU

UPON Newbery's departure Fitch lost no time in carrying out his instructions. Embarking on the Jumna, he floated leisurely down the stream in one of a fleet of boats to Allahabad, noting with interest the ceremonies of the Brahmans at the water's edge, and judging them to be 'a kind of craftie people, worse then the Jewes'. Continuing the voyage, he made a short stay at Benares, and was duly impressed by the busy scenes at the famous ghats there. Patna was the next place of importance that he reached; and from thence he travelled to Tanda, in the district of Malda, having spent on the river no less than five months in all, at the pleasantest time of the year. He had seen 'many faire townes and a countrey very fruitfull', and had noted at Patna the search for alluvial gold and much trade in cotton goods, sugar and opium. Tanda he found also to be a busy commercial emporium, especially for raw cotton and calicoes.

From Tanda he made an excursion northwards to Kuch Bihar, attracted probably by reports of the trade which entered India from China by way of Tibet. This occupied him for a couple of months or more; and on his return he journeyed down the Ganges to Hugli, where a Portuguese trading colony had long been established. There he was probably welcomed as a fellow-European and Christian, without trouble about

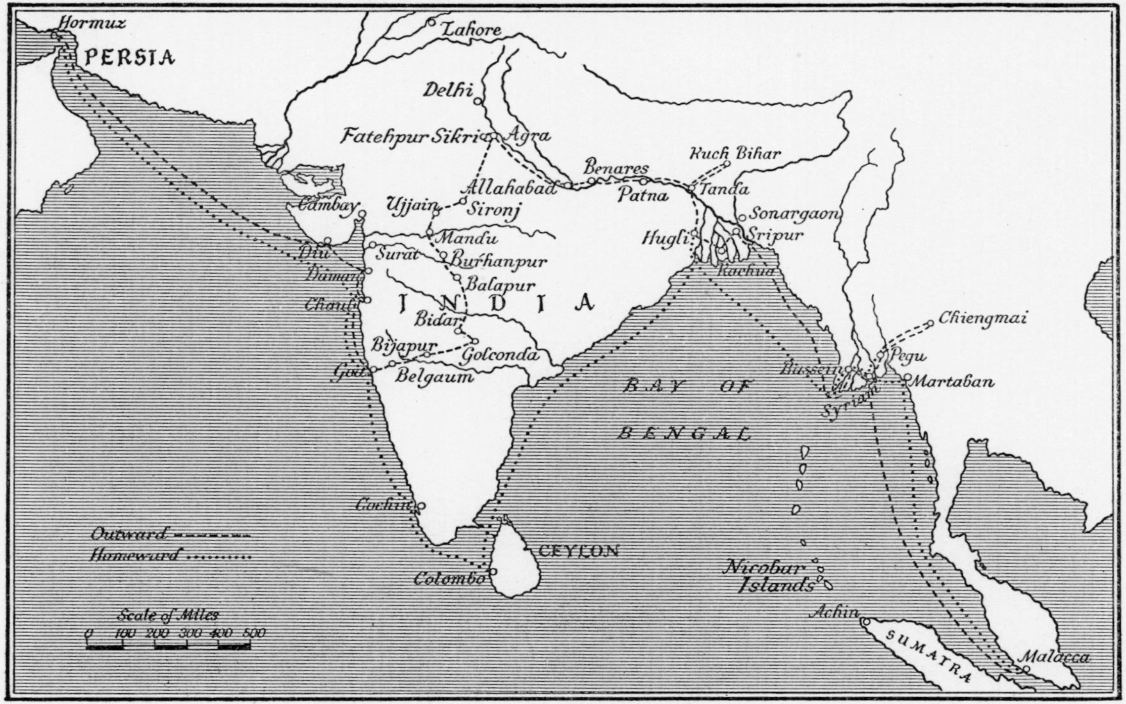

THE WANDERINGS OF FITCH

his nationality, for the Portuguese in Bengal did not recognise the authority of the Viceroy of Goa or any other official, being a law unto themselves. Evidently our traveller had no difficulty in establishing friendly relations and obtaining any help he needed. It was in a vessel belonging to one of these Portuguese traders that he afterwards voyaged to Pegu, and we may assume that it was in association with some of them that he now visited Kachua, Sripur and Sonargaon, in Eastern Bengal. Of course, during these travels, he must have been trading as opportunity offered; for, low as was the cost of living, he could not otherwise have managed on the small capital left with him by Newbery.

Thus trading and gathering knowledge—and incidentally acquiring a complete acquaintance with the Portuguese language—Fitch passed the time until the close of November 1586. Then, there being no sign of Newbery's promised return, he embarked at Sripur for Pegu. Arriving at 'Cosmin' (Kusima, the present-day Bassein), he journeyed by boat along many water-ways to the city of Pegu. Of that city and the royal court he gives a long description, as also of the methods employed for capturing wild elephants. Regarding the products of the country and its commerce with India he made minute enquiries, as was natural; and he has much to say of interest regarding the people, their religion and their customs. His next venture was an expedition to Chiengmai, in the Siamese Shan states, nearly 200 miles north-east of Pegu—a hazardous journey which he relates in his usual matter-of-fact manner. There he found supplies of copper and benzoin, and 'great store of muske, golde, silver and many other things of China worke', brought by 'many marchants out of China'. The country was fruitful, and

Chiengmai itself was 'a very faire and great towne, with faire houses of stone, well peopled'.

In January 1588 he left Pegu and sailed to Malacca, probably in a Portuguese trading-vessel. At that port he stayed seven weeks, gleaning all the information he could about its commerce with China and the Malayan Archipelago. Returning by way of Martaban to the city of Pegu, he remained there until the middle of September, and then sailed from Kusima to Bengal, where he arrived in November.

By this time he had had enough of the East, and his thoughts turned homewards. He was familiar with the Portuguese language and with Portuguese ways; and rather than undertake the long and toilsome journey through Northern India and Persia, he determined to risk the sea route to Portugal[1] by way of Cochin, in spite of the danger of his identity being discovered. So, early in February 1589, he took passage in a crowded ship bound for that port. The voyage was protracted by calms, and those on board suffered much from the heat and lack of water; but after a month at sea they reached Ceylon—'a brave iland, very fruitfull and faire'. A stay of five days having been made (presumably at Colombo), the voyage was resumed, and on 22 March our traveller found himself at Cochin. Unfortunately the last ship of the season for Europe had sailed two days earlier; and Fitch was forced to change his plans and resolve upon returning by way of the Persian Gulf. Even then he had to wait nearly eight months before he could get a passage to Goa. Staying only three days in that dangerous city, he proceeded to Chaul, where, after a delay of over three weeks, he found a vessel which carried him to

[1] This is an inference merely. Fitch's narrative is not clear as to his exact intentions.

Hormuz. Here he was obliged to wait fifty days, in great risk of his life and liberty; but he succeeded in concealing his identity, and at the end of the period got safely on board a ship bound to Basra.

It is characteristic of Fitch's cool determination to see as much as possible that, instead of taking the direct route from Basra to Aleppo, he went thither by way of Baghdad, Mosul, Mardin, Urfa and Bir. Even when he reached Aleppo, he 'stayed certaine moneths for company' before going down to Tripoli. There he found an English ship, which brought him safely to London on 29 April 1591, after an absence of over eight years.

Fitch's relatives—he was evidently a bachelor—had mourned him as dead and had already divided his estate. Just before sailing on his hazardous venture to the East, he had made a will in which he described himself as 'citizen and leatherseller of London' (meaning thereby that he was a member of the Leathersellers' Company), and mentioned a brother Thomas and a sister and niece, both named Frances. In February 1590, seven years having expired and the testator, it was concluded, having died beyond the seas, the document was duly submitted for probate and the estate was administered. The supposed dead man's reappearance, a year later, must have been a complete surprise, and possibly caused some consternation, at least to his executor.

During his 'wonderfull travailes', as Hakluyt called them, we may be sure that Fitch kept no diary. For one thing, if it had recorded in detail his doings throughout those eight years, it would have been portentously long; but probably the chief reason was that, visiting as he did so many Portuguese settlements, it would have been dangerous to have about him any incriminating documents. However, on reaching home, he was doubtless pressed by many, Hakluyt among them, to write down his recollections. This he accordingly did, and presented the narrative to Lord Burghley, the Lord High Treasurer. The traveller was evidently a poor hand with the pen, although his descriptions of the scenes that he had witnessed are often vivid. Hence he eagerly availed himself of the help offered by Thomas Hickock's English version (published in 1588) of the *Viaggio* of Cesare Federici, of whom mention has already been made. Federici's experiences had run largely parallel to those of the English traveller, and the latter to a great extent followed closely the Italian's narrative. When deprived of this support, as for instance in the case of his travels in India—about which we should have welcomed the fullest particulars—Fitch becomes disappointingly meagre and haphazard, dates being conspicuously lacking. However, in spite of all defects, his story is of absorbing interest, and Hakluyt shewed his usual judgement in making it a feature of the second edition of his *Principall Navigations*. Purchas printed it again (with one small omission) in his *Pilgrimes*; and in modern times it has been repeatedly reproduced.

As regards the prospects of further trade, Fitch's report to his employers can hardly have given much encouragement. The neutrality of the Portuguese officials at Hormuz, on which Newbery had counted, had been found to have changed into definite hostility; and no alteration of this attitude could be hoped for as long as Philip of Spain was lord also of Portugal and there was open war between him and Elizabeth. Of the extent to which the waters of the Persian Gulf and the approaches to Western India were dominated by his subjects there could no longer be any doubt; and this left the land route through Persia, of which little was known, as the only possible means of communication between India and the Levant Company's settlements. Moreover, could these difficulties be surmounted, what had India to offer? Obviously, the people in general were too poor to purchase European goods; while for broadcloth, England's prime commodity, there was little or no demand. On the other hand, the belief that the country was full of gold and silver, and that gems might be acquired at cheap rates, had now been proved to be groundless. The pepper of Southern India and the cinnamon of Ceylon could not be procured at first hand in the face of Portuguese hostility. For cotton goods there was as yet no demand in Europe; while raw cotton and indigo were bulky commodities for transport overland, and it was cheaper to buy them in Syria or Egypt than to send Englishmen to fetch them from India itself. So the Levant Company made no further move in this direction, though, as already mentioned (p. 74), it took the precaution to exclude possible competitors by obtaining in its new charter (January 1592) the extension of its monopoly to cover the trade through Turkey to the East Indies. In that charter we find Fitch named as a member of the Company.

Fitch had evidently not brought home a fortune, for ere long he was back again in the Levant. In August 1596 he was trading at Aleppo, where his fellow-merchants elected him to the post of consul when it fell vacant. This appointment had in fact been offered to him by the Company before he left London; but he had then refused it, and now accepted it with much reluctance. He did not hold it long, however, for in March 1597 the Company, while conceding that he was 'a sufficient man' for the post, cancelled the appointment and sent out another person, on the ground that election by the merchants on the spot was an insufferable encroachment upon the Company's prerogatives. Presumably Fitch thereupon returned to England, for Hakluyt speaks of him (about 1599) as 'living here in London'. On 1 October 1600 the new East India Company decided to consult him on the subject of the lading of its ships for the first voyage; and at the end of 1606 the same body referred to him for the proper titles to be used in the royal letters then being prepared for various Eastern potentates.

We hear nothing more of him until October 1611, when he executed a second and final will. This was signed on the 3rd and proved on the 15th of that month; hence his death must have occurred between those two dates. He belonged at the time to the parish of St. Katherine Cree, the church of which is in Leadenhall Street, London; but the parish registers of the period are no longer extant. If, as is likely, he was buried in that church, any monument it may have contained to his memory was probably destroyed when the building was re-erected in 1628–30. But no monument was needed to keep his memory green. His unaffected narrative, enshrined in Hakluyt's pages, is the best possible memorial to one who, in his self-reliance, enterprise and courage, belonged to the best type of England's merchant adventurers.

By the courtesy of Mr. George F. Sutton, M.A., Clerk to the Leathersellers' Company, I have been favoured with some new and interesting particulars of Fitch's connection with that body. In March 1575 he was lent (from a charitable fund established some years before to aid young members in starting business) a sum of £50 for two years, free of interest. His name occurs in a list of the 'yeomanry' of the Company who were assessed on 3 May 1585 for a payment of 5s. each. In a further assessment made in November 1587 his name is omitted; as we know, he was still in the East and, nothing having been heard of him for some years, his death was evidently assumed. In 1599–1600 he is recorded as having paid £10 to the Company as a fine for not serving the office of warden of the yeomanry, and about this time he was admitted to the livery. He was renter warden for the year 1608–9, and on 17 October 1608 was elected an assistant. From time to time his name occurs as contributing to various loans raised by the Company from its members, for an adventure into Virginia, the plantation in Ireland, and other purposes. He was elected a warden on 6 August 1611, and was sworn and admitted on the 23rd of that month; but he was dead by 21 October, when another assistant was chosen warden in his place. Fitch bequeathed to the Company a dozen gilt spoons (which are no longer in its possession), and his executor, in forwarding for that purpose the sum of £8, added £3 : 6 : 8 'for a drinking for the livery', in memory of their deceased brother. His signature appears more than once in the Company's records, and, since no other specimen of his handwriting has survived, one of these is here reproduced.

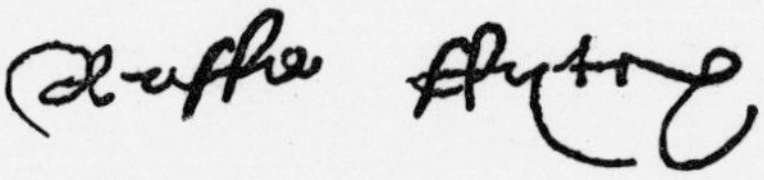

## CHAPTER X

## DAVIS SEEKS THE NORTH-WEST PASSAGE

IN following the career of Ralph Fitch we have been led into another century. We must now retrace our steps and start afresh at the year 1583, when he and his companions disappeared into the East. Until the result of their mission could be known, there was naturally no disposition to make a further attempt in that direction; while the renewed hopes of finding after all a way to China round the coasts of Russia and Siberia had been dashed by the total failure of the expedition sent out in 1580 under Pet and Jackman (see p. 45). Similarly, the ill-success of Fenton's venture accentuated the unwillingness of sober merchants to listen to schemes for a voyage by the Cape route. The political horizon was dark, for the relations between England and Spain were strained almost to breaking-point; while at the same time so tortuous was Elizabeth's diplomacy that, were she to give leave for such a trespass upon the Portuguese preserves, she was quite likely to withdraw permission at the last moment or even to sacrifice the adventurers to Philip's resentment. Moreover, the Cape voyage was known to be long and dangerous; the Indian seas were studded with Portuguese forts and ships, whose determined hostility must now be taken for granted; and finally, some doubt was felt whether the ordinary English merchantman was large enough to navigate successfully the stormy seas that washed the Cape. The vessels employed by the Portuguese were known to be of exceptional size and strength; and although Drake had made his wonderful voyage in a mere cockle-shell, it may well have been thought that he had been exceptionally favoured by fortune.

There remained the alluring theory of the existence of a passage into the Pacific round the north of America. The advocates of this solution were still sanguine, and their case had been strengthened by the discoveries made by Frobisher, who had found in moderately high latitudes two wide inlets—Frobisher Bay and the unexplored strait now known as Hudson's—leading westward, with strongly flowing currents that seemed to come from a mighty ocean.[1] In this very year (1583) Humphrey Gilbert, that enthusiastic believer in the existence of the passage, had projected a colony in Newfoundland, which he hoped would prove a half-way house, and had lost his life in the return journey. His mantle had fallen upon the shoulders of his brother Adrian, who now came forward with a scheme for making a fresh attempt to settle the question whether a practicable route into the Pacific did or did not exist. Legally the monopoly of all such ventures still belonged to the Russia Company; and consequently Adrian Gilbert's first step (March 1583) was to endeavour to enlist the aid of that body. The negotiations, however, came to nothing, and he came to a resolution to disregard any rights that they might have and to solicit a fresh grant from the Queen. He was backed by four men: Dr. John Dee, whose aid, however, was

[1] It was rumoured that the passage had actually been navigated by Cortereal, and that his discovery had been suppressed by the Portuguese for obvious reasons (*Calendar of State Papers, East Indies*, 1513–1616, p. 94).

lost in September 1583, owing to his withdrawal to the Continent; John Davis, a practical and experienced navigator, whose belief in the passage never wavered; Sir Walter Ralegh, the half-brother of the Gilberts and now an especial favourite of the Queen; and the Secretary of State, Sir Francis Walsingham. The influence of the latter two secured the issue, on 6 February 1584, of letters patent to Adrian Gilbert and his associates, 'by the name of the colleagues of the fellowship for the discoverie of the North-West Passage', authorising them to sail 'north-westward, north-eastward, or northward', in search of a passage to China and the Moluccas, and to enjoy the sole profits of any resultant trade, subject to the payment to the Crown of one-tenth of the value of any gold, silver or precious stones brought back. Ralegh further helped by inducing William Sanderson, an eminent and wealthy London merchant who had married Ralegh's niece, to provide most of the funds for the proposed voyage.

The venture was made in two tiny vessels—the *Sunshine*, of fifty or sixty tons, and the *Moonshine*, of thirty-five—Davis himself commanding the former. They sailed from Dartmouth on 7 June 1585. Greenland was safely rounded, and at the end of July Davis anchored at the entrance of a fiord on the western coast, where is now the Danish settlement of Godthaab. This harbour he named Gilbert's Sound, after the chief promoter of the expedition. From thence he shaped a course to the north-west, and on 6 August saw land on the opposite coast in latitude 66° 40′ N., and came to an anchor in an inlet which he christened Exeter Sound. Proceeding southwards from this point, he discovered an opening (Cumberland Gulf), and, 'finding it neither to wyden nor streighten', he took it to be the desired passage. But a strong wind from the north-west prevented him from exploring it, and, as the season was growing late, he turned homewards, reaching Dartmouth at the end of September. Writing to Walsingham three days later, Davis assured him that 'the North-West Passage is a matter nothing doubtfull, but at any tyme almost to be passed; the sea navigable, voyd of yse, the ayre tollerable, and the waters very depe'.

A second expedition was quickly fitted out, consisting of the same two vessels as before, together with a larger ship, the *Mermaid* (120 tons), of which Davis took command, and a tiny pinnace called the *North Star*. A start was made on 7 May 1586. On reaching 60° N. latitude, the *Sunshine* and *North Star* were detached, under Captain Richard Pope, to examine the eastern side of Greenland and search for a passage in that direction. Davis himself, with the other two vessels, pushed up the western coast to a point near his previous anchorage in Gilbert's Sound. There a pinnace, which had been brought out in sections, was put together and launched; and then the voyage was resumed up the Greenland coast. On 2 August a harbour was found at Sukkertoppen, in 66° 30′ N. In order to save expense, Davis decided to send home the *Mermaid* and to continue his explorations in the *Moonshine*, the smaller vessel. She was accordingly repaired and revictualled, and then, leaving her consort preparing for the homeward voyage, on 15 August she weighed anchor and set out across the strait now known by Davis's name. The northern headland of Cumberland Gulf was quickly reached; but bad weather once again prevented the examination of that inlet, and Davis found himself forced to proceed along the coast southwards. A short stay was made in a Labrador roadstead, and on

1 September the homeward voyage was resumed. After coasting along the northern part of Newfoundland and suffering much from a furious storm, the *Moonshine* arrived at Dartmouth about the beginning of October. On the 4th of the same month the *Sunshine* likewise returned. Together with the pinnace she had sailed north-eastwards until Iceland was reached. After a stay of a few days in one of the ports of that island, the two vessels made for the east coast of Greenland, only to be baffled by extensive ice-fields. Skirting southwards along these, Cape Farewell was rounded, and they followed the land northwards until they arrived at Gilbert's Sound (3 August), only to find that Davis had already left. After visiting two other places on the Greenland coast, Captain Pope, at the end of August, commenced the voyage homewards. A few days later the *North Star* was lost sight of in a severe storm, and though the *Sunshine* waited a whole day, she 'could heare no more of them'. The rest of the voyage was uneventful.

Writing to William Sanderson from Exeter on 14 October 1586, Davis declared: 'I have now experience of much of the north-west part of the world, and have brought the passage to that likelihood as that I am assured it must bee in one of foure places, or els not at all. And further, I can assure you, upon the perill of my life, that this voyage may be performed without further charge, nay, with certaine profite to the adventurers, if I may have but your favour in the action.' The profit in view seems to have been from the sale of seal skins, of which the *Sunshine* had brought home a good cargo, of fish, abundance of which had been found by the *Moonshine*, and perhaps of whale oil and furs. As regards the 'foure places' which might prove to be the long-sought passage, these appear to have been Davis Strait, Cumberland Gulf, Frobisher Bay and Hudson Strait; and, as Sir Clements Markham has pointed out,[1] two of them —the first and the last—have been proved by modern research to provide actual routes into the Pacific.

The meagre results of the first two expeditions so discouraged the West Country merchants that they refused to take any part in the fresh venture on which Davis had set his heart. But Sanderson continued steadfast, and by his influence, backed by Walsingham and the Lord Treasurer, sufficient funds were secured in London to set out three vessels, the *Elizabeth*, the *Sunshine* and a pinnace of about twenty tons, called the *Ellen*. Of these the two larger vessels were to devote themselves to fishing, while the pinnace was to be 'for the discoverie'. The three sailed on 19 May 1587, and reached Gilbert's Sound on 16 June. There, as already arranged, the *Elizabeth* and the *Sunshine* were detached to fill their holds with fish, while Davis himself pushed northwards along the coast of Greenland. On 30 June he found himself in latitude 72° 12′ N., the most northerly point he was destined ever to reach. Here the sea to the northward and westward was quite open; and Davis named a lofty cliff 'Sanderson his Hope', as a token that there was every reason to suppose that by this route the passage would be found. Further progress, however, was prevented by a strong northerly wind, and so a course was set across the strait. The progress of the *Ellen* was checked by a great ice-field which she encountered; but she persevered until the western shore was sighted. Turning southwards, the pinnace made her way to Cumberland Gulf. This was now thoroughly explored and proved to be land-locked.

[1] *John Davis*, p. 69.

Then, regaining the open sea, Davis passed down the coast and on 12 August reached an island on the Labrador littoral, to which the name of Darcy was given. After vainly searching for the other two vessels at the appointed rendezvous, on 15 August he 'shaped a course for England in God's name', and arrived at Dartmouth in safety a month later.

Davis, still confident, reported to Sanderson that he had 'bene in 73 degrees, finding the sea all open, and forty leagues betweene land and land. The passage is most probable, the execution easie;' and later he wrote, in his *Worldes Hydrographical Discription* (1595): 'by this last discovery it seemed most manifest that the passage was free and without impediment toward the north'. But the times were unpropitious for an immediate renewal of the search. England was threatened by a mighty fleet known to be preparing in the ports of Spain; and every ship and every seaman was needed for the great struggle, in which Davis worthily played his part as commander of a small vessel named the *Black Dog*. In these years of turmoil and stress no room was left for peaceful exploration, and Davis had to turn to other fields of employment. He had, however, the satisfaction of knowing that he had accomplished much more in the Arctic regions than any of his predecessors, especially as regards detailed and accurate survey of the coasts, and that he had thus prepared the way for others more fortunate than himself in their opportunities.

CHAPTER XI

# THE TWO VOYAGES OF CAVENDISH

THOMAS CAVENDISH or Candish (as he was generally styled), a scion of the well-known family of that name, was born in 1560, and at the early age of twenty-five supplied and commanded a ship in Sir Richard Grenville's Virginia voyage, the colonising aims of which did not preclude a certain amount of privateering in the West Indies at the expense of the Spaniards.

A year later Cavendish planned an expedition into the Pacific, on the model of Drake's famous achievement. There was no difficulty in procuring either funds or men for a voyage that promised rich booty, and the youthful adventurer sailed from Plymouth in July 1586 with three vessels under his command. These were the *Desire* (140 tons), the *Content* (60) and the *Hugh Gallant* (40), manned by crews totalling 123, and victualled for two years. Sierra Leone was reached in about a month, and eleven days were spent there in procuring provisions and water. After a visit to one of the Cape Verde Islands, the fleet proceeded to the coast of Brazil, where a stay was made of three weeks near the island of S. Sebastiano, which lies about 120 miles south-west of Rio de Janeiro. Sailing again on 23 November, they anchored a few weeks later in a Patagonian harbour to which Cavendish gave the name of Port Desire, after his flagship. There they trimmed and repaired their vessels, and then put once more to sea. On 6 January 1587 they entered the Strait of Magellan, and next day took off a Spaniard who was one of the few survivors of the colony of 400 left there by Sarmiento three years earlier. The navigation of the strait occupied them until 24 February, on which day they emerged into the Pacific. Sailing slowly up the coast of Chile, they reached a bay a little to the northward of Valparaiso. While there, a watering party was surprised by the Spaniards and twelve of its number were killed. At Arica two small barks were plundered and a larger vessel was burnt. Several other ships were captured as the squadron passed up the coast, and in May the town of Payta, in Northern Peru, was sacked and burnt. The island of Puna yielded some further booty; but here a dozen men were lost in a skirmish with a Spanish force. Not long after leaving the island, Cavendish emptied and sank his smallest vessel, there not being sufficient men surviving to navigate all three. The remaining two crossed the equator on 12 June, and on the first day of July the coast of Costa Rica came into sight. Soon after this a ship was captured, in which was found a French pilot, whose services proved of great advantage. The ship itself was only in ballast, and was promptly set on fire; while the same fate befell a small vessel captured the next day, on an errand to warn the coast towns of their danger. Raiding and plundering, Cavendish passed along the Mexican littoral, and in the middle of October reached the Cape of S. Lucas, which is the southernmost point of the Californian peninsula.

Off this conspicuous headland the two English vessels hovered for three weeks, keeping a vigilant lookout. From the captured pilot Cavendish had learnt that a great and rich Spanish ship from the Philippines, the *Santa Anna*, was shortly due and would make the cape her landfall. On 4 November a cry arose aboard the *Desire* (which was alone at the time) that a sail was in sight; and soon it was evident that the coveted prize was within grasp. By the afternoon she was overhauled and attacked. Apparently she carried no heavy guns; but nevertheless her crew and passengers, three times as numerous as their assailants, put up a stout resistance. There could, however, be but one issue to such a contest; and after a gallant resistance of five or six hours, the Spanish captain, finding his ship riddled by the English ordnance and ready to sink, surrendered on a promise that the lives of the crew and passengers should be spared. The prize was taken into a harbour on the coast, where the Spaniards were set ashore, with a supply of provisions, and the vessel itself was rummaged and burnt, together with most of its cargo, for which no room could be found in the English ships. The booty included a large quantity of treasure, and the division of this produced a mutiny, which was with difficulty quelled. Some of the prisoners Cavendish took with him; among them a Portuguese, named Nicholas Roderigo, who had lived in China, Japan and the Philippines, and from whom may have been obtained the large map of China mentioned by Hakluyt as having been brought home by Cavendish. A still more valuable prize was the Spanish pilot of the *Santa Anna*, who proved quite willing to guide the Englishmen to the Philippines, secretly hoping that there they would fall into the hands of the Spaniards and he would regain his liberty.

On 19 November the signal was given for departure 'homewardes towardes England'—across the Pacific in the track of Drake. Cavendish's ship, the *Desire*, was soon bowling along with a fair wind from the east-north-east; but her consort, the *Content*, was slow to leave the anchorage, and so, says Pretty, 'we lost her companie and never saw her after'. Week succeeded week as the *Desire* held on her course across the lonely ocean; and then at last, on 3 January 1588, Guam, one of the Ladrone Islands, was sighted. Here provisions were obtained from the natives, who swarmed round the vessel in their canoes with such persistence that they had in the end to be driven off by musket shots. Eleven days later the *Desire* reached the Philippines. The Spanish pilot had prepared a letter, to be smuggled ashore, in which he warned his fellow-countrymen at Manila of the arrival of an English ship and urged an attack. Informed of this by Roderigo, Cavendish acted with stern promptitude, and next morning the corpse of the Spaniard was swinging from the yard-arm. After tarrying some time to take in wood, water and fresh provisions, Cavendish resumed his voyage. Passing through the Philippine archipelago to the south of the great island of Luzon, he then turned south and made for Java. There is some doubt as to the exact course followed, but it would appear that the *Desire* went through the Macassar Strait, between Borneo and Celebes. On 1 March she passed between 'Java Major' and 'Java Minor' (Bali?),[1] and soon afterwards reached a safe anchorage on the south-west coast of Java, believed to have been Wijnkoopers Bay. At this spot Cavendish remained until the middle of March, provisioning his ship for the long voyage home; and then he set a course for the Cape of Good Hope. Nine weeks

[1] Linschoten (Hakluyt Society's edition, vol. i, p. 112) says that Cavendish traversed the Straits of Sunda, between Sumatra and Java; but his authority is doubtful. The track given in Hondius' map of the world (*c.* 1595) goes round the eastern side of Java.

later that famous headland was safely passed, and on 8 June 1588 the *Desire* had the good fortune to sight the island of St. Helena, at which no English ship had hitherto touched. Here it was found that a homeward-bound Portuguese fleet, richly laden, had been missed by twenty days; but as some consolation the new-comers obtained plenty of fruit and fresh meat. After the ship had been cleaned and revictualled, the voyage was resumed. Early in September a Flemish vessel, met near the Lizard, imparted the joyous news of the rout of the Spanish Armada; and on the 9th of that month, after riding out a terrible tempest, 'by the mercifull favour of the Almightie we recovered our long wished port of Plimmouth'. Thus was completed what Hakluyt terms an 'admirable and prosperous voyage . . . round about the circumference of the whole earth'. In a letter addressed to Lord Hunsdon, Cavendish boasted that he had burnt and sunk nineteen ships; had fired and plundered all the Spanish towns at which he had touched; had captured a galleon which was 'one of the richest of merchandize that ever passed those seas'; had obtained intelligence concerning China 'such as hath not bene heard of in these parts'; had ascertained that trade might be freely had in the Moluccas; and, finally, had discovered the island of St. Helena, 'where the Portugals use to relieve themselves' on their homeward voyage. It was indeed a remarkable achievement, especially for so young and so inexperienced a seaman: a feat worthy to be ranked with that of his great predecessor, Drake, and equally favoured by fortune.

The success of Cavendish inspired John Chudleigh of Exeter, a friend of John Davis, to undertake a similar voyage to the South Seas in 1589. This he attempted with three ships and two pinnaces, which left Plymouth on 5 August. The venture proved disastrous, for only two of the vessels succeeded in getting (separately) as far as the Strait of Magellan. Chudleigh died there, with many of his men; whereupon the disheartened survivors set sail for England. Similarly, the crew of the other vessel, the *Delight*, after enduring great misery in the strait, insisted upon returning home. By the time the English Channel was reached, only six men were left alive, and they were forced to anchor near Cherbourg at the end of August 1590. Here a storm drove the ship on shore, where she became a total wreck.

In September of this same year (1590) John Davis headed an equally unsuccessful expedition towards the East Indies. Whether he intended to try the Cape route, or to imitate Cavendish in passing through Magellan's Strait, is not certain. The vessels employed were the *Samaritan* of Dartmouth and a small pinnace; and among those taking part were Randolph Cotton, who afterwards served in Cavendish's second voyage, John Jane (Davis's friend and the chronicler of his voyages) and John Sanderson, whose journal is our only authority. Ill-fortune attended the adventurers throughout. They had several fights with Spanish vessels, in one of which the *Samaritan* was severely damaged. Off Madeira a storm separated her from the pinnace, and it was learnt afterwards that the latter had sunk, though her crew were rescued by another English ship. Davis's own vessel was now so leaky that he had no option but to return, and he was glad to get her safely into Falmouth in February 1591.

Cavendish himself was naturally eager to repeat his success;[1] and in August 1591 he sailed from Plymouth

[1] Robert Parke, in his dedication to Cavendish (dated 1 January 1589) of his translation of Mendoza's *History of China*, says that the explorer was

'for the South Sea, the Philippinas, and the coast of China', with 'three tall ships and two barkes'. He had enlisted the services of John Davis, by promising him facilities for exploring the North-West Passage from the Pacific side; and that experienced seaman took charge of Cavendish's old flagship, the *Desire*. Cavendish himself commanded the *Leicester*, Randolph Cotton the *Dainty*, and a Mr. Cock the *Roebuck*. The remaining vessel was a small one, called the *Black Pinnace*. After a tedious voyage, at the end of November the squadron reached the coast of Brazil, near Cape Frio. The town of Santos was assaulted and taken, in the hope of getting a supply of provisions; but in this they were disappointed. Departing on 24 January 1592, the fleet was soon dispersed by a heavy storm. Cavendish had neglected to appoint a rendezvous; and so Davis made for Port Desire, thinking that his consorts would probably be found there. On his way he picked up the *Roebuck* in a very distressed state. At Port Desire they were joined, after a time, by the pinnace, and finally by the *Leicester*. The *Dainty* had given up the voyage and returned to England. Cavendish, who seems to have become quite unbalanced as the result of his ill-success, now left the *Leicester*, inveighing against all on board her, and took up his quarters with Davis in the *Desire*.

After a brief respite the squadron put once more to sea, and on 8 April, after much bad weather, arrived at Magellan's Strait. Pushing through, they with difficulty reached a cove forty leagues from the outlet into the Pacific, and there they were forced by 'extreeme stormes' to remain until 15 May, short of food and

even then 'preparing againe for the former voyage'. It is worthy of notice that Parke emphasises the benefits likely to accrue to the English cloth industry from the opening up of trading relations with China (by way of the Philippines) as the result of Cavendish's enterprise.

suffering much from the bitter cold. Davis, with his heart set upon the discovery of the North-West Passage, was desirous of persevering; while the men, eager for Spanish spoil, were likewise ready to go on. Cavendish, however, thoroughly discouraged, proposed to turn back and try to make his way into the East Indies by the Cape route. Davis, backed by all the leading members of the expedition, dissuaded him from this mad course, pointing out that the ships were in bad condition, short-handed, and almost destitute of stores and provisions. They could not, however, induce him to continue the voyage into the Pacific, and, going aboard the *Leicester*, he gave orders to make once more for Santos, in Brazil. He was still in a bad humour, and on 20 May at night he altered the course of his own vessel without warning, and by the morning was out of sight. The *Roebuck* also lost company with the remaining two ships.

Davis, concluding that Port Desire was the most likely place in which to find Cavendish, proceeded thither, accompanied by the *Black Pinnace*. After waiting in vain until 6 August, and refitting both vessels as best he could, he persuaded the men to go once again for the strait, in the hope that their missing consorts would be found there. A storm drove them far out of their course to some then unknown islands, which have since received the name of the Falklands. An easterly wind enabled them to recover the entrance of the strait on 18 August, and they pressed on until they were nearly through. After waiting a fortnight for Cavendish and losing many men from the cold, they went out into the Pacific to seek a warmer spot where they might refit. Bad weather drove them back into the strait; and although another attempt was made, during which the

*Black Pinnace* foundered in a storm, on 10 October they were forced to abandon the enterprise, re-thread the strait, and take refuge in Port Desire. On 22 December, having revictualled the ship with salted penguins, they set out for home. The voyage was a terrible one. The dried penguins on which the crew depended for food corrupted in the heat of the tropics; while scurvy was so rampant that at last only Davis himself and one boy remained in good health. When, on 11 June 1593, the ship staggered into Berehaven, on the south-west coast of Ireland, the survivors were so weak that they could not take in sail without the aid of the local fishermen. From thence Davis and a few others went in a fishing-boat to Cornwall, leaving the rest of the crew to guard the vessel until she could be fetched away.

Meanwhile, what had become of Cavendish? As to this, we have but scanty information. He soon picked up the *Roebuck* and both vessels then made for the Brazilian coast. Twenty-five men were slain by a sudden Portuguese attack at the bay of St. Vincent; while an attempt to force a landing at Espirito Santo was defeated with the loss of twenty-five more. Thereupon the crew of the *Roebuck* insisted upon sailing for England. Cavendish vainly tried to induce his own men to go to Magellan's Strait once more; and it was with reluctance that they agreed to seek St. Helena and there refit. The *Leicester* got within two leagues of the island, but could not fetch it, owing to contrary winds. Cavendish then endeavoured to find Ascension, and, missing this, made towards the Cape Verde group. When last we hear of him, his ship was in 8° N. latitude, and he was seriously ill. Probably he died a few days later; but we know nothing for certain, and only infer (from the fact that his farewell letter reached its destination) that the

*Leicester* managed somehow to get to an English port.

It was a sad end to a brilliant career, stained, it is true, by many unworthy actions, yet leaving Cavendish the imperishable glory of having been the second Englishman to circumnavigate the globe. That feat at once recalled and rivalled Drake's great achievement; and it had lasting results. Cavendish's visit to the Philippines shewed how weak was the power of Spain in those vast regions, and excited hopes of getting into touch with China by way of those islands. His return round the Cape gave great encouragement to the advocates of that route. And finally, his call at St. Helena made known to his fellow-countrymen the advantages of that half-way house as a place of refreshment, and was the first link in the chain of events that led to the annexation of the island by Great Britain.

## CHAPTER XII

## LANCASTER PENETRATES TO THE EAST INDIES BY THE CAPE ROUTE

WE have mentioned (p. 110) some of the reasons which appear to have deterred the merchants of London, in pre-Armada days, from favouring an attempt to reach the East by way of the Cape of Good Hope. Before long, however, this attitude underwent a change. The defeat of the Spanish invaders in 1588 gave a great impulse to the spirit of enterprise; the definite outbreak of war had removed some of the political difficulties, and at the same time had narrowed the field of commerce, thus making it urgent to seek fresh markets; while, as regards the route itself, Cavendish's return by that way in a tiny vessel seemed to shew that its dangers had been exaggerated. We may add that the failure of Davis's attempts to find a North-West Passage had damped for the time being all expectations that an easier route to the East would be found in that direction.

It is therefore with no surprise that we discover, in October 1589, a group of London merchants petitioning for encouragement in a project for trying the possibilities of trade with the East by way of the Cape. They pointed out that, without interfering with the Portuguese or Spanish settlements, it should be feasible to open up communication with many rich kingdoms and ports, from Calicut in India itself to China and the Philippines. 'Great benefitte', they said, 'will redound to our countree, as well for the anoyinge of the Spaniards and Portingalls (nowe our enemyes) as also for the ventinge of oure comodities (which, since the beginning of thes late troubles, ys muche decayed), but especially our trade of clotheinge; of which kinde of comodities, and others which our countree dothe yeald, no doubte but a lardge and ample vente wil be founde in those partes.' They proposed to fit out the *Merchant Royal*, the *Susan* and the *Edward Bonaventure* with two or three pinnaces, to be ready by the following December; but they required the issue of a royal warrant that the ships should not be stayed for any reason, and that any booty secured should be quietly enjoyed, subject to the payment of the usual customs dues. Further, they prayed for a commission for the leader of the expedition, to enable him to govern effectually the sailors and soldiers employed, who (as we have seen) were prone to take matters into their own hands when tired of the voyage. Unfortunately, the names of the memorialists are not given, though, from the fact that the ships mentioned were all engaged in the Levant trade, we may safely conclude that the merchants concerned in this new project were interested in that traffic. We are equally ignorant of the answer returned to their petition; but, as no such expedition took place in 1589 or 1590, it would appear that something intervened to discourage the promoters.

In 1591, however, the plan came to fruition. The vessels actually chosen for the task were the *Penelope*, the *Merchant Royal* and the *Edward Bonaventure*, which had already figured in Fenton's voyage. The leader (or 'general', as he was then termed) was George Raymond, of whom we only know that he had distinguished himself in the fight against the Spanish Armada. The

*Merchant Royal* was under the charge of Samuel Foxcroft, who seems to have died early in the voyage; while the *Edward Bonaventure* was commanded by James Lancaster, who had lived in Portugal for several years and knew the language. He had been captain of the same vessel during the Armada struggle, and was therefore well acquainted with her capabilities. As regards the objects of the expedition, we may note that no attempt seems to have been made to trade, and probably, therefore, little cargo was carried, the space thus saved being devoted to stores and the accommodation of extra men. Mention is made of many 'soldiers' as being on board, and prize-taking was kept in view throughout. We conclude, therefore, that the main purpose was a reconnaissance, for the purpose of finding out where trade might be had; while in the background was the hope that sufficient booty would be forthcoming to pay the expenses of the venture.

The ships left Plymouth on 10 April 1591, and made their first landfall at the Canaries. They next sailed in a south-westerly direction towards Brazil, and after crossing the line were fortunate enough to capture a Portuguese caravel which yielded a welcome supply of provisions. In 26° S. latitude a change of wind enabled them to shape a course for the Cape of Good Hope, which was reached at the end of July. Weather conditions being unfavourable and many of the sailors being down with scurvy, Raymond decided to put into Table Bay. After a stay of about a month, preparations were made for departure. Since, however, the mortality in the fleet had been very serious, it was determined to send back the *Merchant Royal*, with fifty men in her, and to distribute the rest of her complement between the other two ships.

After taking in water and provisions the *Penelope* and *Edward Bonaventure* proceeded on their voyage, doubled the Cape, and had got up the south-eastern coast as far as Cape Correntes when 'a mighty storme and extreeme gusts of wind' fell upon them. 'This evening', says one of those on board the *Edward*, 'we saw a great sea breake over our admirall, the *Penelope*, and their light strooke out; and after that we never saw them any more.' Four days later the *Edward*, sadly pursuing her lonely path, was struck by lightning and four of her men were killed and many others injured. Notwithstanding, she continued on her way to Conducia Bay, a little to the northwards of Mozambique, and thence to the Comoro Islands, which had been fixed as the rendezvous in case of separation. There she waited several days, in the hope of being joined by her consort; and then, there being no sign of the missing vessel, Lancaster gave the signal for departure. He had procured a welcome supply of provisions; but on the other hand he had lost the master and sixteen men, who had been surprised and massacred by the natives.

The next place touched at was the island of Zanzibar, where a halt was made from November 1591 to February 1592. Having procured a good supply of fish and other provisions and repelled an attack made by a Portuguese galley, Lancaster laid a course for Cape Comorin, where it was hoped to repay their enemies in kind by capturing some of their vessels bound for Goa. Contrary winds and currents, however, carried the ship so far to the northwards that Lancaster determined to seek either the Red Sea or the island of Socotra, 'both to refresh ourselves and also for some purchase' (*i.e.* booty). But a sudden change of wind enabled him to resume his course for the southern end of the Indian peninsula.

Since we are expressly told that the Indian coast was not sighted, we must conclude that the *Edward* really went round the southern point of Ceylon. From thence she made for the Nicobars, in the hope of obtaining supplies, which were urgently needed. The weather, however, was bad and the master of the ship was out in his reckoning, with the result that the first landfall made (1 June 1592) was the island of Gomez, about three leagues off the north-western point of Sumatra. Failing to obtain a pilot for Achin, they continued their voyage eastwards, and soon arrived at the island of Penang, off the western coast of the Malay Peninsula. There they stayed until the end of August, awaiting the change of monsoon and collecting what food they could procure. Sickness was still rampant among the crew, of whom no less than twenty-six died during this halt; only thirty-four were left, and of these one-third were still unfit for labour. Early in September a fresh start was made. During the stay at Penang four Pegu vessels had been held up. One of them proved to contain a quantity of pepper belonging to some Portuguese, and this was confiscated; the other vessels were released unmolested. Captain Lancaster now stood down the Malacca Strait to the Sembilan Islands (lat. 4° N.), in order to intercept Portuguese shipping using that route. Before long, a vessel from Negapatam, laden with rice, fell into his hands and was emptied and released. On 6 October another Portuguese ship, this time from Goa, was taken and plundered. Then, fearing lest a squadron should be sent from Malacca to attack him, Lancaster decided to go to Junkseylon, an island off the west coast of the Malay Peninsula, in latitude 8° N., and there trim his ship and seek supplies.

On leaving this spot, the *Edward* proceeded westwards to the Nicobars, where a welcome supply of fresh fruit was procured from the inhabitants; and then on 21 November she set sail for Ceylon, which was sighted about 3 December. Rounding the southern point of the island, Lancaster anchored near Point de Galle, intending there to lie in wait for Portuguese shipping bound from Bengal or Pegu to Goa. His men, however, were by this time thoroughly sick of the hardships of the voyage and roundly declared that 'they would take their direct course for England'; and the captain, who was 'lying very sicke, more like to die then to live', was constrained to agree, loth though he was to lose 'all hope of so great possibilities'. On 8 December, therefore, the *Edward* sailed for the Cape of Good Hope. She sighted the African coast in February 1593 and, after being held up for four or five weeks by contrary winds, she rounded the Cape and reached St. Helena (3 April). In a stay of nineteen days the sailors to some extent regained their health and a store of provisions was laid in. On leaving the island Lancaster endeavoured to make for Brazil; but his men, now quite out of hand, insisted upon a direct course for home. This brought the vessel into the Doldrums, where for about six weeks no progress was made; many men fell sick, and the shortness of rations nearly led to a mutiny. In desperation the captain steered for Trinidad. This island was unwittingly passed in the night, and the *Edward* found herself embayed in the neighbouring Gulf of Paria, on the coast of Venezuela; but after struggling for eight days, she succeeded in getting out again. Sailing northwards, she reached the island of Mona, which lies between Puerto Rico and Hayti. Here she fell in with a French ship, which spared her some victuals. Lancaster now decided to make for Newfoundland, where English vessels would doubtless be met with; but a storm drove the *Edward* along the southern coast of Hayti. Passing between that island and Cuba, and then between Cuba and the Bahamas, she made her way through the Florida Channel into the Atlantic and resumed her voyage northwards.

However, after getting as far as the neighbourhood of the Bermudas (17 September), a fresh storm was encountered, which deprived the ship of her foremast and filled her with water. Her victuals were 'utterly spent', and her crew had no other course open to them than to run before the wind to Hayti or some neighbouring island. A short stay at some islands[1] near Puerto Rico gave them water and turtles; and here five of the scanty crew insisted upon remaining ashore, despite all persuasions. Sailing again, the *Edward* reached with difficulty her old anchorage at the island of Mona (about 20 November). Lancaster, with eighteen men, landed to search for provisions, of which they were entirely destitute; whereupon those left aboard (five men and a boy) cut the cable and allowed the ship to drift away. The marooned men endured great hardships for nearly a month, when they managed to attract the attention of a passing vessel, which proved to be from Dieppe. Lancaster and twelve of his companions were taken off, and were divided between their rescuer and another Dieppe ship which had appeared on the scene. Of the seven men who remained on the island, two met with accidental deaths, three (as related below) were slain by the Spaniards, and two were rescued by an English vessel. Lancaster and his men remained aboard the French ships until, after spending about two months in trading on the coast of Hayti, they turned

[1] Referred to as 'the Nueblas or Cloudie Islands'.

homewards and reached Dieppe on 19 April 1594. There Lancaster and his lieutenant, Edmund Barker (our chief authority for the voyage), procured passages for Rye, landing in England on 24 May 1594, after an absence of well over three years.

The fate of the *Edward Bonaventure* is a question of some importance. Sir John Laughton, both in his notice of Lancaster in the *Dictionary of National Biography* and in the notes to his *Defeat of the Spanish Armada* (vol. ii, p. 337), asserted that she returned to England with a valuable cargo. So far as I am aware, the only possible ground for thinking so is the undoubted fact that in 1600–2 a vessel of that name was trading in the Levant; but the repetition of names was quite common, and on investigation we find that the later *Edward Bonaventure* was of 160 tons, as against the 250 of Lancaster's ship. What really happened is scarcely open to doubt. A crew of six was manifestly incapable of navigating the vessel home, and evidently they only managed to get her to Hayti, where she fell into the hands of the Spaniards. This appears from Barker's statement that, of the seven men left behind on the island of Mona at the time of the rescue of Lancaster and his companions, 'three were slaine by the Spaniards which came from Saint Domingo [*i.e.* Hayti], upon knowledge given by our men which went away in the *Edward*'. Further, as regards the fate of the vessel, we have the direct statement, in the account given in Hakluyt of Lancaster's subsequent voyage to Brazil, that she was 'cast away' at Mona; while Purchas explicitly declares that she was 'driven away and lost, not far from Mona'.[1] In the face of these statements, we can only conclude that, of the three ships employed in this memorable voyage, only the *Merchant Royal* re-

[1] *Pilgrimes*, ed. 1625, vol. iv, p. 1825.

turned to England, and she brought home nothing but sick men. The loss of life had been extremely heavy; the booty obtained (and then lost) had been inconsiderable; and the whole of the capital invested had been dissipated. The result was that, despite the fact that Lancaster had penetrated into the Indian seas as far as the Malay Peninsula without effective hindrance on the part of the Portuguese, the promoters were too discouraged to follow up the attempt.

Lancaster himself was nothing daunted by his experiences, and within five months of his return was again at sea with five vessels, provided by London merchants, for a raid upon the Portuguese possessions in Brazil. After taking several prizes near the Canaries, he entered into a partnership with four other English vessels under a Captain Venner. Then, steering for Pernambuco, he stormed the town, and held it until the merchandise which it contained could be safely transferred to the ships. The booty included the rich lading of a carrack which had been cast away in the roads in returning from the East Indies, and the amount was so great that it not only filled the English fleet but left a surplus which Lancaster induced some Dutch and French ships to carry to England on freight terms. This done, the town was evacuated and the squadron sailed for England, arriving safely in the Downs in July 1595. Lancaster was thus richly rewarded for his previous sufferings and losses, and no doubt it was in this way that he laid the foundation of the fortune which, increased by his later voyage to the East, was afterwards devoted to charitable uses.

## CHAPTER XIII

## WOOD ATTEMPTS TO REACH CHINA

THAT the merchants who had provided the funds for Lancaster's ill-fated expedition of 1591–94 should have shewn no inclination to repeat the experiment is easily understood, in view of the losses which they had incurred. We have also to remember that the energies of English seamen were largely absorbed at this time by the naval operations against Spain, notably by the raid upon Cadiz in 1596 under Lord Thomas Howard and the Earl of Essex, and that for such expeditions it was customary to requisition the assistance of the largest and strongest merchantmen available. This of course reduced the number employed in actual trading, and made it more difficult to spare any for the purpose of exploration.

Meanwhile evidence of the great value of the trade between Goa and Lisbon was steadily accumulating. In 1587 Drake, after his successful foray upon the Portuguese and Spanish coasts, fell in, near the Azores, with a homeward-bound Portuguese carrack named the *San Filippe*, and captured her 'without any great resistance'. The value of her cargo was over £108,000. 'This', says Hakluyt, 'was the first carak that ever was taken comming foorth of the East Indies; which the Portugals tooke for an evil signe, because the ship bare the Kings owne name.' He adds that 'the taking of this carak wrought two extraordinary effects in England:

first, that it taught others that caracks were no such bugs but that they might be taken . . . and secondly, in acquainting the English nation more generally with the particularities of the exceeding riches and wealth of the East Indies; whereby themselves and their neighbours of Holland have bene incouraged (being men as skilfull in navigation and of no lesse courage then the Portugals) to share with them in the East Indies, where their strength is nothing so great as heretofore hath bene supposed'. Five years later (1592) another great carrack, the *Madre de Dios*, was waylaid and captured (also near the Azores) by a squadron under Sir John Burgh. She proved to be laden with all manner of oriental wares, to the value of over £140,000. The pious narrator of the action, as reported in Hakluyt, considered its fortunate result to be an instance of 'Gods great favor towards our nation; who, by putting this purchase [*i.e.* prize] into our hands, hath manifestly discovered those secret trades and Indian riches, which hitherto lay strangely hidden and cunningly concealed from us; whereof there was among some few of us some small and unperfect glimse onely, which now is turned into the broad light of full and perfect knowledge. Whereby it should seeme that the will of God for our good is (if our weaknesse could apprehend it) to have us communicate with them in those East Indian treasures, and by the erection of a lawfull traffike to better our meanes to advance true religion and His holy service.' Among the treasures captured was an account in Latin of the kingdom of China and its riches, printed at Macao in 1590. This volume, which was 'inclosed in a case of sweete cedar wood and lapped up almost an hundredfold in fine Calicut cloth, as though it had beene some incomparable jewell', came into the hands of Hakluyt, who afterwards printed a translation of it in his second edition of the *Principall Navigations*. The carrack herself, when taken into Dartmouth, became an object of much curiosity, as being 'farre beyond the mould of the biggest shipping used among us, either for warre or receit', her burden being estimated at not less than 1600 tons. These two sensational successes were followed by a third, which, although it did not bring any material gain to the English, at least inflicted great loss upon their enemies. In June 1594, near the same spot, another huge carrack, the *Cinco Llagas*, was encountered by three ships set out by the Earl of Cumberland. She made an heroic fight of it and, catching fire, was burnt to the water's edge, to the great disappointment of her assailants.

Although, as we have seen, the merchants of London hesitated to make further attempts to establish direct trade with the East, there were others who were sufficiently enterprising to plan in 1596 a voyage to China, by way of Magellan's Strait and the Philippines, in imitation of Cavendish's ventures. Sir Robert Dudley, son of Queen Elizabeth's favourite, was the principal promoter of the scheme, and the execution was committed to Benjamin Wood. The latter was, as Hakluyt tells us, 'a man of approoved skill in navigation'. He had taken part in the expedition of Amadas and Barlow to Virginia in 1584, and in the voyage to the Azores set out by Ralegh two years later. In 1592 we hear of him as being off Cuba, in command of four ships despatched by Lord Thomas Howard. More recently, he had accompanied Dudley in his West India expedition of 1594–95; while (what was more to the purpose) he had been master of one of the vessels employed in Chudleigh's venture of 1589 (see p. 121), and thus had already been as far as Magellan's Strait on the intended route. Two London merchants, Richard Allen and Thomas Bromefield, were engaged as supercargoes, and were furnished with a letter in Latin from the Queen to 'the Great Emperor of China', of which a copy, together with an English version, will be found in Hakluyt's second edition. It is there dated 11 July 1596, though a copy of the original Latin text, preserved in the Public Record Office, gives the date as the 16th of that month.

The three vessels employed were the *Bear*, the *Bear's Whelp* and the *Benjamin*. Of these the first-named was of 200 or 300 tons, while the other two were much smaller. Presumably they left England soon after the date of the royal letter; but unfortunately no detailed account of the voyage is extant. In January and February 1597 they were found on the coast of Barbary and later at the Canaries by a pinnace sent out to Guiana by Ralegh in 1596. So much we learn from Thomas Masham's account, wherein it is expressly stated that Wood was bound 'for the straights of Magellan and China'. After that we have no intelligence of the fleet from any English source. Hakluyt, writing about 1599, could only say that the ships, 'we do suppose, may be arrived upon some part of the coast of China and may there be stayed by the said emperour, or perhaps may have some treacherie wrought against them by the Portugales of Macao or the Spaniards of the Philippinas'. Purchas, a quarter of a century later, imagined that he had discovered some particulars of 'the miserable perishing of the fleet' in an extract from a Spanish letter dated at Puerto Rico on 2 October 1601 (N.S.), which he found among Hakluyt's papers. This document relates the fate of four Englishmen who had reached an island near Puerto Rico, and who were the sole survivors of three ships which had plundered three Portuguese vessels in the East Indies. Of these men, three were stated to have been murdered by some Spaniards who believed them to be possessed of valuables, while the fourth managed to escape to Puerto Rico. It is clear, however, that Purchas was mistaken, for it is obviously impossible that these were survivors of Wood's ship. The story may relate to part of the crew of the *Edward Bonaventure* in Lancaster's disastrous voyage—perhaps those who remained at the 'Nueblas' (see p. 133); but here the discrepancy of dates presents some difficulty.

What appears to be the real story of the voyage has been painstakingly elucidated by the late Mr. Donald W. Ferguson.[1] Quoting from Dutch and Portuguese sources, he shewed that Wood abandoned his intention of going through Magellan's Strait and in lieu thereof followed Lancaster's track round the Cape and up the eastern side of Africa. One of the smaller vessels—probably the *Benjamin*—was lost off the Cape or soon after, and in July 1597 the remaining two were seen passing the Portuguese fortress of Mozambique. A squadron was fitted out and sent in pursuit, but failed to overtake them. The English ships, after watering, like Lancaster, at Conducia Bay, proceeded across the Indian Ocean and (probably in October) reached the coast of India at some point below Goa. They then went down as far as Ceylon, where they captured and plundered two Portuguese merchantmen bound from Goa to Bengal to lade rice. Next, possibly after a cruise in

[1] In his introduction to *The Travels of Pedro Teixeira* (Hakluyt Society, 1902), pp. xliii-lxi, and in an article contributed to the *Geographical Journal* in March 1903.

the Bay of Bengal, they made for the Malacca Strait in search of further booty. They arrived early in January 1598, and in the same month were encountered by a Portuguese fleet. Thereupon a skirmish began, which lasted for eight days without decisive result. Wood's two ships then retired to Old Kedah, on the west coast of the Malay Peninsula, in order to refit. He had now only sufficient men left to work one of his vessels, and therefore he emptied and burnt the smaller. The *Bear* resumed her course northwards, only to be lost off Martaban, or, according to another account, to be stranded and wrecked on the island of Butung, near Kedah. Seven of the survivors (four Englishmen, two negroes and a Frenchman) secured a canoe, in which they trusted themselves to the sea and finally reached the island of Mauritius, then uninhabited. The negroes, being detected in a plot to carry off the boat, threw themselves overboard to escape punishment. The four Englishmen decided to continue their voyage from Mauritius, and were never heard of again; while the Frenchman remained on the island for twenty months, and was taken off in 1601 by a Dutch vessel that happened to call there.

Such was the unfortunate end of Wood's expedition. As will be seen, he had followed closely in the wake of Lancaster, with even less success. In each case the voyage was unduly prolonged, regardless of the fact that the ships of the period, not being double-sheathed, deteriorated rapidly in tropical waters; there was a lack of reserve ship's stores, and an insufficient supply of provisions; while the crews were overcrowded, with the result that the losses from sickness were heavy. These defects, however, were all remediable; and on the other hand there was some encouragement in the fact that the Portuguese had entirely failed to intercept or punish the raiders of their preserves. An optimist could still maintain that little need be feared from enemy action, and that there were no insurmountable obstacles in the way of a successful voyage, if made under a skilful leader and in ships of a good size, suitably equipped.

This view was soon confirmed by the experience of the Dutch, who now appeared on the scene as competitors for Eastern trade. After the fall of Antwerp in 1585 its place as a distributing centre for American and East Indian produce (brought from Seville and Lisbon in Dutch bottoms) had been largely taken by Amsterdam; but the war still raging between King Philip and his revolted subjects of the Netherlands had closed, at least to a considerable extent, the ports of Spain and Portugal to Dutch trade. In these circumstances it was natural that the idea of opening up direct communication with the East should occupy the attention of the merchants of Holland, who were of course in close touch with London and followed with deep interest the attempts made by English navigators to attain that object. In 1592 a company for this purpose was formed at Amsterdam and began the study of ways and means. At first the old idea of finding a north-eastern passage round Asia was entertained, as promising a comparatively short route, entirely free from the danger of hostile action. The result was seen in a series of determined efforts made in that direction during 1594–96, under the leadership of Willem Barentszoon. But these, while yielding some extended geographical knowledge of the regions round Spitzbergen and Novaia Zemlia, had no further success; and the death of the gallant leader discouraged any continuance of the endeavour.

Meanwhile attention had been directed afresh to the

Cape route by the issue of two works by Jan Huyghen van Linschoten. One of these is a book of sailing directions for Eastern waters, based upon the practice of the Portuguese navigators; the other the famous *Itinerario*, which provided full information regarding the Portuguese possessions in the East. Linschoten, after spending six years at Goa, had returned to Holland in 1592, and had thereupon devoted himself to the task of persuading his fellow-countrymen to send ships to the East, particularly to those regions, such as the Malay Archipelago, where the position of the Portuguese was weak. The consequence was the celebrated expedition under Cornelis de Houtman, who, sailing in the spring of 1595, returned safely, with three out of his four ships, in the summer of 1597. He had succeeded in reaching Bantam, the great pepper port on the north-west coast of Java, where he had been heartily welcomed and had made a commercial treaty with the authorities. True, he had lost one of his ships and two-thirds of his men; while the small cargo brought home failed to pay the expenses of the venture. But he had shewn the way, and had opened up illimitable possibilities of future commerce; and this was enough to inflame the enthusiasm of his fellow-countrymen. At once new companies were formed in various towns, with the result that no less than twenty-two ships left Holland in 1598 for the East, followed by nearly double the number during the next three years. It was believed that the enterprise and skill of Dutch merchants and mariners had solved the problem at which their English rivals had worked so long with scant success. The threat to England's Levant trade was patent; and after some hesitation steps to counter it were taken by the merchants of London.

CHAPTER XIV

# THE FOUNDATION OF THE EAST INDIA COMPANY

IF the merchants of London were slow to imitate their Dutch rivals in making use of the Cape route to the East, it is not difficult to conjecture their reasons. Trade was very depressed at this period, particularly about 1596–97, owing to a series of bad harvests. Moreover, many of those who were chiefly interested were engaged in the Levant traffic, and naturally would have preferred to see the trade in pepper and spices keep to that route rather than to follow it into fresh channels. Probably they hoped that the Dutch success would prove to be a mere flash in the pan; and certainly the very moderate results obtained by Houtman's fleet of 1595–97 gave them a fair excuse for waiting to see how the fleets of 1598 would fare, before committing themselves to action. The answer came in July 1599, when four ships of the eight sent out under Jakob Corneliszoon van Neck returned to Holland richly laden; while soon a rumour spread that the Dutch were buying ships in English ports for a further and greater effort. Clearly the time had come for English merchants to endeavour to secure a share in the new commerce or else relinquish all hope of competing in the pepper and spice trade. Moreover, it was well known that the death of Philip II in September 1598 had disposed the Queen and her advisers to seek a termination of the long war with Spain; and since the question of prohibiting the English from trespassing further upon the Portuguese preserves would inevitably arise in any negotiations for peace, it was clearly advisable to peg out a claim beforehand. After striving so long to establish a direct trade with the East, it would indeed be hard if the prize should be carried off by the Dutch and the merchants of England should be barred by treaty from competing with them.

In passing we may note that the interest taken in the subject of Eastern trade was shewn by the appearance in 1598 of an English translation of Linschoten's great work—a project urged upon the publisher, a year earlier, by Hakluyt, whose keen eye had at once detected the importance of the information which it contained. Hakluyt himself, we find, took a lively interest in the new venture and was indefatigable in furnishing information to its promoters. He was rewarded by a gift from the new company of £10, together with an additional sum of 30s. for maps which he had provided.

Allusion should perhaps be made to the statement of some modern writers that the formation of the East India Company was directly due to the fact that the Dutch had raised the London price of pepper from 3s. to 6s. and 8s. the pound. The germ of this story is to be found in Stow's *Chronicle*,[1] where, under the year 1597, he records that 'this yeare pepper was sold for eight shillings the pound'. Anderson, in his *Origin of Commerce*,[2] developed this statement into a theory that 'our own Turkey merchants first, and the Dutch East India Company next', kept up the price at 8s., and that this determined Queen Elizabeth 'to enter her people directly upon a commerce to East-India'. Later, David

[1] 1611, p. 403.

[2] 1764, vol. i, p. 449.

Macpherson[1] placed the whole blame for the increased price upon 'the monopolizing avarice' of the Dutch, and declared that this provoked the merchants of London to renew their attempts to obtain supplies at first hand. The story is of course absurd in alleging that this was the determining factor in the establishment of the East India Company, though a retail price of 8s. a pound for pepper may well have encouraged the advocates of direct intercourse with the sources of supply.

We are on firm ground with the first volume of Court Minutes of the new company. It begins with a list, dated 22 September 1599, of subscriptions for 'the pretended [*i.e.* intended] voiage to the Easte Indias'. This list was headed by the Lord Mayor (Sir Stephen Soame, who was a member of the Levant Company) and a number of the aldermen, and amounted to the large sum of £30,133 : 6 : 8—equivalent to about £300,000 in modern currency. A meeting of the subscribers was held two days later, and it is interesting to note that, of the fifty-seven persons named as attending (amongst others), one-third at least can be identified as connected with the Levant Company. Their object was declared to be 'for the honour of our native cuntrey and for th' advauncement of trade of merchaundize within this realme of England', to 'set forthe a vyage this present year [*i.e.* before Lady Day following] to the Est Indies and other the ilandes and cuntries therabouts', provided the Queen's permission could be obtained. Fifteen 'Comitties or Directours' were elected (seven of whom were members of the Levant Company), together with two treasurers; and it was resolved to solicit Her Majesty for a grant of 'sole priviledg . . .

[1] *History of the European Commerce with India*, 1812, p. 77.

for soe manie yeres as can be obteyned and for such ymmunyties and freedomes of custome and other tollerations and favors as may be gotten'. On 25 September it was more definitely decided to submit a petition to the Privy Council, asking that the adventurers should be incorporated, 'for that the trade of the Indias, being so farre remote from hence, cannot be traded but in a joint and a unyted stock' (in contrast to the Levant Company, which was a 'regulated' body). They further requested that a monopoly of the trade should be granted to the new company; that it should be allowed freedom from customs for the first six voyages; that permission should be accorded to carry out foreign money; and that a guarantee should be given that the ships of the first voyage, when ready, 'be not staied uppon anie pretence'.

At first the omens seemed favourable; the Lords of the Council received the petition graciously and 'promysed ther furtheraunce to Her Majestie for the obteyning' of the desired privileges. But soon these hopes were dashed. A deputation summoned to attend the Council on 17 October, 'to receave Ther Honors order for our further proceadinge', returned with the news that the impending negotiations with Spain had proved a fatal stumbling-block; for the Council refused to give any assurance that the voyage would be permitted, it being held 'more beneficiall for the generall state of merchaundize to enterteyne a peace, then that the same shuld be hindred by the standing with the Spanishe comissioners for the mainteyning of this trade to forgoe the oportunety of the concluding of the peace'. Upon this clear intimation of the Queen's attitude the adventurers decided to 'proceade noe further in the matter for this yere'.

Although Elizabeth and her advisers had deemed it necessary to keep their hands entirely free, it soon became evident that they fully appreciated the importance of obtaining direct access to the Eastern markets and were determined not to yield to Spanish or Portuguese pretensions in this respect. After some delay the negotiations for peace commenced at Boulogne in the early summer of 1600. The English commissioners had been furnished with a memorandum drawn up on behalf of the merchants interested in the subject, together with a report thereon by Fulke Greville, the treasurer of the navy. These documents gave particulars of the many regions in the East which were not under the control of either Spain or Portugal, and to which (it was held) the English had every right to trade if they so desired. In June the commissioners asked for specific instructions on the point of English voyages to the East Indies, and were told in reply not to yield to any restrictions in that respect, but rather to press that the subject should be passed over in silence, as had been done in the recent French treaty with Spain. In the following month the negotiations broke down completely, ostensibly on a question of precedence.

The way was thus cleared for the renewal of the East India project. In the middle of September 1600 the Privy Council wrote to the leaders of the movement, urging them to proceed and assuring them that the desired privileges would be granted and that their ships would be allowed to sail without hindrance. Thus encouraged, the former subscribers were called to a meeting at Founders' Hall[1] on the 23rd of the same

[1] Situated at the north end of Founders' Court, in Lothbury (which runs along the northern side of the Bank of England). The hall was destroyed in the Fire of 1666.

month. They assembled 'in full and ample number', and unanimously resolved to 'goe forward in the said viage'. Its management was entrusted to seventeen 'Committees', of whom eight had been members of the body elected a year before. Among the new-comers we may note the names of James Lancaster, John Eldred (the former traveller, now Treasurer of the Levant Company) and Alderman Thomas Smythe (the Governor of that association). The close connection between the two companies is further emphasised by the fact that Richard Wright, Smythe's chief assistant, acted as secretary to both; while the volume containing the earliest minutes of the East India Company includes also a number of letters written on behalf of the Levant Company.

The Committees set immediately to work. Their first recruit was our old friend John Davis, who had just returned from a voyage to Achin and the Malay Peninsula as pilot-major in Houtman's second fleet, which left Holland in the spring of 1598. He was an obvious choice for a similar post in the expedition now under preparation, and he threw himself heartily into the work of fitting out the fleet. For the position of 'General' or chief commander the Lord High Treasurer (Lord Buckhurst) recommended the engagement of Sir Edward Michelborne, who had served in the Low Countries and was a friend of the Earl of Essex. But the Committees in reply begged to be allowed 'to sort ther busines with men of ther owne qualety . . . lest the suspition of the imployment of gents . . . do dryve a great number of the adventurers to withdrawe ther contributions'; and they decided unanimously to give the post to James Lancaster. Four ships were purchased from various owners and put into dock to be refitted;

and since time was pressing, a barrel of beer a day was provided 'for the better holding together of the workemen from running from ther worke to drinke'. Arrangements were at the same time made for the purchase of provisions and stores, and also of merchandise, consisting of manufactured woollens, iron, tin and lead. Moreover, as it was recognised that these would not suffice for the acquisition of return cargoes, enquiries were set on foot in all directions for rials of eight—the Spanish coins which were in general currency throughout the East.

With an eye to the future a draft charter was drawn up and submitted to the Privy Council. At a general meeting held on 28 October it was announced that the patent was already in the hands of the Attorney-General for completion, and it was resolved that the name of Alderman Smythe should be submitted for inclusion therein as the first Governor of the Company. At the same time, in order to comply with the provisions of the patent, additional Committees were elected to make up the number to twenty-four. The actual date of the charter was 31 December 1600, and nine days later it was read to the members at a meeting convened for that purpose. By its terms the existing adventurers, and others whom they should afterwards admit, were granted a monopoly of the trade for a period of fifteen years, subject to determination by the Crown at an earlier date should this be deemed expedient. They were incorporated by the title of 'The Governor and Company of Merchants of London Trading into the East Indies', and were granted the privileges usual in such cases; the management was put into the hands of a Governor and twenty-four Committees, to be elected yearly; freedom from customs on exports was granted for the first four voyages; goods imported might be exported (within thirteen months) without paying further duties; foreign silver coin or bullion might be carried out, to the value of £30,000 yearly, provided that a fifth part of this should have been coined for the purpose in the royal mint;[1] and finally, subject to exception in cases of special emergency, a guarantee was given that six ships and six pinnaces would be allowed to sail each year without hindrance.

No reference was made in the charter to any capital; and the statement, sometimes made, that the Company started with such and such an amount of capital is based upon a misapprehension. As a corporate body it possessed no capital. It was merely an association of individuals who had been granted, collectively, a monopoly of the trade with the East, and the provision of the means of carrying on that trade was left to be arranged by the members themselves. In point of fact, the necessary funds were raised by a succession of voluntary subscriptions among the members, at first for special 'Voyages', and later for 'Joint Stocks' operating over long periods. Each 'Voyage' or 'Joint Stock' kept its accounts separate from the rest, and was in time wound up and the profits distributed. A member of the Company might be interested in several of these ventures, or he might refrain altogether from subscribing. What he could not do was to trade to the East on his own account, since it had been decided that all trading must

[1] In accordance with this provision, the first fleet carried out a supply of coins specially struck (now known as 'portcullis money'), intended to be equivalent to the rial of eight and its subordinates. It was found, however, that so unfamiliar a currency was not acceptable in the East; and for later expeditions the Company procured from time to time exemption from the requirement. For the story of this curious experiment see my *John Company*, p. 62.

be on co-operative principles and under the supervision of the governing body.

The financing of the first voyage gave much trouble. In the first flush of excitement money was freely promised; but when it came to paying up the calls, several of the subscribers drew back, alleging that the ships would certainly be stayed for political reasons. Thereupon the Committees applied to the Privy Council, who renewed their assurances that no such action was to be feared, and ordered that the names of the recusants should be submitted to them. The veiled threat doubtless had some effect; but on 9 January 1601 it was reported that the outlay upon the voyage had already exceeded the receipts by £4000 or £5000, and it was consequently determined to call for ten per cent. more from each subscriber. Two days later an order was made by the Privy Council that, unless the 'persons refusers' paid their overdue contributions by the following Saturday, they should be committed to prison. On 10 February it was found necessary to levy a further ten per cent., making up the original £200 share to £240. Notwithstanding, on the 6th of the following month it was announced that the Company owed about £9000 and that the arrears came to nearly £7000. Recourse was again had to the Privy Council, who on 10 April ordered the defaulters to appear before them, to be punished for their 'obstinacye and perversenes'; and this was followed up on the 28th by the issue of a warrant for the commitment of four persons to the Marshalsea, unless they paid within four days. In the end these recalcitrants appear to have made good their obligations; though three others (including Sir Edward Michelborne) were disfranchised for failing to pay their subscriptions.

The amount actually spent upon the first expedition cannot be determined with absolute accuracy. The account given by Purchas of the first voyage says that the stock subscribed was £72,000. On the other hand, the list of 'bills of adventure' (*i.e.* share certificates) given at the end of the first court-book yields a total of £63,460. This, however, goes only to April 1602, and therefore takes no notice of the subsequent calls made on account of Weymouth's voyage to the north-west. An account compiled in 1620 states that the amount actually received from the adventurers was £68,373, whereof £21,742 was sent out in money and £6860 in goods, while £39,771 was spent on shipping, stores, etc. On the other hand, a statement drawn up at the East India House in 1654 gave the total subscribed for the first voyage as only £57,473 : 6 : 8. It is possible that this figure represents merely the original subscription, apart from the twenty per cent. subsequently levied. Making this adjustment, and allowing a few hundreds for defaults, we reach a result agreeing roughly with the 1620 figure, which may be taken as substantially correct.

CHAPTER XV

## THE COMPANY'S FIRST VOYAGE

THE fleet which now set out for the East numbered five vessels in all. Lancaster's flagship (on board of which was John Davis) was the *Red Dragon*, which had been bought from the Earl of Cumberland for £3700. She had been specially built for that nobleman in 1595, for use in the raids he was making upon the Spaniards in the West Indies and elsewhere; and the Queen, in launching her, had given her the name of *The Scourge of Malice*—an appellation which, now that she was bound upon a more peaceful errand, her new owners changed to *The Red Dragon*.[1] Her tonnage was variously estimated at from 600 to 900 tons. When bought, her armament consisted of 38 guns; and her crew numbered about 200. Her three consorts were the *Hector* (300 tons and 108 men), the *Ascension* (260 tons and 82 men) and the *Susan* (240 tons and 88 men); these three had been employed for some time in the Levant trade, and each was armed with 24 guns. All four vessels, it may be noted, had had their bottoms coated with cement, in order to preserve them from worms. In addition, a small victualler, named the *Gift*, was sent to carry additional stores and provisions; this, when the fleet had been out five months and had consumed

[1] This title may possibly have been suggested by Cumberland himself, who had possessed, some years previously, a vessel bearing that name.

enough of its own stores to take in her lading, was emptied and turned adrift.

The ships left Woolwich on 13 February 1601, but were so delayed by contrary winds that it was not until early in April that the Channel was left behind. The first landfall was at the Canaries; after which, keeping in their ignorance too close to the African coast, they fell into the Doldrums and were becalmed for a whole month. A captured Portuguese vessel provided a welcome supply of provisions; but when at last (9 September) Table Bay was reached, the crews had been so ravaged by scurvy that Lancaster had to send his own men aboard the other ships to work them into the roadstead. The reason why the *Dragon's* complement was in a comparatively healthy state was that Lancaster had dosed them regularly with lemon-juice; and it is strange that his discovery of the value of this fruit as an antiscorbutic was largely ignored by subsequent navigators.[1]

After a stay of seven weeks, the fleet put once more to sea. Since leaving England more than a fifth of the men had died; but the rest were in good health and a plentiful supply of provisions had been secured. After running along the eastern side of Madagascar, contrary winds and a fresh outbreak of scurvy forced them to anchor in Antongil Bay, on the north-east coast of that island. Here they remained from Christmas Day until 6 March 1602. Then their eastward course was resumed, and about two months later they reached the Nicobar Islands. After staying for three weeks to trim their ships and take in water, etc., a fresh start was made; and on

[1] It was certainly used in the Third and Fifth Voyages (*Court Minutes*, 3 February 1607 and 13 February 1609), and probably therefore in the Second and Fourth.

5 June the fleet anchored in the road of Achin, at the northern end of the island of Sumatra.

The Dutch had already stationed some factors at that port, and these at once came on board to welcome the English General and invite him to take up his abode in their house. Having done so, Lancaster sent word to the King, Ala-uddin Shah, that he had brought him a letter from 'the most famous Queene of England', and solicited an audience. This was granted, and the royal letter was delivered with all due ceremony, accompanied by some valuable presents provided by the Company. The King, who regarded the activities of the Portuguese as threatening the existence of his state, was delighted at the arrival of the English, and readily agreed to grant them facilities for trade, including exemption from all customs dues. In one respect Lancaster was disappointed; he found that, owing to a bad season in the preceding year, pepper was scarce and therefore expensive. Anxious to lose no opportunity of filling his ships, he sent the *Susan*, under the charge of Henry Middleton, to Priaman, on the west coast of the island, where pepper and spices were said to be more plentiful.

The goods procurable at Achin itself had not so far sufficed to fill even one of the remaining ships; and Lancaster accordingly decided to try whether further cargo could be secured at the expense of the Portuguese vessels using his old hunting-ground, the Straits of Malacca. In this scheme he was willingly abetted by the King, who at once agreed to detain a Portuguese envoy then at his court, lest he should give warning at Malacca of the intentions of the English. The result of the foray was the easy capture of a great vessel from San Thomé, on the eastern coast of India, and the transfer to the

English ships of a large quantity of calicoes and other merchandise. Then, feeling 'much bound to God, that had eased him of a very heavy care', Lancaster returned to Achin (24 October 1602). After receiving from the King his reply to the Queen's letter and a return present, he departed with his three ships on 9 November. Two days later the *Ascension*, fully laden, was despatched to England; while the *Dragon* and the *Hector* made their way to Priaman, where they found the *Susan* lading pepper and spices. Instructing Middleton to complete his cargo as quickly as possible, and then to follow the *Ascension*, Lancaster passed on, threaded the Straits of Sunda, and on 16 December dropped anchor at Bantam, on the north-west coast of Java.

Bantam, which for long afterwards continued to be the headquarters of English trade in the Malay Archipelago, was a flourishing centre of commerce at this time, having not only a large exportation of pepper grown in the neighbouring districts but also a considerable transit trade from all parts of the East. It had a numerous Chinese colony and was a regular resort of junks from that country. Thus it was in all respects superior to Achin, both for the sale and for the purchase of goods. The reigning monarch was a minor, and the actual administration was in the hands of a protector. Lancaster presented to the King a letter from Queen Elizabeth and a number of valuable articles, and in response obtained permission to trade freely, and to leave a number of merchants 'to settle a factorie [1]

[1] At this period the term 'factory' denoted either (1) a group of merchants established at a foreign centre for regular trading, or (2) the building in which they dwelt and carried on business. The practice was very ancient, and was an inevitable outcome of the trading conditions then prevalent. While in general use throughout Europe (familiar examples are the Hanse factories in London and Bergen), in the East the maintenance of such 'factories' was

against the returne of the next shipping out of England'. A brisk sale of the new-comers' wares (including the captured piece-goods) resulted, and sufficient pepper was obtained to lade both ships. The goods yet unsold were left in the hands of a body of factors, together with a pinnace in which an attempt was to be immediately made to reach the Banda Islands and there procure a stock of spices for the next fleet. Then, after receiving from the boy king a letter to Queen Elizabeth, 'with many kind countenances and good words', on 20 February 1603 Lancaster departed for England.

A voyage of seven months, mostly through tropical seas, in a ship of those days, must have been a trying experience, even under the best conditions. But when the ship had been two years out and her spars and rigging were worn and unreliable; when her men were few and sickly, and her provisions both scanty and stale; when she was full of loose pepper, which permeated all parts of the vessel: the discomfort must have been almost unendurable. All that was needed to crown the unhappiness on board was bad weather; and this the *Dragon* and *Hector* had in full measure. As the two vessels approached the Cape a furious storm fell upon them, with the result that they 'were so shaken that they were leakie all the voyage after'. A few days later, in another tempest the *Dragon* lost her rudder, and 'drave up and downe in the sea like a wracke, which way

indispensable as a condition of profitable commerce. The arrival of a foreign ship, with a cargo which must of necessity be disposed of, and a return cargo purchased, within narrow limits of time, simply invited combinations on the part of the local merchants to force down prices in the one case and to raise them in the other. The only remedy was to keep agents on the spot all the year round, to sell their own goods as opportunity offered, and to purchase the produce of the country at the appropriate season, and hold it in readiness for the next ship.

soever the wind carried her'. The mizen mast was taken down and put overboard as a means of steering; but it pounded the stern so heavily that it had to be hastily withdrawn. It was then cut up and converted into a rudder, which a brief interval of calm enabled the crew to fix. In a few hours, however, this substitute was unshipped, and all but two of the rudder-irons were carried away. In despair his men now crowded round Lancaster, demanding that the ship should be abandoned and that they should all take refuge in the *Hector*, which was loyally standing by. But the General would not hear of any such course, declaring that he would 'yet abide Gods leasure, to see what mercie He will shew us', and that he was confident of saving both ship and goods. Fearing lest his crew should endeavour to enforce their demand by open mutiny, he determined to send away his consort; and going down into his cabin, he wrote two letters. One was to the Company, saying that he would do his utmost to save the *Dragon* and her cargo, despite the sore straits in which he found himself;[1] the other was to the master of the *Hector*,[2] ordering him 'to depart and leave him there'. The master, however, 'was an honest man and a good man, and loved the Generall well, and was lothe to leave him in so great distresse'. Therefore, when next morning Lancaster looked out over the waste of waters, to his amazement he saw the *Hector* in attendance as usual. 'These men regard no commission', was his comment; but he made no further attempt to enforce

[1] He added that 'the passage to the East India lieth in 62½ degrees by the north-west on the America side'. This suggests that the difficulties and delays of the Cape route had convinced him that the discovery of a north-west passage was the only satisfactory solution.

[2] Alexander Cole. He was drowned in Table Bay on the outward voyage of the next fleet.

their departure, and soon a period of calm weather enabled a temporary rudder to be fixed. The two ships now made for St. Helena, which to their great joy was sighted on 16 June. Here they stayed nearly three weeks, refitting the vessels as best they might and laying in a stock of provisions. The rest of the voyage was uneventful. Passing by Ascension, the Cape Verde Islands and the Azores without attempting to touch at any of these places, the pair reached the Downs on 11 September 1603. The *Ascension* had got home in the preceding June, and the *Susan* had also arrived in safety.

The venture had been a success, in so far that all four ships had returned with full ladings; but financially the results of the great expenditure which had been incurred were scarcely satisfactory. The loss of the Court Minutes from the middle of 1603 to the end of 1606 leaves us nothing to rely upon save scattered references, and from these we glean that the position was one of great difficulty. The money subscribed for the voyage had all been spent; and when the *Ascension* arrived in the Thames, £2000 had to be borrowed before her mariners could be paid off; while some of the leading members of the Company had to give their personal bonds to the customs officials before the cargo was released. It might be thought that the sale of the goods brought home offered a ready solution of the difficulty. This, however, was by no means easy. With the accession of James I had synchronised a more than usually virulent outbreak of plague in London, and trade was at a standstill. The home market was in any case a limited one; while exportation offered small prospect of relief, seeing that the Dutch had equally large or larger stocks to dispose of. From the *Ascension* alone were landed 210,000 lb. of pepper, 1100 lb. of cloves, 6030 lb. of cinnamon and 4080 lb. of gumlac. When the cargoes of the other three ships were added, the problem of finding buyers for such huge quantities must have seemed almost insuperable. In this dilemma the Company resolved that the only suitable course was to divide the pepper among its members by way of dividend, at the rate of 2s. a pound. The result was that the ensuing competition to sell drove down the price to 1s. 2d., and some of the adventurers could not get rid of their stock of pepper for six or seven years.[1]

To complicate matters further, the royal exchequer had on hand a large mass of pepper (probably the result of the capture of a Portuguese carrack in the previous year[2]); and in November 1603 the Lord Treasurer wrote to the Company intimating that an embargo was intended on the sale of all other pepper until His Majesty's stock was disposed of. In reply, the Committees declared that such a course would raise a clamour, both among the adventurers and among the still unpaid sailors, and would utterly ruin the prospect of a second voyage being undertaken. A further proposal from the Lord Treasurer that both stocks should be sold *pari passu* was rejected as impracticable, as so much of the Company's pepper had already been divided; and we gather that in the end matters were left to take their course.

Since we take our leave of Lancaster at this point, it may be well to record a few facts regarding his later life, to supplement those given in the *Dictionary of National Biography*. The value of his achievement was recognised by the bestowal upon him of a knighthood (2 October

[1] *Court Minutes*, 29 August and 8 October 1623.

[2] See Monson's *Naval Tracts* (Navy Records Society), vol. ii, appendix C.

1603), probably upon the occasion of his presentation to King James of the letters brought from the Kings of Achin and Bantam. Although he now retired from active service, he continued to take the liveliest interest in the Company's concerns. The loss of some of the Court Minutes volumes prevents us from ascertaining the extent of his participation in the direction; but we find him acting as a Committee in 1606–7 and again in 1617–18, and in other years he was frequently consulted in cases of difficulty. He was a strong supporter of schemes for the discovery of the North-West Passage, as is witnessed by the name of Lancaster Sound, given by Baffin to an inlet discovered by him in 1616. Concerning his private life at this period we know little, save that he resided in a large house, with garden, situated on the eastern side of Bevis Marks, backing on the city wall.[1] It had been originally a hospice for aged priests, and was then known as the Papey; this was suppressed at the Reformation and the house became a private dwelling, numbering among its subsequent tenants Sir Francis Walsingham. In February 1612 Lancaster was nominated as alderman for Cordwainer Ward, but failed to secure election. His death occurred in 1618 (probably in May). Apparently he had never married, and his wealth was bequeathed to charitable uses, partly for the benefit of his native town of Basingstoke. A portrait of him, copied from one belonging to Mrs. Christie Miller, hangs in the hall of the Skinners' Company, of which he was a member. It has been reproduced in J. F. Wadmore's history of that body, and it forms a fitting memorial of one who played so prominent a part in the founding of English trade to the East Indies.

[1] Close by the western end of the present Goring Street.

## CHAPTER XVI

## THE COMPANY'S SECOND VOYAGE

DESPITE the difficulty that had been experienced in raising funds for Lancaster's fleet, in July 1601 the Company began to consider the necessity of preparing a further expedition, to second him and continue the trade. On 13 September a general court was held, at which it was resolved to circulate a subscription list for this purpose, with a minimum of £100. The result was disappointing, for the total of the sums offered did not exceed £11,000—a quite insufficient amount. This backwardness created a bad impression at court, and on 12 October the Privy Council addressed a letter of remonstrance to the Company, holding up the example of the Dutch and reminding the members that others were ready, 'in your default', to send out ships; adding significantly that they could not shelter themselves under their charter if they did not fully use the privileges granted by it. This warning, however, fell upon deaf ears, and the Committees were perforce obliged to let the matter drop, pending the return of the ships already sent out.

One cause of the hesitation shewn was probably the fact that the members of the Company were being urged to provide money for an expedition which it had been decided to set out for the discovery of the North-West Passage. It seems that the exportation of treasure in the First Voyage had provoked much unfavourable comment; while the Eastern markets yet in sight afforded but slender opportunities for selling English goods. It was judged advisable, therefore, to seek a way to the East which would not only be shorter but would bring the ships to 'the countries of Cataia and China . . . which in all likelihood will aforth a most liberall vent of English clothes and kersies, to the generall advancement of the trafficke of merchandize of this realme of England'. A wrangle followed with the Russia Company, which claimed the sole right of such discovery, or at least of any advantages that might result therefrom. In December 1601 the Privy Council intervened in the dispute; and in the end the Russia Company came round, and agreed that the expedition should be a joint one. Towards the expenses the East India Company determined to make a levy of a shilling in the pound, as a minimum subscription, on the adventurers in the First Voyage, on penalty of a fine of five times that amount, to be deducted from each man's existing stock. Subsequently it was arranged that all money so subscribed should be reckoned as part of the stock of the First Voyage and should participate in any profits that might accrue from Lancaster's operations. With the funds thus collected two pinnaces were equipped and despatched, under an agreement with George Weymouth, the commander, that he should not return for at least a year and that he should then receive £500, on proof that he had reached China or Japan; otherwise, he was to have no claim to remuneration. The result was an absolute failure. Weymouth started at the beginning of May 1602, and reached Warwick's Foreland towards the end of June. He succeeded in penetrating for a considerable distance into the strait now known as Hudson's, but on emerging again he was driven south by contrary winds. After a time his men grew mutinous, and he was forced to abandon the enterprise and return home. A scheme was mooted for sending him out again to continue the search; but on 26 January 1603 it was resolved at a general court that the pinnaces should be sold and the attempt 'utterlie geaven over'.[1]

The return of Lancaster's ships, in the summer and autumn of that year, made it necessary to take immediate steps to continue the trade. Since part of the stock of the First Voyage had been left at Bantam for sale, it was obviously to the interest of the existing shareholders to despatch another fleet; and they were accordingly persuaded to subscribe a further sum of £60,450, in order to equip the same four ships. The cost of outfit, victuals, etc., was £48,150; while £11,160 was sent out in rials of eight, and £1142 in goods. The 'General' appointed was Henry Middleton, who had recently brought home the *Susan*.

The fleet sailed on 25 March 1604. Middleton had been instructed to pass the Cape without calling there; but by the middle of July scurvy had made such ravages among his men that he unwillingly agreed to put into Table Bay. This caused a month's delay; after which all went prosperously, save for a further outbreak of scurvy, and two days before Christmas the fleet anchored in the road of Bantam. The factors left there by Lancaster had a sorry tale to tell. The pinnace had been duly despatched to the Bandas, but had been

[1] In 1606 the Russia and East India Companies again collaborated in setting out a small vessel for the same discovery, under John Knight, who had already explored the western coast of Greenland in a Danish expedition. He sailed on 18 April, and reached the coast of Labrador two months later. On 26 June a party, including Knight, landed and disappeared, having, it was surmised, been attacked and killed by the natives. The survivors turned homewards, and arrived at Dartmouth on 24 September.

forced to return, after battling for nearly two months against contrary winds. Thereafter the factors had led a miserable existence, decimated by sickness and distracted by dread of fire and thieves, by brawls with the Hollanders, and by the exactions of the Javanese officials. Middleton's arrival changed all this, and the factory became the scene of the busiest activity. The authorities at home had no wish to be flooded a second time with pepper, though they recognised that this commodity must necessarily form the staple of any cargo procured at Bantam. They had therefore instructed Middleton to send back from that port only two of his ships; while he, with the other two, was to proceed to the Moluccas in search of cloves and nutmegs. It was now decided that the two vessels to go home should be the *Hector* and the *Susan*, and that those to go to the eastwards should be the *Dragon* and the *Ascension*. With these two Middleton sailed accordingly on 18 January 1605; the other two completed their ladings, and left Bantam on 4 March.

The *Dragon* and her consort anchored off Amboina on 10 February. The island was at this time under the control of the Portuguese; and, on its being pointed out that peace had been concluded between the two countries, the Governor, Gaspar de Melo, willingly agreed to permit the English to trade. On the 11th, however, five Dutch ships arrived and demanded the surrender of the Portuguese fort. After a brief resistance the Governor capitulated, and Amboina passed under the dominance of the Hollanders. They at once made it clear that no trade would be allowed on the part of the English, and Middleton had no option but to depart. His instructions contemplated his taking both his vessels to the islands of Banda, the centre of the production of nutmegs; but, against the advice of all his colleagues, he determined to send the *Ascension* thither alone, while he himself, in the *Dragon*, stood northwards for the Moluccas proper, lying to the west of Gilolo. Accordingly, on leaving Amboina (18 February) the two parted.

After a tedious voyage, Middleton found himself on 22 March off the island of Tidore, which was then under the domination of the Portuguese. Here he hoped to find as friendly treatment as had been offered by that nation at Amboina. As he approached the island, however, he saw two galleys being chased by seven others, and in imminent danger of being captured; instinctively taking the weaker side, he rescued the nearer of the two and drove off the pursuers. This galley proved to contain the King of Ternate and three Dutch merchants, who informed Middleton that the fleet from which they had been so opportunely saved belonged to Tidore, there being a standing feud between the two islands. It was of course well known to the English that Sir Francis Drake, some twenty-six years earlier, had been warmly welcomed at Ternate; and having now rendered a signal service to its monarch, Middleton was easily persuaded to escort the fugitives thither. He was, however, still bent upon trying his fortune at Tidore; and, after being feasted by the King of Ternate, who promised him free trade, both there and at the island of Maquian, he proceeded on his way, leaving a few merchants behind to purchase cloves.

At Tidore the Portuguese received the English very cordially, and offered no objection to their buying cloves from the natives. On 21 April, having secured a fair quantity and hearing that a hostile Dutch fleet was bearing down upon the island, Middleton made sail for

Maquian, passing through the Dutch squadron on his way. Failing to get any cloves at that island, he returned to Tidore, where the Dutch were still riding before the Portuguese castle, accompanied by the King of Ternate and his forces. There the English were spectators of the Dutch assault (9 May), which resulted in the capture of the fort, after an heroic resistance. Middleton then exerted himself to secure good terms for the vanquished Portuguese, and to effect a pacification between the Kings of Ternate and Tidore. The first was easily accomplished, but, as regards the second, his intervention bore little fruit. The Dutch, too, though outwardly polite, made no secret of the fact that they suspected him (not without reason, it would seem[1]) of having sold ammunition to the Portuguese, thus assisting them to prolong their resistance.

Reports from the merchants left at Ternate were far from satisfactory, and at last Middleton asked the King point blank whether he intended to permit the continuance of the factory there or not. After some hesitation the King confessed that, in soliciting aid from the Hollanders, he had promised them a monopoly of trade in his dominions, and that they were now holding him to his promise. There was nothing to be done but to fetch away the English factors; and so on 21 May the *Dragon* left Tidore and proceeded to Ternate for that purpose. On her arrival further negotiations followed, both with the King and with the Dutch, but these failed to lead to a favourable result; and on 18 June Middleton took his departure. After calling again at Maquian and buying a few cloves, the *Dragon* made her way back to Bantam, which was reached on 24 July 1605.

[1] See *Histoire de la Conquete des Isles Moluques . . . traduit de l'Espagnol d'Argensola* (Amsterdam, 1706), vol. iii, p. 60.

On the 16th of the following month the *Ascension* returned thither from the Bandas. Our information concerning her experiences there is very scanty; but it appears that she reached the group without difficulty on 20 February, and stayed until 21 July, being well treated and presumably acquiring a good stock of spices. Preparations were now made for the homeward voyage of the two vessels. Gabriel Towerson was appointed to be head of the factory at Bantam, and formal leave was taken of the King and of the Dutch residents, who appear to have been on very friendly terms with Middleton. Then, on 6 October 1605, the *Dragon* and *Ascension* set sail for England. Early in December the two lost company, and Middleton determined to take the *Dragon* into Table Bay. On nearing the roadstead he overtook the *Hector*,[1] in great distress. She had only fourteen men left in her, and these were preparing to run the vessel ashore, as the only hope of saving their lives. She was now helped into the bay; and there, on 27 December, they were joined by the *Ascension*. After refitting so far as they were able, a fresh start was made. The rest of the voyage, which included a short stay at St. Helena, was uneventful, and on 6 May 1606 the three ships anchored in the Downs, after an absence of over two years.

In the interval at least two events of importance to the East India Company had happened. The first was the conclusion, in August 1604, of peace with Spain and Portugal. During the negotiations the Spanish commissioners demanded the exclusion of English traders from the Indies; but meeting with a stubborn resistance, they withdrew this stipulation, and the

[1] Her consort, the *Susan*, which had left Bantam with a crew of forty-seven only (many of them sick), was never heard of again.

treaty contained no reference to the point. The dispute was thus left undecided. The Spaniards and Portuguese persisted in their claim to exclude all others from their spheres of influence; the English remained determined not to admit any such right, while recognising that it was hopeless to attempt to trade at any place in the East that was actually in the possession of their rivals.

The second event to be noticed was the grant by King James, on 25 June 1604, of a licence to Sir Edward Michelborne 'and to his associates and companye' to set out ships 'to discover the countries and domynions of Cathaia, China, Japan, Corea and Cambaia, and the islands and countries thereunto adjoyning, and to marchandize and trade with the said severall countries and people inhabiting the said places, not as yet frequented and traded unto by anie of our subjects . . . any restraint, graunt or charter whatsoever to the contrarie . . . notwithstanding'. This flagrant disregard of the charter granted by Queen Elizabeth must have excited deep resentment amongst the leaders of the struggling East India Company; but they were powerless to prevent it, and Michelborne departed in December 1604 with a small vessel (the *Tiger*) and a pinnace, accompanied by John Davis as pilot. Disregarding the limitations in his licence, Michelborne made an unsuccessful attempt to trade at Priaman, in Sumatra, and then proceeded to Bantam. He next set out for Patani, on the eastern coast of the Malay Peninsula. On the way, a leaky vessel belonging to a party of Japanese pirates was met and assisted; in return for which kind action the pirates attempted to seize the *Tiger*. After much stubborn fighting they were foiled, but with the loss of Davis and many of the crew (27

December 1605). Disheartened by this unfortunate incident, after a short cruise Michelborne turned homewards, and reached Portsmouth on 9 July 1606. During the earlier part of the voyage he had overhauled several native vessels, including a large Chinese junk bound for Bantam; and these piratical proceedings not only brought odium upon the English name but endangered the lives of the Company's servants at Bantam and elsewhere. The Company commenced a suit against Michelborne in the Admiralty Court, but in July 1607 decided to drop it, on account of the great expense and uncertain issue.

Middleton's voyage had been on the whole distinctly successful. The loss of the *Susan* was to some extent neutralised by the valuable nature of the cargoes of the other three vessels; and when, in 1609, the accounts of the combined First and Second Voyages were finally cleared, the adventurers had received back their capital and a profit of ninety-five per cent. Middleton's crowning achievement had been his success in reaching the Moluccas and there trading; and though there was ground for disquietude in the monopolising tendencies of the Dutch, whose bold policy of allying themselves with the native chiefs against the Portuguese, in return for the privilege of absorbing all foreign trade, had now been fully displayed, it was hoped that they would hesitate to offend the English, or that in any case means would be found to surmount this obstacle. As a mark of royal satisfaction with his intrepid and skilful conduct of the expedition, Middleton was knighted by King James at Greenwich on 25 May 1606.

One result of the plethora of spices brought home in the Second Voyage appears to have been the promotion of an export trade in this commodity. There was a difficulty in the way, in the shape of a recent act of parliament, prohibiting the sale of any spices, drugs, etc., unless first 'garbled' (*i.e.* cleansed and sifted), on pain of forfeiture of the goods. The Company therefore submitted a petition to King James, representing that its stock of spices was 'more then this land can utter in manie yeares', and that unless it could be disposed of, the equipment of a fresh fleet would be seriously hampered. The consequence was the grant of letters patent (9 August 1606), exempting from the operation of the act, for a period of three months, all such spices as the Company might sell wholesale for transportation abroad.

## CHAPTER XVII

# MIDNALL TRAVELS THROUGH PERSIA TO INDIA

THE reader will recall that in 1583 Newbery, on his last journey eastwards, had planned to proceed from Basra to Bushire by sea and then continue by land through Persia and Afghanistan to Northern India; he was, however, obliged to abandon this route for lack of a suitable interpreter. We have now to turn our attention to another remarkable journey, in which John Midnall or Mildenhall (like Newbery, a Levant merchant) made his way entirely over land from Mesopotamia to the Punjab, and, again like Newbery, reached the imperial court and interviewed the Mughal Emperor, Akbar.

Our chief authority consists of two documents written by Midnall himself—one a memorandum giving a brief account of his outward journey as far as Kandahar, the other a letter (probably addressed to Richard Staper), written at Kazvin on his homeward way, detailing his experiences at the Indian court. Both these documents were found among Hakluyt's papers by the Rev. Samuel Purchas, who published them in his *Pilgrimes*. In addition, some useful supplementary information is given in a narrative by Midnall's fellow-traveller, the Rev. John Cartwright, in his work entitled *The Preacher's Travels*.

Of Midnall's earlier career all we know is that he

had been 'servant' to Richard Staper and that he was at Constantinople early in 1598. In the same year he must have returned to England, for it was from London that he started (February 1599) in the *Hector* for Constantinople, where he arrived at the end of October. Apparently he had then no idea of trying to make his way to India, for he stayed in that city, 'about my merchandize', until the beginning of May 1600.[1] In March he had contemplated a venture to Cairo;[2] but he changed his mind and in May proceeded to Aleppo, where he remained until 7 July, and then set out for Persia and India. There is no evidence that he was employed for this purpose by any group of merchants; while the statement that he was sent by Queen Elizabeth as an ambassador is palpably absurd. Although in India he played the rôle of a messenger from his sovereign, this was clearly assumed for the purpose of obtaining more easily the concessions he was seeking. A not improbable explanation of his enterprise is that it was suggested by the news, received at Constantinople, of the abortive attempt made in 1599 to set out an expedition to the East Indies by the Cape route. Sooner or later such a venture was bound to be undertaken; and if in the interim Midnall could secure a grant of trading privileges in India, he might expect to reap a handsome reward for his pains.

A companion, for at least part of the way, was found in the Rev. John Cartwright, who happened to be in Aleppo at the time. This cleric was not in the employment of the Levant Company as chaplain, but had

[1] During his stay at Constantinople, a youth named Birkhead had 'his feet tasted [*i.e.* beaten] for being accused to caule John Midnall cuckold' (Sanderson, p. 197). This suggests that domestic unhappiness had had some share in hastening Midnall's return to the East.

[2] Brit. Mus. *Lansdowne MS*. 241, f. 75.

recently come out from England, apparently on a journey of curiosity. Setting out in a caravan numbering 600 persons, the pair crossed the Euphrates at Bir, and proceeded by way of Orfah to Diarbekr, and thence through Bitlis, Van and Nakhichevan to Julfa, on the Persian frontier. According to Midnall's own account, from Julfa they went by way of Sultanieh to Kazvin. Cartwright, on the other hand, declares that they journeyed from Julfa northwards to Shemakha, Derbend and Arrash, and then went to Tabriz and so to Kazvin. I am inclined to accept his statement, and to conclude that Midnall had some reasons of his own for trying to conceal this portion of his route. He may perhaps have had in mind the possibility of reviving the trade through Russia into Persia. From Kazvin, after a month's stay, the two travelled on through Kum to Kashan. There they separated, Cartwright continuing his journey to Isfahan,[1] while Midnall took the road for Yezd.[2] From thence Kerman was the next stage; and from Kerman he proceeded through Sistan to Kandahar (which was then an appanage of India), and so to Lahore. Presumably he had made the journey from Kashan with a caravan, or a series of caravans; and the inordinate time taken was perhaps due to the necessity of waiting for suitable opportunities of passage, as well as to long periods spent in buying and selling, to augment the funds at his disposal.

[1] From the Persian capital Cartwright returned to Aleppo by way of Shiraz, Susa and Mosul. He was afterwards (1602) employed by the East India Company as chaplain in Weymouth's voyage to the north-west, the failure of which was by many imputed to the reverend gentleman's cowardly encouragement of the mutinous seamen in their determination to return.

[2] Cartwright (p. 70) says that Midnall had a companion named John Parrot, who died when they reached Lahore. No other evidence has been found, and, since Midnall makes no allusion to the matter, the correctness of this story is to be doubted.

Midnall tells us that he arrived at Lahore in the year 1603, but does not indicate either the day or the month. It seems evident that he quitted Indian territory again some time before the death of Akbar in October 1605, for he makes no mention of that important event. Since a Jesuit from personal knowledge afterwards referred to him as having 'lien in Agra three yeeres', he must have arrived very early in 1603. According to his own account, on advising the Emperor that he had reached his dominions, Midnall was by his orders escorted to Agra, and was there accorded an interview, at which he presented Akbar with twenty-nine horses (presumably brought from Persia for the purpose) and a number of jewels. Asked to specify his wishes, he declared that the Queen his mistress was desirous that her subjects should be granted facilities for trade similar to those enjoyed by the Portuguese; and he added that, since the English and the Portuguese were at war, it was hoped that, if the former took any ships or ports belonging to the latter, the Emperor would not interfere. To these demands no demur was made at the time; and soon afterwards Akbar sent Midnall a return present 'in money to the value of five hundred pound sterling'. After some delay an imperial *farman* (order) was offered to him, granting all his requests, 'saving they had left out the taking of the ships and the ports of the Portugals'. On discovering this, Midnall refused to accept the document, insisting upon his full demand.

Thus the matter rested for six or seven months. Midnall attributed his rebuff to the intrigues of certain Jesuits at the imperial court; but although it was doubtless true that these were exerting all their influence against him, it seems that Akbar's principal advisers also viewed his proposals with suspicion, and were

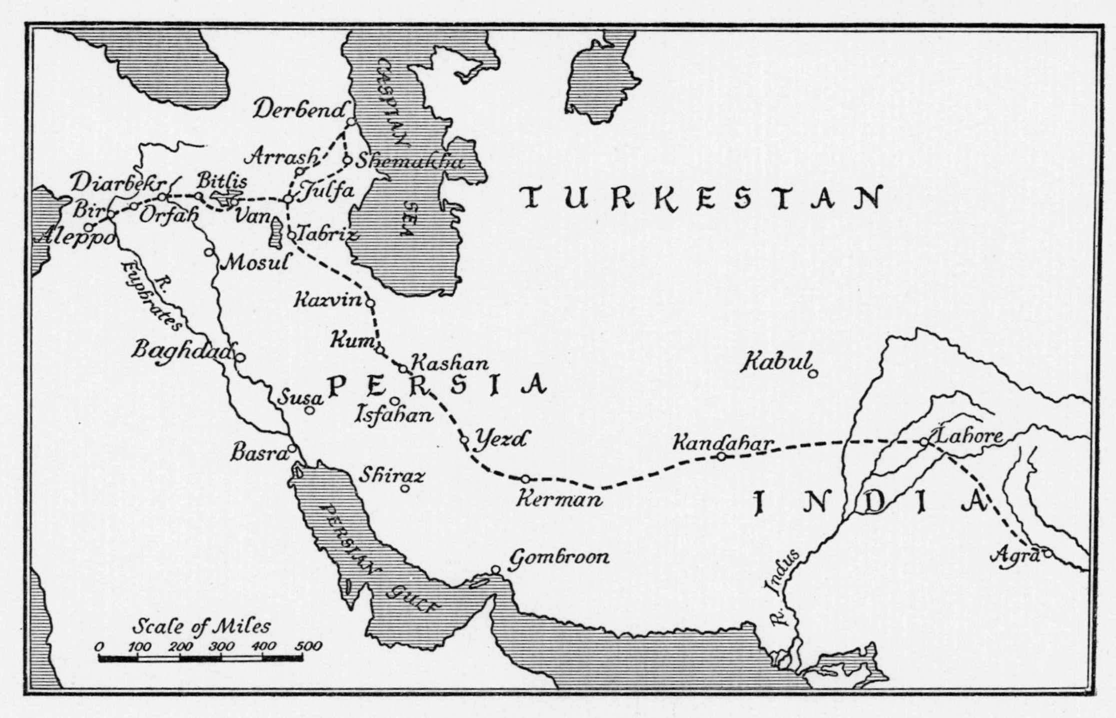


THE JOURNEY OF MIDNALL

unwilling to risk a breach with the Portuguese, of whose power at sea they were fully conscious. It is possible, moreover, that what Midnall was really endeavouring to secure was that the Emperor should veto any attack by the Portuguese upon English vessels visiting his ports; and if so, it is quite comprehensible that Akbar should see no reason for giving any undertaking of the sort. However, if our traveller's story is to be believed, he succeeded at length in overcoming all opposition. Having learnt enough Persian to enable him to dispense with an interpreter, he demanded and obtained an interview with the Emperor; and at this he confronted and confuted the Jesuits, and removed the monarch's scruples by declaring that it was the intention of the English sovereign to send an ambassador, with rich presents, to reside at the imperial court, where he would be, in effect, a hostage for the peaceable behaviour of his countrymen. Thereupon, we are assured, Akbar gave orders that 'whatsoever priviledges or commandements I would have' were to be granted without delay or question. 'And so, within thirtie dayes after, I had them signed to my owne contentment and (as I hope) to the profit of my nation.' He goes on to say that he thereupon went to Akbar's son and destined successor, Prince Salim (afterwards the emperor Jahangir), and from him obtained 'the like commandements'.

These precious documents once in his possession, Midnall quitted Agra and started on his homeward way. He appears to have returned by the same route as he had come, at least as far as Kazvin, from whence he wrote the letter of 3 October 1606 already mentioned. In this he said that his intention was to make his way home by way of Russia, as he feared to go by Baghdad, lest some harm should have been plotted against him by two Italian merchants whom he had found at Agra. He was evidently as leisurely in returning as he had been in going, for on 21 June 1608 he had not yet reached England. On that day letters from him to Richard Staper were read to the Committees of the East India Company, giving particulars of the privileges he had obtained and offering them, together with his own services, for a sum of £1500. Consideration of the matter was deferred, pending Midnall's arrival in London, or at least in the Netherlands.

Nothing more is heard of the subject until 23 May 1609, when Midnall's proposals were again brought forward; and a week later some members of the directorate were deputed to confer with him about them, though at the same time his demands were pronounced to be unreasonable and he himself was considered to be fit only for employment in a subordinate capacity. Evidently the concessions which he had obtained were judged to be of small practical importance, especially as the Company was expecting to hear news shortly of the success of William Hawkins, who (as related in a subsequent chapter) had been despatched to the court of the new emperor with letters from King James. Soon, however, the Committees were startled to learn that Midnall had presented to the King a petition representing that he had spent ten years in travel and had obtained, at a great cost, privileges for trade in India; and praying that, since the East India Company would pay no attention to his claims, he and his associates might be permitted to exploit the said grant. This petition the Lord Treasurer had referred to Sir Walter Cope and three merchants, of whom at least two were friends of Midnall, and had instructed them to deal with the East India Company and report the upshot. The Company at once appointed four representatives to confer with the said committee; and these were apparently successful in opposing the grant, for nothing more is heard on the subject. It would seem that thereupon there was some idea of getting rid of Midnall by sending him out to the East in the Company's service, and in October 1609 he was actually nominated as a factor; but, possibly because his demands as to remuneration were not acceptable, it was decided not to engage him, as being 'for divers respects . . . not fittinge to be ymployed in the service of the Companie'.

Hereupon, it would seem, Midnall determined to return once more to the Levant; for we next hear of him in a letter from Sir Thomas Glover, the English ambassador at Constantinople, dated 19 May 1610. This shews that Midnall had conceived a scheme for going by sea to Trebizond, and thence through Georgia into Persia, hoping thus to open up a new commercial route to the latter country. With this object in view, he hired a small vessel in which he embarked at Constantinople with two other Englishmen and a stock of goods and money. Immediately after his departure, however, he was denounced by some foreign trade rivals as being a Persian spy, although the only reason alleged was that he could speak Persian. He was thereupon pursued and overtaken. On his being brought back to the Turkish capital, his goods and money were confiscated on the unproved charge; and it was only in consequence of the energetic intervention of the English ambassador that he was cleared and his stock restored to him.

Midnall's next step was to try his fortune once again in India. For that purpose he set out from Aleppo, carrying with him a stock, part of which belonged to Richard Staper and other London merchants. The English colony at Aleppo suspected him of an intention to embezzle these goods, and sent two of their number in pursuit. He was overtaken before he had quitted Persian territory, and was induced to return to Isfahan; there he made over the goods in dispute to Richard Newman, one of his pursuers, who carried them back to Aleppo. The other merchant, Richard Steel, agreed to accompany Midnall in his venture, and the pair set out for India together. They duly reached Lahore, where they separated; Steel going on to the imperial court, which was then at Ajmer, in Rajputana, while Midnall, who was ill, followed him by slow stages, finally reaching that town in April 1614.

After lingering for two months, Midnall died. Purchas repeats some gossip about his having learnt 'the art of poysoning, by which he made away three other Englishmen in Persia, to make himself master of the whole stock, but . . . himselfe tasted of the same cup and was exceedingly swelled, but continued his life many moneths with antidotes'. The story is scarcely a probable one, and we may safely assume that the death was due to natural causes. Midnall had declared himself a Roman Catholic, and his body was conveyed to Agra and interred in the Catholic cemetery there. His tombstone still exists in good preservation, and is the oldest English monument of the kind in India. Thus ended the career of a self-reliant and enterprising adventurer, who managed twice to reach India overland, and was the only Englishman who is known to have visited the courts of both the great Akbar and his successor, Jahangir.

CHAPTER XVIII

# THE COMPANY'S SHIPS REACH ARABIA AND INDIA

BY the close of 1606 the East India Company's charter had run for six out of the fifteen years for which it had been granted. The progress made during that period had been disappointingly slow. Only two small fleets had been sent out, and only one factory had been established, namely at Bantam. The effort seemed puny compared with the achievements of the Dutch, whose 'United East India Company' (into which the existing companies had been federated in March 1602) was covering the Indian Ocean with its fleets and threatening to displace the loose Portuguese monopoly in favour of one far more complete and aggressive. Moreover, the voyages already made had had little success in respect of their chief aim, namely to extend the markets for English manufactures. As yet the main result had been to procure at cheaper rates spices and pepper, and this only at the cost of a great exportation of treasure. Clearly, if it was to survive, the Company must seek in other directions for markets which would take goods in lieu of money, or at least provide a wider choice of return cargoes. As we have seen, two attempts to get to China by the north-west had failed utterly;[1]

[1] On 9 January 1607 a royal licence was issued to Richard Penkevell and his associates (who were to be incorporated under the title of 'the Colleagues of the Fellowship for the Discovery of the North Passage') to find a route

and attention was fixed upon India itself, access to which would perhaps be more feasible now that peace had been concluded with the Iberian powers. True, the Portuguese had not abated one jot of their claim to monopolise the Indian seas; but it was faintly hoped that, if only for political reasons, they would hesitate to attack English merchantmen making for the ports of the independent Indian princes, who in their turn might resent any such interference with the trade of their subjects.

It was resolved, therefore, that the fleet of 1607 (Third Voyage) should not only continue the trade with Java, but should endeavour on its way to open up commercial relations with the dominions of the Mughal Emperor, or at least with the Red Sea ports, which were much frequented by vessels from Western India. A fresh stock of £53,500 was raised, of which £28,620 was spent on shipping, etc., and £7280 on cargo, while £17,600 was sent out in money. The *Dragon*, the *Hector* and the estimated stock of goods remaining at Bantam, were purchased from the previous adventurers; and a pinnace of 115 tons, named the *Consent*, was bought to form part of the expedition. For the post of 'General' William Keeling was chosen, who in Middleton's voyage had commanded, first the *Susan*, and then the *Hector*. As 'Lieutenant-General' and commander of the *Hector* a new-comer, William Hawkins, was appointed, and it was resolved to entrust to him, 'in reguarde of his experience[1] and languadg', the duty of delivering His

China, Cathay, the Moluccas, etc., by the north, north-east or north-west, the said grant to be valid for seven years (*Calendar of State Papers, East Indies, 1513–1616*, no. 358). Nothing, however, appears to have resulted from this project.

[1] What this experience was remains a mystery. We know from Hawkins himself that he had been in the West Indies; yet this was scarcely a qualifica-

Majesty's letters and the Company's presents to 'the princes and governours' in India and Arabia. The command of the pinnace was given to David Middleton, a younger brother of Sir Henry. The instructions, in the preparation of which Sir James Lancaster took a prominent part, were of a very detailed character. The ships were to avoid stopping at the Cape, watering instead at St. Augustine's Bay, on the south-west coast of Madagascar, and, if necessary, again at Zanzibar or the Comoro Islands. After that, they were to make for the island of Sokotra,[1] where a pilot should be sought. Then, if the season permitted, they were to proceed to Aden, open up trade, and, if possible, leave a factory. Should sufficient cargo be obtained, the *Hector* was to go straight home, while the other two vessels were to make for Bantam. If time allowed, they were to call on the way on the coast of Gujarat, in order to enquire there into the possibility of 'a mayntenance of a trade in those parts heereafter, in saffetie from the daunger of the Portingales or other enymies; endevouring alsoe to learne whether the Kinge of Cambaya or Suratt[2] or any of his havens be in subjection to the Portugalls, and

tion for negotiations in the East. The fact that he spoke Turkish and was familiar with oriental ways suggests that he had served in the Mediterranean, but no trace of him has been found in the extant records of the Levant Company. Sir Clements Markham (*The Hawkins' Voyages*, p. xliv) confidently identified him with the William Hawkins who was a nephew of the famous Sir John and served in Fenton's voyage of 1582–83 as second in command. In reality, however, as Sir John Laughton pointed out in the *Dictionary of National Biography* (s.n.), what little evidence there is tends to a contrary conclusion, and there are no grounds for thinking that the Hawkins who went to India had ever been a sailor. The fact that he was placed in charge of the *Hector* does not imply that he was responsible for the navigation of the vessel, for that was the province of the master.

[1] A large island lying about 130 miles east of Cape Guardafui. It was noted for the production of aloes Socotrina.

[2] In ignorance of Akbar's death, the royal letter carried out was addressed to him as 'Kinge of Suratt'.

what havens of his are not'. In the event of the fleet being unable to reach Aden in the first instance, all three ships were to sail to the Gujarat coast; and there, if such a course appeared safe, the *Hector* and *Consent* were to be left to trade, while the *Dragon* proceeded to Bantam. Should all go well at Surat, the *Consent* was to remain there to lade for England, and the *Hector* was to try to obtain a cargo at Aden; failing which, she should go on to Bantam.

After considerable delay in getting down the Channel, the three ships left Plymouth in the middle of April 1607. The *Consent* got away four days before the other two, and was never overtaken. The *Dragon* and *Hector*, after calling at the Cape Verde Islands, met with contrary winds and were forced to put into Sierra Leone for water. After leaving, they made but slow progress, and on 17 December both vessels were glad to anchor in Table Bay. Further delay was caused by calling at St. Augustine's, and Sokotra was not reached until April 1608—more than a year from the commencement of the voyage. A Gujarat ship which was found there gave Keeling encouraging reports of trade prospects at Aden, as well as useful information about the navigation to that place and to Surat; and accordingly at the end of April an attempt was made to reach Aden, but the ships were driven back by contrary winds. After waiting some time, it was agreed to abandon that plan and proceed separately to the eastwards. Keeling therefore sailed in the *Dragon* for Bantam, and Hawkins in the *Hector* departed for Surat. On 17 August the latter sighted the coast of India near Diu, and a week later (24 August 1608) she anchored off the mouth of the Tapti. An English vessel had at last reached an Indian port.

The mouth of the river was found to be blocked by a bar of sand, too shallow for the *Hector* to cross; but the roadstead outside was safe enough during fair weather. A messenger sent to the Governor of Surat, which lies about fourteen miles up the river, returned with an invitation, and Hawkins accordingly went up by boat to that city. His request for permission to establish a factory there was referred to a higher official, Mukarrab Khan, who was in charge of the administration of the Gujarat ports and was then at Cambay. His reply was that the English might sell the goods they had brought, but that for the settling of a permanent trade the consent of the Emperor must be procured. Accordingly Hawkins determined to proceed to Agra, present King James's letter, and negotiate for the requisite concessions. Meanwhile, on 5 October he despatched the *Hector* to Bantam, remaining at Surat with one factor (William Finch) and a couple of servants.

The Portuguese, alarmed by this intrusion into a region which they had so long had to themselves, at once took steps to counteract his projects. Even before the departure of the *Hector*, some of their lighter vessels, hovering in the Tapti, surprised and captured two boats in which the English were conveying goods down the river to their ship. Hawkins demanded restitution, but was met with insults and a defiant declaration that 'these seas belonged unto the King of Portugall, and none ought to come here without his license'. According to his own account, the Portuguese laid various plots to murder him; while to Mukarrab Khan and other officials they urged that any concession made to the new-comers would entail not only the ruin of the trade between Goa and Gujarat, but active reprisals on Mughal shipping. Nothing daunted, Hawkins, leaving

Finch in charge at Surat, started on 1 February 1609 for Agra, where he arrived in the middle of April. The news of his coming had of course preceded him, and he was at once sent for by the emperor Jahangir, who probably supposed him to be the ambassador promised by Midnall four years before. Hawkins, when presenting the letter which he had brought from his sovereign, had nothing to offer by way of gift but a little broadcloth; but his explanation that the presents brought from England had been detained at Surat by Mukarrab Khan was smilingly accepted, and he was bidden 'most heartily welcome'. Jahangir appears to have been favourably impressed by his visitor, especially by the fact that he spoke Turkish, which was well understood at the Mughal court; and in the days that followed the two had repeated interviews, and Hawkins found himself 'in great favour . . . to the griefe of all mine enemies'. The Emperor pressed him to remain at court as a resident ambassador, and promised that in such case he would grant all his requests for trading concessions; and without much reluctance the Englishman agreed, 'seeing it was beneficiall both to my nation and myselfe'. Thereupon he was made captain of 400 horse, was married to an Armenian maiden chosen by the Emperor, and took his place among the grandees of the court, living and dressing in Muhammadan fashion. Meanwhile, as Hawkins tells us, 'the Jesuites and Portugalls slept not, but by all meanes sought my overthrow; and, to say the truth, the principall Mahumetans neere the king envyed much that a Christian should bee so nigh unto him'; and the authorities at Goa stirred up the Gujarat officials to represent that the trade of that province would suffer seriously if the English were allowed to gain a footing. Jahangir, however, continued to shew kindness to his visitor, though the latter could not by any means secure the promised grant of privileges.

We must now look back for a while to London, where, under the energetic guidance of Sir Thomas Smythe,[1] the East India Company had entered upon a policy of sending out ships regularly each year. Accordingly in 1607 a stock of £33,000 was raised for a Fourth Voyage; and with this money the *Ascension*, which had been bought from the adventurers in the First and Second Voyages, and the *Union* (formerly known as the *Merchant Bonaventure*) were equipped and despatched under Alexander Sharpie, who had had some experience of the Levant trade. Sailing in March 1608, the two vessels got separated after leaving Table Bay. The *Union* found her way to Sumatra and procured a cargo; but by the time she reached the Channel on her homeward way almost all her crew had died, with the result that she drifted on to the coast of Brittany and had to be abandoned. The *Ascension* succeeded in reaching Aden on 7 April 1609, only to find that it was a place of garrison rather than of trade, and that its Turkish Governor was both rapacious and treacherous. Negotiations with the Pasha of the Yemen failed to produce permission to establish a factory at Mokha with-

[1] Nominated as Governor in the charter, Smythe's first period of office was abruptly terminated in the spring of 1601 by his committal to the Tower on a charge of complicity in the rebellion of the Earl of Essex; and although released after a while, he remained in retirement during the rest of Elizabeth's reign. After being knighted by the new sovereign in May 1603, he was elected Governor in the following July. A year later his services were not available, owing to his employment on a special mission to Russia; but in July 1605 he reassumed the chair. During 1606–7 the post was held by Sir William Romney. Then, in July 1607, Smythe was once more elected, and he remained in office for fourteen years. From 1600 to 1621 his house in Philpot Lane continued to be the headquarters of the Company.

out express authorisation from Constantinople, and a visit to that port had no satisfactory result. The *Ascension* then made for Surat. When nearing her destination, she had the misfortune to run upon a sandbank, where she became a total wreck. Luckily the weather was fine, and the crew managed to reach the land in their boats and to make their way to the English factory at Surat, where their arrival caused both surprise and trouble, owing to their unruliness.

The news of the approach of the *Ascension* had been promptly sent by Finch to Hawkins at Agra, and the latter made use of the intelligence to obtain from the Emperor a *farman* for English trade at Surat, 'so firmely for our good and so free as heart could wish'. Immediately after its despatch a further letter from Finch announced the loss of the vessel; whereupon Hawkins procured a second order that the survivors should be well treated and assisted to recover, if possible, the cargo from the wreck. In December 1609 a number of the Englishmen made their appearance at Agra, where their disorderly behaviour did nothing to improve either the general reputation of the nation or Hawkins's position at court. This was further shaken by the loss of the presents Jahangir had expected to receive by the *Ascension*, and by Hawkins's continued feud with Mukarrab Khan, who had influential friends at court and was much in favour with his master. The energetic remonstrances of the Portuguese and the arguments of the Gujarat officials, who contended that the tenuous commerce of the English could be no compensation for the loss of the existing trade with Goa, were having a powerful effect upon the capricious Emperor; and when, on being ordered to Goa to purchase a particularly fine ruby for sale there, Mukarrab

Khan declared it necessary that he should be able to assure the Viceroy that the English would not be admitted, Jahangir readily gave a promise to that effect.

Once Mukarrab Khan had started, Hawkins made a fresh application, with the result that the fickle Emperor changed his mind and declared that the English should be allowed to trade. Apprised of this by the vigilant Jesuits, Mukarrab Khan sent back word that in such case it would be useless for him to proceed to Goa; whereupon Jahangir 'went againe from his word, esteeming a few toyes which the fathers had promised him more then his honour', and the promised *farman* was withheld. To add to his vexation, the juggling of the Wazir deprived Hawkins of any benefit from the pension allotted to him, and in addition he was ousted from the place of honour he had hitherto enjoyed at court. This last mortification was largely his own fault. Jahangir, in one of his fitful attempts to cure himself of his propensity to drunkenness, had given orders that nobody should come into his presence smelling of liquor. Hawkins, who had the same weakness, one day offended against this regulation and was denounced in the face of the court. The Emperor, 'consideringe that he was a stranger', contented himself with a reprimand; but the consequence was that the Englishman lost his position and 'went not soe often to courte'. Determined, as he says, 'either to be well in or well out', Hawkins petitioned that he should either be reinstated or be given leave to depart; whereupon Jahangir, by this time thoroughly tired of his troublesome visitor, promptly ordered that he should be given his passports. To a request for an answer to the royal letter which he had brought, the Wazir returned a disdainful refusal.

Hawkins now prepared for departure. The Jesuits at Agra, 'only to rid me out of the country', readily agreed to procure a safe-conduct from the Viceroy to enable him to go home by way of Cambay, Goa and Lisbon. However, while awaiting this document, he found that the situation had taken a more favourable turn. Mukarrab Khan returned from Goa in some disgust with the Portuguese and without the ruby, which he declared was false; while a change of Wazirs replaced an enemy by a friend. Still more important was the news that an English fleet, under Sir Henry Middleton (the Company's Sixth Voyage), was on its way to the Gujarat coast. When, towards the close of September 1611, these vessels reached the bar of Surat, Hawkins at once applied for a *farman* to enable them to trade. The Emperor, influenced no doubt by the hope that they were bringing him the oft-promised present of European curiosities, at first granted his request. Reminded, however, by a courtier that this would entail 'the utter overthrow of his sea coasts and people' by a breach with 'his ancient friends the Portugals', he retracted the concession; at the same time assuring Hawkins that, if he would remain in his service, he should receive in full the allowance previously granted to him. The envoy answered with dignity that it was useless for him to remain, 'unlesse the English should come unto his ports according to promise'; while, as for his own maintenance, 'my king would not see me want'.

Having thus burnt his boats, Hawkins, accompanied by his Armenian wife, quitted Agra on 2 November 1611, and reached Cambay towards the close of the year. His intention still was to go home by way of Goa; but on receiving an invitation from Middleton to join him at Swally, he changed his mind, and on 26 January 1612 he got safely aboard the English fleet. He participated in the subsequent voyage to the Red Sea and thence to Bantam, where he and his wife took passage in the *Thomas* for England in January 1613. The ship with much difficulty reached home in the autumn of that year, but without Hawkins, who had died, 'on the Irish shoare', towards the close of the voyage.

To judge by his own account and by the verdict of his contemporaries, Hawkins was a man of many faults of character. He was evidently arrogant and tactless; while, apart from his intemperance, he was accused of being 'very fickle in his resolution, as alsoe in his religion'. Sir Thomas Roe, who had no personal acquaintance with him, concluded that he was no better than 'a vayne fool'. It must be conceded, however, that for over two years he maintained in a spirited fashion a very difficult position, and spared no effort to carry out the mission entrusted to him. Despite his final discomfiture, he made an impression at the Mughal court which contributed in no small degree to weaken the influence of the Portuguese and to prepare the way for the establishment of his fellow-countrymen in India.

Before concluding this chapter, it may be well to give a fuller account of the proceedings of Middleton's fleet of the Sixth Voyage. This represented a further effort on the part of the Company to follow up the trade in a vigorous fashion. In this resolve the adventurers had been greatly encouraged by the prospect of a widening trade and by the grant of a fresh charter from King James, on 31 May 1609, by which (subject to revocation at the pleasure of the Crown) the Company's monopoly was extended indefinitely. A capital of over £80,000 was thereupon subscribed, and three vessels were prepared for a new expedition. Of these, one was a pinnace of 100 tons, named the *Darling*, bought from Sir Edward Michelborne; the other two had been specially built for the Company, and were of 1000 and 240 tons respectively, the former being the largest merchantman yet constructed in an English dockyard. King James himself, accompanied by the Prince of Wales, attended the launching at Deptford, and bestowed upon the two vessels the names of the *Trade's Increase* and the *Peppercorn*. The monarch was in high good humour, and presented Sir Thomas Smythe with a 'very fayre chayne of goulde, with a jewell wherein was the kinges picture'. Both ships, however, disgraced themselves by refusing to budge from the stocks, and His Majesty departed 'somewhate discontente'. By hard work on the part of the shipwrights the pair were got into the river some days later in ignominious silence. It was an ill-omened beginning.

Sir Henry Middleton was induced to take command of the fleet as 'General', while for the charge of the *Peppercorn* Nicholas Downton was selected. All that was known of the proceedings of the fleets previously despatched was that Hawkins had been left at Surat and that an English ship (concluded to be the *Ascension*) had visited Mokha. Middleton was therefore instructed, if the season permitted, to call at the Red Sea ports before proceeding to Surat. As before, Aden was found to be hopeless for trade purposes; while at Mokha, after being lulled into security by fair promises, Middleton and several of his companions were seized by the Governor and imprisoned. After nearly six months' captivity, they managed to escape to the *Darling* (15 May 1611); and in revenge Middleton blockaded the port until he had exacted some compensation for the outrage. He then resumed his voyage for India, and arrived at the bar of Surat on 26 September. A swarm of Portuguese light vessels, dodging among the sandbanks, for a long time prevented all communication with the shore, and it was not until the beginning of November that an anchorage —afterwards famous as 'Swally Hole'—was discovered, where deep water enabled the vessels to anchor close to the shore and thus to command the landing-place with their ordnance. Even then the Portuguese attacked a party which had ventured to land; but a few volleys from the ships soon put them to rout.

The news that letters and presents had arrived from the King of England for the Emperor soon brought upon the scene Hawkins's old enemy, Mukarrab Khan. In his usual crafty manner he held out hopes that the settlement of a factory at Surat would be permitted; but he had no intention of displeasing the Portuguese by making such a concession, and his real purpose was to acquire as much of the English merchandise as suited his convenience, and especially to get hold of curiosities likely to please his master's taste. When this was accomplished, he threw off the mask and abruptly commanded the new-comers to be gone. On 9 February 1612 the fleet set sail accordingly, having wasted over four months to little or no purpose. Middleton felt deeply aggrieved at the duplicity with which he had been treated, and was seriously alarmed at the loss likely to accrue to his employers, since a considerable proportion of his goods—velvets, vermilion, quicksilver, etc.—had been specially provided for sale in India or Arabia. The monsoon would not yet permit of his going on to Bantam; and he decided to spend the interim in the Red Sea, and there revenge himself upon the Indian shipping. If the Mughal's subjects would not be friends and permit peaceable trading, they should learn that the power of the English was no less to be dreaded than that of the Portuguese. Accordingly, after leaving the *Peppercorn* off Aden to capture any Indian vessels visiting that port, Middleton entered the Red Sea and proceeded to lay hands on all the Indian shipping he could find. An unexpected complication now occurred. A fresh fleet from England, under John Saris (the Company's Eighth Voyage), was lying at Mokha, and, being provided with a permit obtained from Constantinople, had every hope of profitable trade. Middleton, however, had already commenced hostilities, and Saris had no option but to withdraw. Concerned only with the interests of his particular group of shareholders, he felt much resentment at the action of the rival 'General'; but he could do nothing to stop him, and in the end he was persuaded to join in the enterprise, on condition that he should have a share of the booty. By the time the *Peppercorn* arrived, bringing a number of prizes, the English had under their control an imposing array of Indian 'junks'; and from these they took such goods as they pleased, giving in exchange their own commodities, at rates fixed by themselves. In addition, such of the vessels as belonged to Gujarat ports were forced to pay large sums as ransom before being released. From the Turks no additional compensation could be exacted, though the damage done to the Mokha trade was in itself a heavy punishment. Having now glutted his vengeance, Middleton set sail on 16 August 1612 for Sumatra and Java, reaching Bantam three days before Christmas.

Early in the following February Downton took home the *Peppercorn* with a lading of pepper. The hull of the *Trade's Increase* was riddled by worms and extensive repairs were found to be necessary. Whilst these were being carried on, Sir Henry Middleton, worn out by anxiety and dispirited by the failure of his voyage, died at Bantam (24 May 1613). Soon after, all hope of refitting his ship was abandoned; and she was finally burnt by the Javanese in October or November 1614.

## CHAPTER XIX

## KEELING AND DAVID MIDDLETON IN THE BANDAS

WHILST in India itself the efforts of the English to gain a footing were being frustrated by the opposition of the Portuguese, farther to the east the Company's servants were being no less obstructed by the Dutch. To fair and open competition no objection could have been taken; but the manifest aim of the Hollanders was to secure complete control of the chief sources of production of the more valuable spices, and to exclude all other Europeans from the trade—the Spaniards and Portuguese by open violence (since a state of war still subsisted), the English under pretext of treaty rights. This policy naturally excited great indignation among the English merchants, who, in common with the bulk of their compatriots, were inclined to look upon the Dutch as an inferior nation, owing its very existence to the aid received from Queen Elizabeth in its revolt against Spain. However, neither the factors themselves nor their employers in London had any definite policy to oppose to the well-laid schemes of their competitors; and during these early years they devoted their energies mainly to securing cargoes where and how they could, leaving the future to take care of itself.

Mention has already been made of the despatch of the *Consent*, the smallest of the three vessels employed in the Company's Third Voyage. Under the command of David Middleton, she reached Bantam on 14 November 1607, and soon after sailed for the Moluccas for cloves, arriving there early in January 1608. Middleton found that the political situation had changed considerably since his brother Henry left the islands in June 1605, for the Spaniards at Manila had come to the help of their Portuguese allies, and the King of Ternate, with his Dutch confederates, had experienced a severe reverse. The appearance of an English ship gave rise to hopes that she would join the Spaniards and their native allies in opposing the Hollanders, or would at least make a show of so doing. But Middleton of course refused to take sides, and was accordingly informed, after some delay, that no trade would be permitted. Sailing on 14 March, he called at the island of Buton, where he met with a friendly reception and procured a supply of cloves from a Javanese junk lying at anchor there. He reached Bantam on 22 May. By various means he had secured, despite all difficulties, a good lading; and with this he set sail for England on 15 July 1608, reaching Dartmouth in the following January.

The fortunes of the other two vessels of the same fleet we have already followed to the point where Captain Keeling departed from Sokotra in the *Dragon*, leaving the *Hector* to visit Surat and then come on to Bantam. The former vessel called at Priaman, in Sumatra, where nearly two months were spent in buying pepper, and then proceeded to Bantam, which was reached early in October 1608. It was Keeling's intention to proceed to the Moluccas, to obtain a cargo of cloves; but the seamen declared that the *Dragon* was too much worn to stand a lengthened stay in Eastern waters and that to adopt this course would imperil her ultimate return to England. It was decided, therefore, that she should go home as speedily as possible, and that a pinnace should then be despatched in her stead to the Bandas, carrying two of the Bantam factors, who should remain there until the following season and provide nutmegs and mace against the arrival of a subsequent ship. Accordingly, early in December 1608, Keeling departed in the *Dragon* for England. Whilst working through the Straits of Sunda, he met the *Hector*, captainless, owing to the fact that Hawkins, as we have seen, had remained in India. Feeling that he could not evade the responsibility of seeing to her disposal, Keeling turned back with her to Bantam. There he placed Gabriel Towerson in charge of the *Dragon* and sent her, just before Christmas, to England, where she arrived in safety nine months later.

Keeling himself took over the command of the *Hector*, and at the beginning of 1609 started in her for the Moluccas. He was, however, baffled by winds and currents, and altered his course for the Bandas, where he anchored off Neira on 8 February. The Dutch factors on that island shewed a friendly front and entertained Keeling in their house until he could arrange for the building of a special dwelling. The natives also welcomed the new arrivals, and the purchase of cloves went on busily, both at Neira and at Wai.[1] Suddenly there came a change. In Europe, events had for some time been shaping towards the conclusion of a truce in the long war between Spain and the United Provinces; and the Dutch East India Company, foreseeing that this agreement would probably be on the basis of the retention by the contracting parties of their respective

[1] Wai and Run are used in these pages for the more customary Pulo Wai and Pulo Run. Pulo is merely the Malay word for 'island'.

conquests up to the time of its ratification, had sent out instructions to strain every nerve to bring the Moluccas and the Bandas under subjection as quickly as possible. With this object Admiral Verhoeff, in March 1609, appeared at Neira with a powerful fleet and demanded leave to build a fortress in a situation which would command the anchorage. Naturally the Bandanese refused, perceiving that such a concession would mean the loss of their independence. Keeling, not unwilling to fish in troubled waters, suggested secretly to the

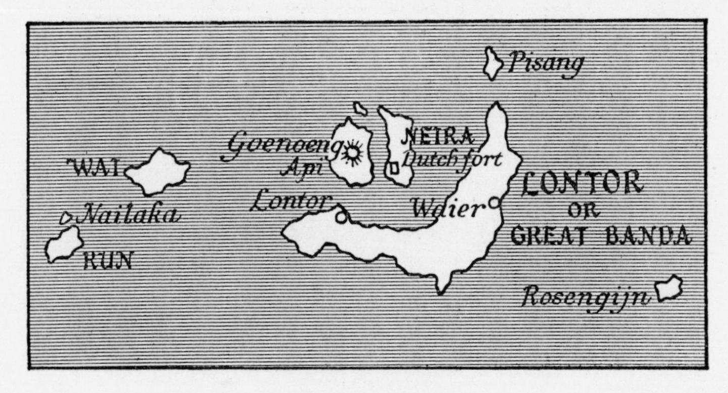


THE BANDA ISLANDS

chiefs, as a means of avoiding such a fate, 'the formall delivering of Banda to the use and in the name of His Majestie of England our soveraigne, before the Hollanders did land or begin their purposed fort'; but, though 'they seemed to like well thereof', they had no mind to surrender their territory to any European power, and so nothing was concluded. In the middle of April the Dutch landed, 1200 strong, and, brushing aside all resistance, began to erect a strong fortification. The natives could do nothing to prevent this; but they maintained an attitude of determined hostility, and Verhoeff, drawn into a parley, was murdered, together with a number of his men. At length, however, further resistance appeared so hopeless that an agreement was concluded (31 July 1609) by which the Bandanese sullenly acquiesced in the maintenance of the fort and undertook to sell their spices to none but the Dutch. The treaty, nevertheless, was only effective as regards Neira, Lontor and Goenoeng Api, since the outlying islands persisted in their hostility, and the Dutch as yet had not sufficient strength to subdue them.

Preoccupied by their difficulties with the Bandanese, the Hollanders for a time paid but scant attention to Keeling's endeavours to purchase a lading for his vessel; but once an agreement was in sight they promptly notified him that they had conquered Neira and its dependencies and that he must depart within five days. His only reply was a verbal one, that he would go when his ship was fully laden, and not before. In their anxiety to be rid of him, the Dutch offered him a letter of credit on Bantam for the amount of the debts still due to him by native purchasers of his goods; and having obtained this, and all the cargo he was likely to get, he sailed for Bantam. He had intended to call at Macassar on his way, but, having no pilot and being warned that the coast was dangerous, he desisted when within half a day's sail of that port. Bantam was reached towards the end of August, and early in October Keeling departed in the *Hector* for England, arriving in the Downs on 10 May 1610.[1]

Meanwhile at home David Middleton's success in his expedition in the *Consent* had led to his immediate employment as commander of a larger vessel, the *Ex-*

[1] On his way he is supposed to have discovered and named the (Cocos-) Keeling Islands, since rendered famous by the destruction there of the German cruiser *Emden* during the late war.

*pedition* (240 tons). This, the Company's Fifth Voyage, was really a branch of the Third, though the accounts were temporarily kept distinct. Quitting the Channel in April 1609, the ship had a prosperous voyage to Bantam, where she anchored on 7 December. No time was lost, for eleven days later Middleton sailed for the Moluccas. Calling at Botun, he was assured by its chief that a large stock of goods, collected by him for trade with the English, had been destroyed in a recent fire; whereupon Middleton, disappointed, resumed his voyage. Contrary winds and currents prevented him from reaching the Moluccas, and he made his way instead to the Bandas, where he came to an anchor off Lontor on 5 February 1610.

The arrival of yet another English ship greatly annoyed the Dutch, who at once sent a message to Middleton, demanding that he should bring his vessel into the road of Neira and shew his authority for venturing into their jurisdiction. The English captain, who had no mind to place his ship under the guns of the Dutch fort, took a high tone, refusing to shew his commission, and declaring that he had been sent expressly by the King of England and the Prince of Wales to fetch spices from the Bandas, and that he would ride where he pleased. He next endeavoured to negotiate with the people of the neighbouring islands for a lading. Those of Lontor, mindful of the recent treaty, referred him to the Dutch authorities, without whose permission they could not venture to trade with him. He then made overtures to the inhabitants of the more distant islands of Wai and Run, who were still defying the domination of the Hollanders. The latter in exasperation decided to use force to get rid of the intruder, and sent him an ultimatum to that effect. Middleton now judged it prudent to visit the Dutch commander and exhibit his commission from the King, though he would only allow his own name and the royal signature to be seen, refusing to allow a perusal of the rest of the document. Words passed, 'some sharpe, and some sweet'; but the Dutch were evidently anxious to avoid pushing matters to an extremity, and treated the Englishman with a show of friendliness. Middleton, on his part, knowing that the spot in which his vessel was riding was in fact a dangerous one, agreed to bring her into the usual roadstead near the fort. He then tried to bribe the leading Dutch officials to connive at his purchase of a lading; but they assured him that they dared not permit him to trade, especially as they had two large ships of their own to fill and comparatively few spices had yet been collected. Thereupon he departed, ostensibly for the Moluccas, but in reality for Wai, where he hoped to procure a supply of nutmegs and mace, despite the Dutch. However, the currents carried the *Expedition* past the island, and she was forced to bear up for Ceram, where she anchored in a harbour on the southern coast. By means of a pinnace Middleton got over to Wai, where he induced the natives to sell him spices, and apparently encouraged them to hold out against the Dutch, adding vague promises of English help in the future. His boats made frequent passages between the island and his ship, and a considerable amount of cargo was gradually acquired. Meanwhile the Hollanders at Neira watched his proceedings with deep resentment, but without actively interfering, as they were not strong enough to make an attack upon Wai with any prospect of success. An assault upon the *Expedition* seems to have been contemplated. But she was in a difficult position to reach, and possibly the Dutch authorities were in some doubt as to the wisdom of taking extreme measures, which might cause complications in Europe.

Having now secured a good lading, Middleton proceeded to Bantam, leaving a smaller vessel to collect a further supply of spices at Wai and then follow him. For a time he was uncertain as to his future course. He contemplated a visit to Sukadana, in Borneo, where, according to report, diamonds were procurable. In the end, however, he decided that it would be more prudent to go home at once, and leave the Sukadana venture to be undertaken by the factors at Bantam. He sailed accordingly on 16 November 1610, and appears to have reached England in the early summer of the following year.

It had now become abundantly evident to the leaders of the East India Company that they had to face a determined effort on the part of the Netherlanders to monopolise the commerce of the Far East. The recent conclusion of a truce with Spain for twelve years would greatly assist them in such a purpose, and enable the Dutch East India Company to use its vast resources to this end, unhampered by conflicts with the Spaniards and the Portuguese. In this extremity the English Company turned to its government for support, and in November 1611 addressed a petition to the Lord Treasurer Salisbury, setting forth the 'uncyvell and inhumaine wrongs' their servants had sustained at the hands of the Dutch, and assuring him that these, if continued, must necessarily force the petitioners 'to give over the trade ther, which is the cheif end the Hollander aymeth at'. His Lordship was begged to intervene with the States-General 'for redresse in these injuryous courses', and to secure for the English Company 'fredome of trade' and 'reciprocall kindnes'.

Thereupon Sir Ralph Winwood, the English ambassador at the Hague, was instructed to make representations on the subject. He did so, and was promised an investigation of the complaints; though, in reporting this to Salisbury, he added that the Dutch East India Company was a very powerful body, which was not likely to pay much attention to the orders of the States-General, if these jeopardised its own interests. In effect, the only result of the promised investigation was to produce a multitude of recriminatory charges against the conduct of the servants of the English Company; and Winwood concluded that the only hopeful remedy was to conclude, if possible, an agreement between the two companies for joint trade in the East. For such a course the merchants on either side had little liking. The two governments, on the other hand, anxious to remove all causes of friction, pressed the proposal, with the result that conferences took place in London (1613) and at the Hague (1615). Nothing was achieved at either meeting. The Dutch stood resolutely upon the rights granted to them in the treaties concluded with the natives, and complained of the unreasonableness of the English in expecting to share free of cost in a commerce which had been snatched from the Portuguese and Spaniards at a vast expense, and was being safeguarded in the same way—for the truce was proving a dead letter in the East. To this the English replied that they had traded in the Moluccas long before the Dutch—alluding to the voyages of Drake and Cavendish—and that hostilities with other powers ought not to be made a pretext for limiting the commerce of a friendly nation. They insisted that they had a natural right to free and unrestricted intercourse with those parts, and none but a declared enemy could debar them from this. As for paying any part of the expenditure already incurred by the Dutch and joining them in further warlike measures, they scouted the notion. On this point King James, who was much concerned to keep on friendly terms with the Spanish monarch, agreed entirely with his subjects; and since the Dutch made such co-operation an indispensable condition, the negotiations broke down.

CHAPTER XX

## THE TRADE IS EXTENDED TO THE COROMANDEL COAST AND TO SIAM

EXPERIENCE soon shewed that in the Malay Archipelago, while there was little or no demand for European manufactures, there was a vast consumption of the calicoes, plain or printed, produced in India, especially those of its eastern (Coromandel) coast, and that, in bartering for spices, the trader who brought these piece-goods was even more welcome than one who offered ready money. From an early date the Portuguese merchants settled at Negapatam and San Thomé (now a suburb of Madras) regularly shipped cotton goods to Malacca and the Spice Islands; and soon after their arrival in the Eastern seas, the Dutch took steps to establish themselves on the Indian littoral for the same purpose. By 1606 they had founded factories both at Masulipatam and at Petapoli, the chief ports of the Muhammadan kingdom of Golconda, the coast of which extended from the Penner river on the south to the Godavari delta on the north. In 1608 a footing was obtained at Tegnapatam in the Hindu country lying to the southwards, whence came most of the printed calicoes so popular in the Far East. Two years later still, an agreement was concluded with the raja of that region (known in the seaports as 'King of Vellore') by which the Dutch were allowed to establish a factory at Pulicat and were promised that no other

Europeans should be admitted to trade there. As the result of a Portuguese attack, they were permitted to fortify this last station, which before long became the headquarters of the Dutch on the Coromandel Coast.

In their turn the English began to direct their attention to the same quarter. In November 1609 the directorate in London received an offer from a Dutchman styling himself 'Florence Devyne' (probably a pseudonym), who stated that he had served on the Coromandel Coast and was willing to co-operate in an English attempt to open up trade in those parts. The loss of the Court Minutes of the period deprives us of exact information as to the course of the negotiations; but we know that in March 1610 a preliminary agreement was reached between the Company and two Dutch merchants, Pieter Willemszoon Floris[1] and Lucas Antheuniszoon. This provisional arrangement was superseded by a definite agreement, dated 13 December 1610, by which the two Dutchmen undertook to join in an expedition to the Coromandel Coast and other parts, themselves contributing capital to the extent of £1500 and being remunerated on a scale varying according to the profits made. For this Seventh Voyage of the Company a stock of about £15,000 was subscribed; and a vessel called the *Globe* was purchased and placed under the charge of Anthony Hippon, who had been master of the *Dragon*. All matters of trade were committed to the two Dutchmen and to an English merchant named Robert Brown, who had already

[1] Possibly the 'Florence Devyne' already mentioned, who had now added 'Floris' to his real name by way of disguise. Both he and Antheuniszoon had been in the service of the Dutch Company and were well acquainted with the Coromandel trade. The strictness with which that body was enforcing its prohibition of private trade on the part of its employees was probably one of the reasons why these two transferred their services to its rival.

served at Bantam. It seems, however, to have been well understood that the main function of the latter was to look after the interests of his employers, and that the real direction of the voyage was to be left in the hands of Floris and Antheuniszoon. It may be added that both proved themselves entirely worthy of the trust reposed in them.

The *Globe* sailed from the Downs early in February 1611, sighted Ceylon at the beginning of August, and, running up the Coromandel Coast, anchored off Pulicat. Floris had learnt, from a Portuguese boat encountered near San Thomé, that his fellow-countrymen had established themselves at Pulicat, and he judged it advisable to ascertain whether similar facilities for English trade would be accorded there. He and Brown landed in miserable guise, for in passing through the surf their skiff overturned, and it was in a half-drowned condition that they presented themselves to the group of native officials awaiting them on the beach. The result of their negotiations was far from satisfactory. The Dutch merchants were resolute in their insistence upon the monopoly that they had secured; while the local authorities would not venture to disregard the Raja's grant. An application to the latter for permission to trade elsewhere in his dominions would probably have been successful; but Floris decided that he could not spare the necessary time. So the *Globe* passed on to Petapoli. There Brown and Antheuniszoon remained to purchase calicoes, while Floris proceeded in the ship to Masulipatam. No difficulty was experienced in obtaining permission to establish a factory, and all concerned were soon busy trying to sell their English goods and buying piece-goods for the eastwards. Brown, who had long been ailing, died in the early part of September.

Several months were spent in this way; and then the *Globe* sailed for Bantam, which was reached on 26 April 1612. Departing again at the beginning of June, Floris and Antheuniszoon took the ship to Patani, a port on the eastern side of the Malay Peninsula, where there was a considerable amount of transit trade. At this place they were well received by the Queen,[1] who readily gave them permission to trade on the same terms as the Dutch. Floris remained, with seven assistants, at Patani; while Antheuniszoon departed in the *Globe* at the beginning of August for Siam. The mouth of the Menam river was reached a fortnight later, and Antheuniszoon, accompanied by Adam Denton and Thomas Essington (who had succeeded to the command of the *Globe* upon the death of Hippon), went up the river to Ayuthia, the capital of Siam, with a letter from King James and suitable presents. They easily procured leave to trade, and were allotted a house close to the Dutch factory. There Antheuniszoon, with a few companions, remained to dispose of their stock of goods—no easy task, for the markets were depressed, owing to civil wars—while the *Globe* returned to Patani. Siam, we may note, was entirely fresh ground for the English, though their Dutch competitors were already well established there. Its importance lay chiefly in its trade with China and Japan, particularly the former country, whence came supplies of raw silk, silk goods and porcelain; while the local

[1] Described by Floris as 'a comely olde woman . . . tall of person and full of majestie; having in all the Indies not seene many lyke unto hir'. In spite of her regal dignity, she appears to have been a merry soul; for, on a subsequent occasion, after watching the efforts of her professional dancers, she commanded 'all the gentilitie' to dance, and then 'both wee and the Hollanders muste do lykewyse, wherewith the olde queene was muche rejoyced'. She was also a 'good sport', for, although she was about sixty years of age, 'shee woulde go on hunting of wilde buffes and bulls', to the surprise of her European visitors.

markets provided also opportunities for the purchase of the dye-wood known as 'brazil', aloes-wood, benzoin, tin, hides and skins.

Floris had had small success in disposing of his merchandise at Patani, owing to the competition of the Dutch and other traders; and, as a result, he had little or no cargo ready. The season, moreover, was too far advanced to leave much hope of reaching the Coromandel Coast; and it was resolved that the *Globe* should stay where she was until the spring. In January 1613 arrived intelligence from Antheuniszoon at Ayuthia that he had sold a good part of his stock; whereupon Denton was despatched thither in a native vessel to announce that a further supply would follow. Accordingly the *Globe* shortly afterwards sailed for Siam. Antheuniszoon had sent two of his staff, Thomas Samuel and Thomas Driver, on a hazardous inland journey to Chiengmai, in the Shan district, some 350 miles to the northwards,[1] hoping that there would be found a lucrative market for the calicoes and yarn they carried with them. But nothing had been heard of the result of the venture when Antheuniszoon sent the *Globe* back to Patani, with 13,000 rials of eight in money and goods. With this capital and the proceeds of sales

[1] They were not the first of their nation to visit this distant mart, for (as we have seen) Ralph Fitch had reached it from Pegu some twenty-five years earlier. Driver returned before long to Ayuthia, bringing in gold the proceeds of the sale of part of the stock. Samuel stayed to sell the remainder, with the result that he was still at Chiengmai when the town was captured (1615) by the King of Pegu. The conqueror took the Englishman and his goods back with him to his capital, where Samuel died soon after his arrival. On the news being brought to Masulipatam, Antheuniszoon despatched a couple of factors by sea to Pegu, to claim the Company's goods. They returned in 1620, bringing the remnants of Samuel's stock and a letter from the King, inviting the English to trade in his country. This, however, was ignored; and it was not until 1647 that a short-lived factory was established at Syriam, the chief port of Pegu.

at Patani itself, Floris provided a cargo; and on 22 October 1613 the vessel sailed for the Coromandel Coast, leaving three men behind to continue the trade.

At Masulipatam Floris found the *James*, which had been equipped, on a separate subscription of nearly £20,000 (the Company's Ninth Voyage), to follow in the track of the *Globe*. The *James* was under the command of Edmund Marlow, a headstrong and quarrelsome fellow, with whom it was not easy to co-operate. She had left England in February 1612, but spent much time at Bantam and did not reach Pulicat until June 1613. Repulsed there (as Floris had been), Marlow went on to Petapoli, and there left a party of nine to trade; while he himself took the ship to Masulipatam. About a month after the arrival of the *Globe*, the *James* departed for Petapoli, where Marlow picked up the merchants he had stationed there and sailed early in February 1614 for Bantam.

The *Globe* needed extensive overhauling before she could venture upon further voyaging, and for this purpose she was taken to Narasapur, a shipbuilding centre at the mouth of the Godavari. Meanwhile Floris busied himself in procuring a cargo of indigo, cinnamon, cotton-yarn and piece-goods, intending to complete her lading for England by buying pepper at Bantam. An interesting episode of his stay at Masulipatam was the arrival of letters from the local authorities at Pulicat, who had repented of their previous churlishness and invited the English to settle at their port. Floris, however, was preoccupied with the success of his own venture, now drawing to a close, and gave them no encouragement. He reminded them that they had repulsed both the *Globe* and the *James*, and declared that the English could not visit Pulicat again without a safe-conduct. This did not end the matter, for at the end of July 1614 fresh envoys arrived, bringing a letter from the Raja of Vellore, 'written uppon a leafe of golde, wherein hee excused the former faulte done to us in Paleacatte, desiring that nowe wee woulde come into his countrie and chuse a place to our beste lyking, and that there wee shoulde builde a howse or castle according to our owne lyking, with other privileges more mentioned in the same. Hee gave mee [Floris] a towne of aboute 400 pagodas yearely revenue, with promise to do more at my comming thether.' Floris detained the messengers until nearly the close of the year, by which time news had arrived that the Raja was dead and that a civil war was feared. This finally determined Floris not to entertain the overtures, and he dismissed the envoys accordingly.

The *Globe*, having completed her repairs, returned to Masulipatam in October 1614. The goods provided for her were soon put aboard, and all that remained was to get in the money owing on sale transactions. The chief debtor was the Governor, whose tyrannous behaviour in other matters had already tried Floris's temper. Finding that all his applications for payment were unheeded, with the obvious intention of forcing him to sail without the money, the Dutchman resolved to take strong measures. Watching his opportunity, he seized the Governor's son and carried him on board the *Globe* as a hostage, 'in spite' (wrote one of the English merchants) 'of 1000 of his people, to the Companies benifitt, the honor of our king and countrey, and to the great countents of all the Moores'. The Governor raged, but, seeing no remedy, at last invoked the intercession of the Dutch chief; and upon payment of the money due Floris released his prisoner. Then on 8 December he sailed from Masulipatam. At Bantam he found the *James*, which had returned from a voyage to Patani. The latter vessel departed for England at the end of January, and was followed by the *Globe* a few weeks later. The two met at Table Bay, and arrived together in England towards the end of August 1615. Marlow had died during the voyage, and Floris himself was in a very weak condition. Brought to London in a litter, he survived only about three weeks, dying a few days before Michaelmas.

His partner, Antheuniszoon, did not return to England until three years later. He had remained at Ayuthia until September 1615, when he proceeded to Patani in a coasting vessel. At the latter port he embarked in the *Solomon* for Masulipatam. On his arrival there, he sent the *Solomon* to Narasapur for repairs, and meanwhile set to work to purchase goods for Bantam and England. The refitting of the ship took longer than had been anticipated, and then much time was lost in getting her over the bar, with the result that the monsoon for Bantam was missed for that year. At length, in June 1617, Antheuniszoon wound up his business and quitted Masulipatam, leaving behind him a small factory under Adam Denton. By way of Bantam he reached London in September 1618, and proceeded to give the Company an account of his stewardship. The result was entirely satisfactory. When a final settlement of the Seventh Voyage was worked out, it was found that a profit of 218 per cent. had been secured; while, as a more permanent outcome, factories had been settled in Siam and the Malay Peninsula and on the Coromandel Coast. Those in Siam and at Patani lasted only until 1623, when, in the general contraction of the Company's operations, they were dissolved as unprofitable. But Masulipatam became an important centre of English trade; and the formation of a factory there proved to be the first link in a chain of events that led to the establishment of British supremacy over the whole of India.

## CHAPTER XXI

## THE ESTABLISHMENT OF ENGLISH TRADE WITH JAPAN

THE romantic story of William Adams, the first Englishman to reach Japan, has often been narrated, and for our present purpose a brief summary will suffice. Born at Gillingham, near Chatham, and apprenticed to a Limehouse shipbuilder, he served in Queen Elizabeth's navy as master and pilot, and also made several voyages to the Mediterranean. His competence in navigation led to his appointment as pilot-major of a fleet of five ships despatched from Holland to the East Indies in 1598 under Jacques Mahu. Failing, owing to a late start, to make sufficient headway to pass by the Cape route, the fleet stretched over to the coast of Brazil, and, after much suffering and loss of time, got through the Strait of Magellan and out into the Pacific (September 1599). There they were scattered by storms; and Adams' vessel and another, having met again on the coast of Chile, made a bold attempt to cross the ocean and reach Japan. A tempest separated the pair, and only the one guided by the Englishman succeeded in its quest, casting anchor near 'Bongo'[1] on 19 April 1600. All but twenty-four of the original complement had died, and of the survivors three-fourths were sick. The arrival of a foreign ship naturally created a sensation,

[1] The Oita of the present day, on the north-eastern coast of the island of Kiu-shiu.

and Adams was soon summoned to Osaka by the great Iyeyasu, who, under the title of Shogun ('General'), was the actual ruler of Japan, though nominally still the servant of the much venerated Mikado.[1] According to Adams' own story, the Jesuits and the Portuguese did their best to induce the Shogun to put him to death as an intruder. But Iyeyasu was not to be persuaded to take this ruthless course, and after a short imprisonment the Englishman was released and ordered to bring the ship round to Yedo, to which city the Shogun was then proceeding. There the vessel was confiscated; the survivors being given allowances and left to their own devices, though forbidden to leave the country without permission. After a time two of the Dutchmen were authorised to proceed to Patani, carrying an invitation to their fellow-countrymen to open trade with Japan; and in 1609 a Dutch ship was sent to Hirado, on the north-west coast of Kiu-shiu, where a factory was established. Meanwhile Adams had settled down in the country and had married a Japanese wife. Iyeyasu, who was a man of broad sympathies and enlightened opinions, shewed him much favour, which was increased when, at his command, the Englishman constructed for him a couple of small vessels of European pattern. As a result Adams was granted an estate near Yedo, of considerable value. Emboldened by such a mark of approval, he besought the Shogun to allow him to return to his own country, but this was firmly refused.

From time to time Adams made attempts to communicate with his friends and relatives in England, but apparently none of his early letters reached its destination. However, the fact that he was in Japan and 'in

[1] The English factors always spoke of the Shogun as 'Emperor', while the Mikado they regarded as the 'Pope' of Japan.

greate favour with the Kinge' became known in London from Dutch sources, and the East India Company determined to imitate its rivals by endeavouring to open up communication with that country. When the *Globe* was despatched, early in 1611, it carried out a letter from James I to 'the greate Kinge of Japan', asking for trading facilities; and this the leaders of the expedition were instructed to forward 'from the most convenient place you shall arrive att', using for that purpose some country vessel, in which also factors were to be sent with a stock of merchandise. No opportunity was found of carrying out these instructions in full; but in July 1612 Floris forwarded to Adams, by a Dutch pinnace bound from Patani for Hirado, two letters which he had brought out from England, and also a reply to one which Adams had addressed to the English factors at Bantam in the preceding October. In one of these letters Sir Thomas Smythe, the Governor of the Company, announced its intention of sending a ship to Japan to establish commercial relations.

This promise was redeemed a few months after the departure of the *Globe*, when the *Clove*, *Hector* and *Thomas* sailed for the East under John Saris on the Company's Eighth Voyage. It is true that the fleet had an extensive programme—the Red Sea, Surat, Sumatra, the Bandas and Japan—and that its instructions provided that all three ships might return without going farther than India, should full cargoes be forthcoming; but Japan was clearly one of its chief objectives, and it carried out for this purpose yet another letter from King James to the 'Emperour' of that country. The choice of Saris as leader points in the same direction, for he had recently returned from Bantam, after spending several years at that port, where he must have gleaned from the Dutch much information regarding Japan and its possibilities.

The fleet sailed in the middle of April 1611, and made in the first instance for the Red Sea. Of its proceedings in that quarter something has already been said on p. 196; nor need we linger on its subsequent voyage

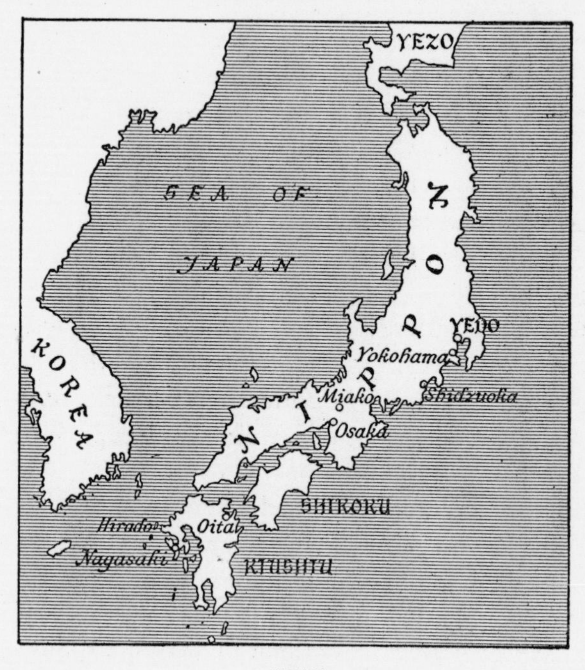


JAPAN

to Bantam, which was reached in October 1612. From that port Saris sent home the *Hector* and the *Thomas* in January 1613, with the goods already collected; while he himself, in the *Clove*, sailed in the same month for the Moluccas and Japan. In passing through the former group he managed to secure a small quantity of cloves, in spite of the opposition first of the Dutch and then of the Spaniards. Continuing his voyage, he reached the shores of Japan without difficulty and, guided by some fishermen met with off Nagasaki, anchored at Hirado on 12 June 1613. There he was cordially welcomed by the local authorities, and a house for a factory was at once hired in the town. Adams arrived at the end of July, and was eagerly questioned as to the prospects for trade. He held out no great hopes, for, as he had already informed the Bantam factors, the country was well supplied with woollen goods, which were brought in abundance by both the Dutch and the Spaniards. In his view the chief hope of profit lay in establishing trade with China, the products of which always fetched good prices in Japan; and he thought that the eastern parts of the island-empire offered better chances of profit than the western, as being less open to Dutch competition. Evidently there was from the first no great sympathy between Adams and Saris. Possibly the rough old sailor did not like the authoritative bearing of the merchant-captain, who in his turn thought that Adams had become in effect 'a naturalised Japanner' and was not sufficiently eager to advance the interests of his fellow-countrymen. They differed especially as regards the Dutch. It was natural that Adams, who had come out in a Dutch fleet at a time when the two countries were on good terms, should feel nothing but friendliness for the Hollanders; while Saris and his colleagues, on the other hand, were exasperated by what they deemed the unfair treatment the English had suffered at their hands in the Moluccas and the Bandas, and were disposed to retaliate so far as lay in their power.

Adams, however, was quite willing to do what he could to obtain a grant of privileges for his fellow-countrymen; and in August he and Saris set out for the court with this end in view. Iyeyasu, as far back as

1605, had resigned the direction of affairs to his son, Hidetada, though he still retained a considerable control over the administration. It was to the father's residence at Sumpu (now Shidzuoka) that the English party first bent their steps. To him the letter from King James was duly presented, and in return a formal grant of permission to trade freely in all parts of Japan was willingly accorded. Next they went on to the court of Hidetada, who made no difficulty about confirming his father's grant. Iyeyasu seems to have understood that the English would settle at Yedo, a course which, as we have seen, had been warmly recommended by Adams; but Saris and his colleagues, on his return, decided to keep their headquarters at Hirado, which was convenient for shipping from Bantam and Siam, and might, it was hoped, prove a stepping-stone to China. In taking this decision they were ill-advised. At Yedo they would have been near the Shogun's court and away from Dutch competition; while Adams would doubtless have assisted more willingly and effectively had the factory been near his home and family.

Saris got back to Hirado on 6 November 1613, and a month later departed in the *Clove* on his homeward voyage. He left at Hirado a factory of seven Englishmen, under the charge of Richard Cocks; and among them was Adams, who had been engaged as Cocks's chief assistant at a salary of £100 a year. In accordance with the Company's instructions Saris had offered Adams a passage home; but this the latter refused, although during the recent visit to court he had sought for and obtained the Shogun's permission to leave the country. His ostensible reason for changing his mind was resentment at the way in which he had been treated by Saris. But we may surmise that, when it came to the point, he could not bring himself to quit his Japanese family and his comfortable circumstances in a land to which he had grown accustomed, for an uncertain future in the dim fatherland. Moreover, he had a cherished scheme for making a voyage to the northwards, in the hope of discovering the eastern outlet of the North-East Passage, and to this project Iyeyasu had promised his assistance. In a letter sent by the *Clove*, Adams pressed this plan upon the East India Company, offering his services towards its realisation; and he had thus a good excuse for awaiting a reply before deciding whether or not to go home. As a matter of fact, the Company ignored his proposal; and when, in 1616, his agreement expired, he left its service and traded on his own account. He died on 16 May 1620, leaving one-half of his estate to his English and one-half to his Japanese family. His memory is still revered in Japan, and his tomb (or cenotaph) near Yedo remains an object of interest, both to the inhabitants of the city and to European visitors.

The commerce thus established lasted for only ten years. From the first it was unremunerative. English lead, as in many other parts of the Indies, was in fair demand, but broadcloth and calicoes found little favour; while the Dutch, on their part, spared no effort to spoil their easygoing rivals' market by underselling them. A certain amount of trade was done with Cochin China and Siam by means of small vessels, but with little result. Cocks made many efforts, through local Chinese merchants, to obtain permission to open up trade with China, with an equal lack of success. Meanwhile in Japan itself English commerce was carried on under ever-increasing difficulties. In 1616 Iyeyasu died; and Hidetada, now absolute, soon began to shew reactionary tendencies in the matter of the admission of foreigners. Cocks and Adams solicited a fresh grant of privileges, but could obtain only permission to continue their trade at Hirado itself, and had to withdraw from all their other stations. Then began a systematic persecution of the Japanese Christians and the Jesuit missionaries; and although the Dutch and English escaped, on the plea that they were not Catholics, they suffered from the effects of the general dislike of Europeans and European influence. A further cause of trouble was the rapidly widening breach between the Hollanders and the English in the East, which naturally had its repercussions in Japan; and the open warfare that ensued between the two nations in 1619–20 for a time isolated the small English community at Hirado. The subsequent agreement of the Dutch and English Companies seemed to promise better treatment for Cocks and his colleagues, but fresh dissensions soon broke out. At length the English council at Batavia determined, on 25 April 1623, to dissolve the factory in Japan, and sent a vessel to Hirado to fetch away the factors and their goods. At the end of the year Cocks and his assistants embarked in that ship, and a month later reached Batavia. There Cocks was severely censured for his mismanagement of affairs, and was sent home in disgrace. He died on his homeward voyage and thus in all probability escaped an equally unfavourable reception at the hands of his employers in London. The East India Company declared later that they had expended £40,000 on the factory, with little or no return.

The reopening of trade with Japan was more than once contemplated. In 1658 a ship was actually prepared for that purpose, but in the end the scheme was abandoned, largely because fresh hostilities with Holland were feared. Fourteen years later an attempt was actually made, and the *Return* reached Nagasaki in June 1673, only to find the prospect hopeless. The Dutch, who had been allowed by the Japanese to continue their trade, though under the severest restrictions, did their utmost to prevent any concession being made to their rivals; and their artful representation that the English king was married to a Portuguese princess so prejudiced the Shogun against the new-comers that he utterly refused to permit them to settle. Later schemes for the same purpose failed to come to fruition, and the English remained under the ban until the general opening of the country to foreign commerce in comparatively recent times.

CHAPTER XXII

## FURTHER ATTEMPTS TO FIND A PASSAGE BY THE NORTH

BEFORE pursuing further the development of English commerce in the East itself, it seems desirable to look back to England, where, between 1607 and 1616, a series of expeditions kept up an almost continuous search for a shorter route to the Indies through the northern seas. The reasons that made the idea so attractive have already been explained; and it may be added that the experience gained in the East India Company's first two voyages had not lessened the conviction that the way by the Cape of Good Hope was too long and too dangerous to be followed, except as a matter of necessity. Lancaster had taken fourteen months to reach an Eastern port and seven to return; Middleton's outward voyage had lasted nine months and his homeward seven; while from start to finish these two fleets had been away, in the one case over two years and a half, in the other only about six months less. The results of such protracted voyages were a heavy loss of life among the sailors, great deterioration of the ships employed, and a large drain upon the merchants' funds for repairs, stores and wages. It is not surprising, therefore, to find that the East India Company helped to finance projects for discovering an alternative route, and that Smythe, Lancaster and other important members of that body took a prominent share in the direction of such enterprises.

We have already (p. 165) glanced at the expedition sent out in 1606 to the north-west, under John Knight, at the joint expense of the Russia and East India Companies. Its failure did not discourage a further attempt, though this time only the former body was responsible. The leader of the new venture was Henry Hudson; and his plan was to test the practicability of the scheme advocated long before by Robert Thorne (see p. 6), of sailing straight across the pole to the 'islands of spicery'. Embarking in a small vessel bearing the encouraging title of *The Hopeful*, he left Gravesend at the beginning of May 1607, and ran up the eastern coast of Greenland until the ice barrier forced him eastwards. Towards the end of June he sighted the western side of Spitzbergen. Coasting northwards along that island, he finally struck out to the north-east; but impenetrable masses of ice barred his progress and left no hope of finding a passage in that direction. Hudson made another attempt to pierce the ice barrier on the Greenland side, and then turned homewards. On his way back to the Thames, which was reached in mid-September, he discovered the lonely island now known as Jan Mayen.

In the following year Hudson was again sent out by the Russia Company, this time in a definitely north-east direction. Passing the North Cape early in June 1608, he tried in vain to round the northern extremity of Novaia Zemlia. He next coasted down the western side of that island, intending to pass through the Kara Strait; but failing in this, and meeting with bad weather, he turned westwards. He seems to have entertained the idea of going round Greenland and making an endeavour to run up Davis Strait. Contrary winds made this impossible, and so Hudson set a course for home, getting back to Gravesend towards the end of August.

His next voyage was in the service of the Dutch East India Company, which was as eager as its English rival to find an easier way to the Spice Islands and was building great hopes upon the discovery of a North-East Passage. Hudson sailed from Amsterdam in the spring of 1609 in a small vessel called the *Halve Maan*. Apparently his intention was to pass through the strait that separates the island of Vaigats from the mainland; but he soon abandoned the attempt, under circumstances that are still mysterious, though it has been inferred that his crew were mutinous. Acting, it would seem, in defiance of the instructions which he had received, he proceeded to cross the Atlantic to Nova Scotia, and then went southwards as far as 35°. Turning north again, he searched the American coast carefully as far as Sandy Hook, including Chesapeake and Delaware Bays. Rumours—apparently based upon Indian reports of the great inland lakes—had reached England that a channel through the continent existed somewhere about latitude 40°; and Hudson had been drawn to this quarter by the hope that here, in temperate latitudes, would be found the long-sought North-West Passage. Having satisfied himself that this was not so, he proceeded to ascend the river that now bears his name, reaching a point near the site of the present city of Albany. Then, in the autumn, he sailed homewards.

The hopes of Hudson and his supporters now concentrated upon the strait which has since borne his name. It had already been partially explored by Weymouth, and was known to be a broad inlet stretching indefinitely westwards, and promising therefore to prove the desired way into the Pacific. In 1610 a strong syndicate was formed, headed by Sir Thomas Smythe and supported by both the Russia and the East India Companies; and in April Hudson was despatched in that direction, in command of the *Discovery*, of fifty-five tons. Early in August he succeeded in penetrating through the strait into Hudson's Bay, and until the end of October he carefully examined its eastern side down to the southern portion of James Bay. Here, at some spot near the mouth of the Moose river, the explorers were forced to spend the winter and the first half of 1611. Food was very scarce and discontent was rife, not only among the crew but among the officers. Hudson was by nature impetuous and irritable. At an earlier date he had displaced his mate, Robert Juet, in favour of Robert Bylot; and he had had a violent quarrel with his clerk, Henry Green. Now, when about to leave the winter quarters, he made another change, appointing John King to be mate in place of Bylot. The result of all this was that, when the mutiny took place, Green and Juet were among the ringleaders, and Bylot gave his commander no active support. Hudson's intentions seem to have been to secure a fresh supply of food, by shooting and salting down birds, and then to spend the rest of the summer in exploration. His crew, on the other hand, were determined to get home as quickly as possible, and, knowing that their captain would be violently opposed to this course, they planned to achieve their end by force. Hudson, who suspected nothing of this, was seized one morning as he stepped out of his cabin, and was thrust into the shallop, together with his son, King (the new mate) and six others, some of whom were sick. The mutineers then sailed callously away, leaving their commander and his companions to perish miserably.

The eleven men remaining on board elected Bylot as master, and a course was shaped for home. Retribution soon fell upon some at least of the evildoers. On five of their number landing to barter for venison, they were suddenly attacked by the Eskimos, with the result that Green was killed outright and the other four were mortally wounded. Juet died on the homeward voyage, and the five survivors, after great privations, only just managed to get their vessel into the harbour of Berehaven, in Ireland. On making their way to London, they were clapped into prison; but after a time they were released, having contrived to throw the blame of the outbreak on Juet and Green, who were both dead. Nothing was ever heard of the fate of Hudson and his companions; but there is little doubt that death by starvation soon put an end to their sufferings. Such was the sad fate of one of the most eminent of the early Arctic explorers. His memory is preserved for all time by the bay, strait and river that still bear his name; and although, as others have pointed out, none of these was actually discovered by him in the first instance, yet his careful exploration of them fully justified the honour thus bestowed upon him.

The knowledge that had been gained of the existence of a large sheet of water, of which only the eastern shore had been examined, stimulated the despatch of a fresh expedition in 1612. This was placed under the command of Thomas Button, who had been in the West Indies with Captain Newport; he had also served in the Royal Navy, and knew how to handle a troublesome crew. Two ships were employed, the *Resolution*, of which Button himself took charge, and the *Discovery*, under John Ingram; and among those employed in the voyage were Robert Bylot and another of the survivors of

Hudson's ill-fated venture. Sailing early in May 1612, Button explored the northern portion of Hudson's Bay, and followed its western shore down to Port Nelson, where he wintered. In the ensuing summer he continued his examination of the bay, and satisfied himself that there was no outlet on the western side. He then returned to England and made his report. With the rest of his career, spent in the Royal Navy and rewarded with a knighthood, we are not here concerned.

Meanwhile the promoters of Hudson's and Button's voyages, confident that these were about to be crowned by a great discovery, had obtained from King James, on 26 July 1612, a grant of incorporation, under the style of 'The Governor and Company of Merchants of London Discoverers of the North-West Passage', with Sir Thomas Smythe as the first governor. This body was to enjoy the sole benefit of the expected trade with Tartary, China, Japan and the islands of the Pacific by way of the passage supposed to have been discovered. Certain privileges were given to the promoters of Hudson's expedition; while the customs revenue for one whole year was granted by the Crown to Button and his associates. In the list of original members we note the names of Richard Hakluyt, Robert Bylot and William Gibbons—a relative of Button and a member of his expedition.

In 1614 this company fitted out the *Discovery* and despatched it, under the aforesaid Gibbons, with Bylot as his assistant, to follow up the explorations already made by Button. But the vessel got no farther than the coast of Labrador, where it spent most of its time, blocked by ice, in a harbour long known as 'Gibbons his Hole', though it now bears the more dignified title of Hamilton Inlet. In 1615 the *Discovery* was again sent out, this time under the charge of Bylot, with a certain William Baffin as mate,[1] who had in 1612 taken part in an expedition to the west coast of Greenland under James Hall, and had since been twice to Spitzbergen in the whaling fleets of the Russia Company. Sailing in March, the vessel, after some trouble with ice, passed through Hudson Strait into what was afterwards named Fox Channel, lying between Southampton Island on the west and Baffin Land (a much later designation) on the east. Before getting far into this fresh piece of water, progress was rendered impossible by a barrier of ice; and since the lead gave indications of shoaling and land was visible on all sides, it was concluded that the explorers were only at the mouth of a large bay, with no outlet in a northerly direction. They therefore turned homewards, arriving at Plymouth on 8 September 1615. Baffin was still confident that a passage existed, but he now thought that it must be sought up Davis Strait, and not by way of Hudson Strait.

The Company of the North-West Passage determined to persevere in the quest, and in the spring of 1616 the *Discovery* again set forth, under the command, as before, of Bylot, with Baffin as pilot. By the end of May, Sanderson his Hope (Davis's farthest point) had been safely reached. Proceeding northwards along the Greenland coast, the *Discovery* had got a little beyond Whale Sound, when its progress was barred by ice in lat. 78°. There was no alternative but to turn west and then south. In running down the western side, two

[1] Baffin's fame as an Arctic explorer, and the fact that he wrote the account of the voyage, have somewhat obscured Bylot's position as the leader of the enterprise; and the same is true of the 1616 expedition, in which again Bylot was in command. He is, however, adequately noticed in the *Dictionary of National Biography*.

large openings were discovered and named Jones Sound and Lancaster Sound respectively. Crossing to the Greenland coast, a short stay was made in a harbour there, and then a prosperous run home crowned a memorable voyage, which had made a notable addition to geographical knowledge. The result, however, was not encouraging. Baffin's own conclusion was that what had been discovered was 'no other then a great bay' (Baffin Bay) and that 'there is no passage nor hope of passage in the north of Davis Straights'. He himself gave up further Arctic exploration and, as we shall see, entered the service of the East India Company, with some hope that an opportunity might occur of attempting the passage from the Pacific side; while the company for which he had made his voyages abandoned the quest and petered out. The search was often renewed in later times; but with these endeavours we have here no further concern.

CHAPTER XXIII

# A FOOTING IS OBTAINED IN WESTERN INDIA

IN previous chapters we have followed the fortunes of the English pioneers in the dominions of the Great Mogul down to February 1612, when Sir Henry Middleton and his fleet, after an apparently irreparable breach with the local authorities, left Surat and proceeded to widen that breach by making a forced levy upon the Indian vessels found in the Red Sea. At that very time, however, Captain Thomas Best, with the old *Dragon* and a much smaller vessel, the *Hosiander* [1] (the Company's Tenth Voyage), was on his way from England to Surat, furnished with a special authorisation from King James to conclude a treaty of commerce with the 'King of the Magolls or any his deputies'; and, as it turned out, the breach was easily closed, despite the efforts of the Portuguese to keep it open.

On reaching the Indian coast (early in September 1612) Best received a letter, left behind by Middleton, warning any new-comers that the Indians had proved treacherous and that there was no likelihood of trade on a permanent basis. But since a small party of merchants, sent up to Surat, found an apparently cordial reception, it was decided to venture some goods ashore. Hardly

[1] This curious appellation is the Graecised form of the name of Andreas Hosemann or Heiligmann (1498–1552), the German founder of a Protestant sect whose doctrines found wide support.

had these been taken up to Surat when news arrived in that city of Middleton's violent dealings in the Red Sea. The profound agitation thus caused dismayed the English factors, who expected instant expulsion; but on the contrary the incident proved to be distinctly to their advantage. The Red Sea traffic was vital to Surat, and of hardly less importance to the Mughal empire in general; for, apart from its commercial value, it was the chief vehicle of the pilgrimage traffic to the holy places of Islam, so dear to all Muhammadans. The demonstration that this all-important traffic lay at the mercy of the foreigner—for the Indian ships were practically defenceless—made the Gujarat authorities realise how dangerous it was to play fast and loose with the English traders, even though any encouragement given to them should offend the Portuguese. So they glossed the matter over and continued to shew courtesy to Thomas Aldworth, the chief of the factors at Surat, merely soliciting his intervention with his employers for compensation for the losses sustained by the Indian traders—a course which he readily promised to take.

Best himself was very doubtful as to the sincerity of the Indians, and was inclined to withdraw the factory and sail away; but Aldworth and his colleagues opposed this plan, believing strongly in the possibility of making arrangements for a permanent establishment. Moreover, the fleet had brought out a large stock of goods specially chosen for the Indian markets, and Best knew that the home authorities were counting much upon the success of the venture. For these reasons he grudgingly consented to stay. In the middle of October the official in charge of the whole province of Gujarat arrived at Swally and had a long conference with the English captain, as the result of which a preliminary agreement was concluded, with a promise that this should be confirmed by a *farman* from the Emperor in due course. The agreement provided, among other things, that no reprisals should be made against the English for the proceedings of Middleton: that trade should be freely permitted, subject to the payment of the usual customs duties: that protection should be given to the Englishmen and their goods whilst on Indian territory, and that, should this prove ineffectual, any seizures made by the Portuguese should either be recovered or compensation given:[1] that an English representative should be stationed at the Mughal court: and finally, that within forty days a sealed confirmation by the Emperor of these articles should be obtained from Agra and delivered to the English.

Whilst awaiting the promised confirmation, Best learnt that four Portuguese galleons had left Goa to attempt the capture of his two vessels; and at the end of November this squadron arrived at Swally, accompanied by twenty-five 'frigates'. There followed a series of determined fights, in which the advantage rested with the English. The Portuguese were weak in gunners, and their only hope lay in pouring on board the English vessels their mass of soldiers. But their agile opponents easily avoided this danger, and meanwhile the English guns caused terrible losses aboard the crowded galleons. Then Best, conscious of the difficulty of manœuvring in shallow waters, set sail, hoping to draw the galleons after him and 'to have banged yt out with them' on more favourable terms. The Portuguese, however, had had enough for the time being

[1] As before, the Portuguese 'frigates' (small armed vessels, propelled by oars) had been active in the Tapti, intercepting the English boats, and had actually captured and taken to Goa two of the merchants.

and retired to refit. The English ships, finding that they were not pursued, went over to the coast of Kathiawar for a supply of water and fresh provisions. Whilst there, on 22 December their pertinacious opponents appeared once more in sight. Best at once cleared for action, and next morning attacked the two largest vessels. 'The *Dragon*,' wrote the surgeon of the *Hosiander*, 'being ahead, steered from one to another, and gave them such banges as maid ther verie sides crack; for we neyther of us never shott butt [we] were so neere we could nott misse. We [in the *Hosiander*] still steered after the *Dragon*, and when she was with one, we weere with another; and the truth is we did so teare them thatt some of them weere glad to cutt cables and be gone.' In a second encounter the English ordnance did equal havoc; and then Best, finding himself short of ammunition and other stores, decided to return to Swally. There he anchored on 27 December, with all the prestige of having, with two merchantmen (one a mere pinnace), repeatedly repelled four warships specially equipped for the purpose.

At Swally, Best found that the imperial *farman* had not arrived; and, thinking that he was being tricked with promises, he ordered the factors to quit Surat and come aboard. Aldworth, however, did not share these doubts, and firmly refused to abandon his post. On 7 January 1613 news came that the expected document was at hand, and a few days later it was delivered with due ceremony. Then, leaving Aldworth in charge of the factory, Best sailed on 17 January for Achin, promising to return in the autumn to fetch away the goods provided for the English market. The Portuguese galleons had again appeared at Swally, and now made a show of pursuing him, but soon desisted. 'Thus we partted from thes valient champians, that had vowed to do such famous acctts, butt yett [were] content [to] give us over, with greatt shame and infamy redounding unto themselves.'

Aldworth and the other factors at Surat were full of hopes of benefits to be derived from the new trade. In a letter sent overland to the Company about a week after Best's departure, they wrote that 'through the whole Indias there cannot bee any place more benifitiall for our country then this, beeinge the onely key to open all the rich and best trade of the Indias; and for sale of our commodities, espesially our cloath, itt exceedes all others, insoemuch our hope is you shall not neede to send any more mony heather, for heere and in the neighbour citties wil bee yeerly sould above a thowsand broade-cloathes and five hundred peeces of Devon keirsies, for ready monies; and (beeinge sorted accordinge to our advise, heerewith sente you) will double ittselfe'. Quicksilver, vermilion, ivory, sword-blades and lead would, they affirmed, prove very profitable; while, 'as for the commodities of this country, viz. indicoes, callicoes, cotten yarne, and divers other commodities, [these] will, by our computation, yeald three for one att home att least'. They added that 'heere are allsoe divers druges, wherein wee have little experience'. The sole danger was from the hostility of the Portuguese; and this, if it could not be removed by negotiations at Madrid, must be countered by the use of fleets strong enough to meet force by force.

Animated by these anticipations of success, Aldworth despatched a merchant named Canning to Agra, where he was to present a royal letter to the Emperor, and to induce him to send a reply, accompanied by a solemn confirmation of the agreement already concluded. Canning duly arrived at Agra, and was allowed to deliver King James's letter; but the Jesuits at court were careful to depreciate his credentials, and his incautious admission that the presents which he had brought came really from the Company, not from the King, still further discredited him. Jahangir paid far more attention to a cornet player who had come in Canning's suite, for his instrument was a novelty, and the Emperor's delight in its martial music created profound disquiet among the Jesuits, who produced a European conjurer as a counter attraction. As regards all matters of business the English envoy was referred to Mukarrab Khan, Hawkins's opponent, who was still in charge of the Gujarat ports, and from him he could not obtain a definite answer on any point.

Canning died of dysentery on 27 May 1613; whereupon the Surat factors sent up Thomas Kerridge to take his place. He arrived in August, and after some delay secured an interview with the Emperor, who, however, took no interest in anything but the Englishman's headgear,[1] which in consequence had to be sacrificed to the monarch's love of novelties. Kerridge was not allowed to broach the subject of his errand, but was told that all matters of foreign trade were in the hands of Mukarrab Khan. With some trouble he obtained admission to that functionary, only to be met with bitter complaints concerning Middleton's depredations on the Indian shipping. Kerridge excused these as justifiable retaliation for the treatment experienced at Surat, but held out some hopes that the Com-

[1] Kerridge himself terms it 'a hat'; but since he says that it was new and that he had just bought it in Agra (for sixteen rupees), it must have been a turban. The English merchants usually adopted Indian costume, at least when travelling; and Hawkins, while at Agra, wore regularly the garb of a Muhammadan noble.

pany would make restitution, if a peaceable commerce were once established. Mukarrab Khan then changed his tone, and made some vague promises; but he refused to procure the Emperor's signature to a new agreement, saying that this was unnecessary; nor would he undertake that a reply should be sent to the letter from the English monarch. Kerridge was much disgusted. 'For good successe', he wrote to Surat, 'I have smale hope, except shippinge come this yeare; as well to curbe the Portingals as to affright this people, whome nothinge butt feare will make honest.'

Of English shipping, however, there was no sign. Best did not carry out his promise to return to Surat, but, after filling the *Dragon* with pepper at Tiku and Bantam, sailed for home in December 1613. At Agra, as in Gujarat, to all appearance Portuguese influence was paramount, and the position of our countrymen was precarious in the extreme. Fortunately for them, however, their enemies were not content to let matters take their course, but endeavoured by open violence to force the Indians to expel the English from their territories once and for all. In September 1613 a Surat vessel of great value, returning from the Red Sea, was seized by some Portuguese frigates and carried off, with all her passengers, in spite of the fact that she was duly furnished with a Portuguese pass. She belonged to the Emperor's mother, and this deepened the affront. Thereupon the enraged monarch closed the Jesuits' chapel, ordered the seizure of all the Portuguese in his dominions, and sent Mukarrab Khan with an army to besiege their settlement at Daman. On his side the Viceroy of Goa threatened to attack Surat, and commenced the preparation of an armada for that enterprise. These acts of hostility naturally caused a revulsion of feeling in favour of the English. 'Had wee now English shippinge here,' wrote the Surat factors in August 1614, 'wee might doe greate good in matter of trade, which now is debarred to the people of this country, haveinge none to deale with them. They all here much wish for the comminge of our English shipps, not onely for trade but to help them, for, as they say, the comminge of our shipps will much daunt the Portingalls.' As regards the commercial outlook, however, the factors had to confess that they had been too sanguine in their estimate of the sale of their broadcloth. Once the novelty had worn off, the demand had dropped almost to nothing; and the factors were therefore enquiring into the possibility of sending the surplus to Persia for sale. From court Kerridge wrote (in the following month) a little more hopefully regarding the sale of cloth; but as for his other business he could get no definite answer, being always referred to Mukarrab Khan, who had gone down to the coast.

Such being the state of affairs, it may be imagined with what joy Aldworth and his colleagues learnt that on 15 October 1614 a fleet of four ships, under Nicholas Downton, had anchored at Swally. No less rejoiced was Mukarrab Khan, in spite of his prejudice against the English, for he was dreading the appearance of the threatened squadron from Goa and was conscious that Surat, then unwalled, would be at the mercy of the Portuguese. He at once demanded a promise that Downton would take an active part in the expected hostilities, which in Mukarrab Khan's view had for their sole cause the encouragement given to English trade. Downton, however, was of a cautious nature and was mindful of the clause in his commission by which he was forbidden to commence hostilities with the subjects of other Christian powers, and so he returned a non-committal answer. He let it be known, however, that, if assaulted, he would vigorously defend himself. Mukarrab Khan was deeply incensed; but he dared not quarrel with his only friends. He accordingly permitted the new-comers to land their goods and to take active steps for consolidating their position in the country, including the despatch of a fresh envoy to the court, which was then at Ajmer, in Rajputana. For this service William Edwards, the principal of the newly arrived factors, was detailed; and he started in December, carrying with him yet another letter from King James and an ample supply of handsome presents brought out for the purpose.

Had the Portuguese been satisfied to seek a reconciliation by peaceful methods, they would doubtless have been successful, for all the Gujarat officials, from Mukarrab Khan downwards, were eager for an accommodation, and would gladly have sacrificed for that end the exiguous trade with the English. Luckily, however, the Portuguese Viceroy, Jeronimo de Azevedo, was persuaded that he had an excellent opportunity for crushing the English and dictating terms to the Indians at the same time. Collecting a formidable armament, he sailed northwards for this purpose in January 1615. But he found Downton's fleet snugly ensconced in Swally Hole, protected by sandbanks which his own heavy vessels could not pass. A determined attack by his lighter craft upon the smallest of the English ships was repulsed with great loss to the Portuguese; while subsequent efforts to destroy the enemy by means of fireships were frustrated by Downton's vigilance. Azevedo did not dare to send a force up the river to assault Surat, lest the English should take the offensive during its absence; and after a while he found himself obliged to make an inglorious retreat to Goa.

Meanwhile the Surat factors, profiting by the abnormal cheapness caused by these warlike operations, had acquired a good stock of indigo and calicoes; and when Downton sailed for Bantam, at the beginning of March 1615, one of his vessels (the *Hope*) was completely filled with Indian goods; and as soon as the squadron had got out of danger from a possible Portuguese attack, she quitted her consorts and made the best of her way home. She reached England towards the close of the year, and was the first ship to return direct from an Indian port.

## CHAPTER XXIV

## FACTORIES IN SUMATRA, JAVA, BORNEO AND CELEBES

WE now quit the shores of India and follow the fortunes of Captain Best in his further voyage to Sumatra and Java.

Subsequent to Lancaster's visit to Achin, at the northern extremity of the former island, the English for several years had little or nothing to do with that port, as they found it both easier and cheaper to buy pepper at Tiku or Priaman.[1] It is true that the *Union* called at Achin in 1609 and was well received, despite the efforts of the Dutch to prevent her from trading there. The real cause, however, of the reopening of relations with Achin four years later was the success of its monarch (grandson of the one with whom Lancaster had treated) in extending his power over Tiku and the neighbouring pepper ports, and his adoption of a policy of excluding foreigners from those places and forcing them to confine their trade to Achin itself. This rendered it necessary to undertake fresh negotiations, which would, it was hoped, not only secure permission to resume trade at Tiku and Priaman but also exempt the English from the payment of customs, in accordance with the treaty concluded by Lancaster. For this purpose Best called at Achin in April 1613, and spent three months in treating with the King. With

[1] It should be noted that the Sumatra pepper was of better quality than that procured at Bantam, and in 1614 it was fetching in London 3d. a lb. more.

much difficulty he at last procured permission for a visit to the subordinate ports; but exemption from customs dues was, not unreasonably, refused. He accordingly called at Tiku, and there and at Priaman purchased a supply of pepper, in spite of some obstruction from the local authorities. Proceeding to Bantam, Best completed the lading of the *Dragon*, and set sail for England on 15 December 1613.

In the middle of 1615 the *Thomas*, arriving at Tiku from Bantam, was refused trade, unless licence were first obtained from Achin; and thither she accordingly proceeded. At that port she found the *Hector*, which had called for the same purpose on her way from Surat. The King's policy was unaltered; but he was induced, by means of presents, to allow both vessels to trade at the subordinate ports for limited periods; and thereupon the *Thomas* left factors, both at Achin and at Priaman. In 1616 Captain Keeling, at the cost of further presents, obtained permission to trade at Tiku for a period of two years and no more. Results, however, were far from satisfactory, for the King was an active trader, and his officials at Tiku did all they could to hinder their foreign competitors; while at Achin itself the English had to face the rivalry of the Dutch and the rapacity of the monarch. The development of trade in India rendered the Company's factors unwilling to give up the struggle, since calicoes found a ready sale at the Sumatran ports; but in 1618 they had to confess themselves beaten, and the establishment at Tiku was withdrawn. That at Achin was continued with varying fortunes; but it is not necessary for our present purpose to follow the matter further.

An alternative source of pepper—and one much nearer to Bantam—had been found at Jambi, on the eastern side of Sumatra, to which place two small vessels were despatched in September 1615. Its king readily granted leave to trade, despite the opposition of the Dutch; and a factory was duly established. This settlement continued to be for many years an important means of procuring pepper for the English market, and was not entirely abandoned until about 1681, when Bencoolen, on the other side of the island, became the headquarters of the trade.

In 1616 a merchant named Christopher Sacker was sent in a junk from Patani to Indragiri, a pepper port lying to the northwards of Jambi. He was cordially received by the local chief; and upon applying to the Jambi factory for assistance, George Rix was despatched to co-operate with him. All went well until the time came for return to Patani. Then the chief failed to deliver the pepper that he had contracted to supply; and when Sacker ventured to remonstrate, he was promptly put to death for his insolence. Rix succumbed to illness ten days later, and then the chief took possession of the remaining stock. An Englishman, sent from Jambi in ignorance of the facts, narrowly escaped sharing Sacker's fate, and the goods that he had brought were confiscated. This was an ill-omened beginning; but later a reconciliation appears to have been effected and a regular factory established. This was maintained until 1622, when orders were sent to the merchants to wind up their business and come away. Before this could be effected, their house was set on fire by some natives and, although the factors made their escape to Jambi, it was with the loss of most of their goods. Such was the end of the establishment at Indragiri.

In Java the English headquarters remained at Bantam throughout the period with which we are concerned, though from time to time disputes arose with the Protector, who was the virtual ruler and shewed himself overbearing and oppressive. The Dutch, less patient than their rivals, about the end of 1610 came to terms with the King of Jakatra, a port town lying about fifty miles east of Bantam, and established there a factory which before long became their headquarters, under the name of Batavia. The English also used this port, particularly for refitting and provisioning their ships, and in 1614 they secured permission to establish a regular factory. The jealousy of the Bantam authorities, however, prevented them from proceeding with the project immediately, though they took care to keep on good terms with the Jakatra monarch, and frequently sent vessels thither for repair.[1] By 1617 they had summoned up courage to disregard the protests made at Bantam and to set up a factory at Jakatra. Of its fortunes we shall hear more in another chapter.

As regards other parts of Java, we may note that several attempts were made to open up communication with towns on the north-eastern side. At the beginning of 1615 Jourdain wrote from Bantam to the Company, advising that factories should be established at Japara and Gressik; also in Timor, an island lying farther east, where sandal-wood was procurable. In February of the same year the *Thomasine* was ordered to visit all these places on her return from the Bandas; but she was wrecked after leaving Macassar, and so nothing came of the scheme. About the same time the *Concord* received similar instructions, but found no opportunity of carrying them out. In 1618 Richard Bishop appears to have been sent to Japara with a stock of money and

[1] It was while being careened at Jakatra that the old *Hector* came to an inglorious end, owing to a mishap.

goods; and in February 1619 John Bonfoy is mentioned as having been appointed a factor there. It was a place of some importance, as being the chief port of the Sultan of Mataram, who ruled over the central portion of Java. The hostilities that developed between that monarch and the Dutch had dire results for the English. In May 1619 the Hollanders attacked and burnt Japara, destroying the English factory with the rest of the town and treating the English colours with studied indignity. Before long, however, the settlement must have been re-established, for the *Globe* went thither in November 1620 to fetch boards and provisions, and in March 1621 we hear of William Bennet as being chief at Japara, though in the following year he was sent home, 'for drunkenness and other lewdness'. In 1624 there were two factors there, and a similar number is found in a return dated five years later. The factory lingered at least until 1648, when the Company resolved to dissolve it. The chief reason for retaining it so long appears to have been that it provided facilities for repairing ships employed in the Far East.

The spacious island of Borneo, reputed rich in diamonds, gold (which was washed out of the sands of the rivers), bezoar stones, eagle-wood, benzoin, camphor and other products of commercial value, naturally attracted the notice of the English merchants at an early stage, though, as usual, the Dutch were the first to open up trade in that direction. John Saris, writing from Bantam at the close of 1608, reminded the Company that he had several times called their attention to the success of the Netherlanders in obtaining gold and diamonds at Sukadana, on the south-west coast of Borneo; and it was probably in consequence of his enthusiastic advocacy that Captain Keeling had arranged, in the previous October, that, when the pinnace *Hope* should return from an intended voyage to the Bandas, she should then go to Sukadana, under the charge of Saris himself. Apparently, however, the attempt was never made; and the next we hear upon the subject is in David Middleton's account of his voyage in the *Expedition* (1609–11). He tells us that, when his vessel was about to return, he seriously contemplated remaining behind at Bantam, in order to go in a junk to Sukadana, 'where the Hollanders have made great voyages'. But in the end he decided that his duty was to go home with his ship. He left orders, however, with Augustine Spalding, the chief at Bantam, to arrange for the despatch of an expedition to Sukadana. These instructions were given towards the end of 1610; and from Floris we learn that 'by order of David Middleton a factorie was setled at Succadania, and continued by Master Spalding'. From this we may assume that the English established themselves at that port either in 1611 or 1612, though precise information on the point is lacking. Saris' journal informs us that in December 1612 Captain Alexander Sharpie sailed from Bantam in a small junk for Sukadana, apparently on a trading venture undertaken by order of Sir Henry Middleton on account of the Sixth Voyage. We hear nothing further about him, except that at Jakatra the Dutch searched his vessel; and probably he died, either at Sukadana (if he ever succeeded in reaching that port) or on the way thither.

Some time in 1613 Sir Henry Middleton sent to Sukadana Sophonias,[1] a merchant, and Hugh Greet, a jeweller, both of whom had come out with David Middleton; and we find the pair of them there in July

[1] He was a Russian by birth and is usually called in the records Sophony Cozuck (*i.e.* the Kazak).

of that year. In the following spring the *Darling* was despatched thither from Bantam with a fresh stock of merchandise. She reached her destination at the beginning of April 1614, and found Sophonias and Greet in good health, but very short of money. They had settled a subordinate factory at Sambas, some distance along the coast to the northwards; and this too was short of supplies. Sophonias was now sent thither with a stock of cash in a native boat; and he took the opportunity to explore the possibilities of trade in the Landak region, still farther to the north. With only two Englishmen in his company, he proceeded for some distance inland. Then he was attacked by a large force of Dyaks, and though these were scared off by the Europeans' firearms, it was deemed prudent to abandon the enterprise and return to Sukadana. Nothing daunted, he shortly afterwards renewed the attempt, in a larger boat and with nine Englishmen; but only to be again baffled by the attitude of the natives, who, though outwardly friendly, were obviously waiting for an opportunity to overwhelm the small party. On its return, the *Darling* departed (13 June 1614) for Patani, leaving Nathaniel Courthope in charge at Sukadana.

The factory at Sambas was not of long continuance. A merchant named Cassarian David was sent thither from Sukadana to take charge, arriving in July 1614. After four months' experience, finding that the trade by no means came up to expectation, and having on three occasions narrowly escaped death at the hands of the natives, he determined to abandon the place. Getting leave from the local chief to repair to Sukadana, under the pretext of fetching more goods, he embarked on 25 November in a small junk, and reached the head settlement three weeks later. David then sailed for

Bantam in the same junk, with six more Englishmen; but being foiled by contrary winds, he sailed eastwards along the coast to Banjarmassin, now the capital of Dutch Borneo. At this place he arrived on 10 January 1615, and was welcomed by the inhabitants; and finding the prospects favourable, he remained until the following autumn. Then, having received no supplies, in spite of his appeals, and his cash being exhausted, he was forced to leave his house and his small stock of goods in the hands of the chief and go in a Malay junk to Bantam. It would seem that the factory at Banjarmassin was soon after re-established, but the facts are obscure. A settlement there was certainly in existence in January 1618, when a letter from Bantam spoke scornfully of it as a needless factory; but probably it was withdrawn in the disastrous period that succeeded, when the English and Dutch were in open conflict. In October 1620 we hear that a factor is about to be despatched thither, and after that all is silence.

The establishment at Sukadana continued with varying fortunes, though suffering alike from the competition of the Dutch and the general embarrassment of the Company's affairs in the Far East. At last, in 1622, a force from Java made a sudden descent upon the town, which was captured and sacked. Edward Pike, one of the English factors, was killed by an explosion of gunpowder, and both his compatriots and the Dutch sustained heavy losses. The latter withdrew their factory, and the English appear to have followed suit, for in February 1623 the President at Jakatra reported to the Company that the debts at Sukadana must be looked upon as irrecoverable, the queen having been captured by the Javanese and the natives having fled from the town. This is the last we hear upon the subject.

Macassar, on the western coast of the island of Celebes, was a port of considerable trade throughout the first half of the seventeenth century. It was of special importance by reason of its position as a half-way house between Java and the Spice Islands; and it had with the latter a valuable commerce, sending thither gold and rice and receiving spices in return. As we have already seen, Captain Keeling had made an unsuccessful attempt to reach the port as early as August 1609. In July 1613 Jourdain called there on his way back from Amboina and, finding the king friendly, established a factory, which proved of long continuance. The Dutch had likewise settled there; but before long they quarrelled with the monarch and were forced to quit. Their subsequent conquest of the Bandas diminished the volume of the trade of Macassar, but in a sense increased its importance for European traders, since it still received a considerable supply of cloves, despite all the efforts of the Dutch to prevent this leakage in their monopoly. The Danes, the French, the Portuguese, all resorted thither; but the greatest eyesore of all to the Hollanders was the factory maintained by the British. At last an opportunity of crushing this out of existence was offered by the Anglo-Dutch war of 1665–67. Assembling a strong fleet, they succeeded (November 1667) in forcing the King of Macassar to sign a treaty, by which all other Europeans were to be excluded from his dominions, while the English factors and their goods were to be delivered up for transport to Batavia. Since this was done before the treaty of Breda became operative in the East, all protests proved unavailing, and Macassar passed permanently under the influence of the Dutch.

## CHAPTER XXV

# JOURDAIN VISITS AMBOINA AND CERAM

BY this time friction had developed between the Dutch and English at practically every Eastern port to which the two nationalities resorted; but it was in the Moluccas—using that term in its widest sense—that this antagonism reached its bitterest intensity. In the Bandas the Hollanders, relying upon the treaties which they had forced the inhabitants to sign, claimed the monopoly of the export trade and warned off the English as trespassers. The same restrictive policy was being pursued in Amboina and the larger island of Ceram; while the Sultan of Ternate, who asserted sovereignty over the whole of the Moluccas, was entirely under the influence of the Dutch. To the claims of the latter the English retorted by denying the right of their opponents to thrust them out of a commerce already enjoyed for a considerable period, and declared their intention of ignoring the treaties and of continuing to trade with the natives wherever they found willing buyers and sellers. The consequence was a series of disputes which led by degrees to actual fighting. Had the Hollanders treated the natives with more consideration, they might have won their goodwill and have induced them to accept the position, at least with resignation. But in this respect they did not rise above the level of general European thought in regard to Asiatics; and, conscious of the great expense to which they were being put by the maintenance of fortresses and of fleets of war, the Dutch officials were keen to make the greatest possible profit out of the traffic in spices. Upon the point of the prices to be paid to the cultivators, the agreements they had concluded either said nothing at all or else referred the determination to the Sultan of Ternate, who was their obedient servant. The result was that these prices were gradually beaten down to nearly half the usual rates; while a system of advances (chiefly in cotton cloths, at prices fixed by the Dutch) still further enslaved the unfortunate peasants. Hence arose a deep feeling of resentment among the latter, with a longing to return to the old state of things, when they had been free to sell their produce at their own price to all comers. Though still in awe of the Dutch power, they felt no obligation to stand by the terms of agreements which they regarded as one-sided and oppressive, and they made no scruple of evading them whenever it was safe to do so. The English traders were of course specially welcomed, in the hope that they might be induced to help in throwing off the burden of the Dutch yoke; and it must be admitted that our fellow-countrymen were too often guilty of encouraging these expectations, without any real intention of actively intervening.

A previous chapter has narrated the course of events down to the departure of David Middleton from Ceram in the autumn of 1610. During the next two years the English factors at Bantam were too engrossed in other schemes to make any further move in that direction; but early in 1613 Sir Henry Middleton despatched the *Darling* to Amboina and the Bandas, under the charge of John Jourdain. This remarkable individual, who for the next six years was to be the protagonist of the struggle against the Dutch, had come out to the East five years earlier in the *Ascension*, and had been wrecked in that vessel on the coast of Gujarat in the autumn of 1609. After spending some time at Surat, he joined Hawkins at Agra towards the close of 1610, only to be compelled to quit the capital in the following summer, when the English envoy fell into disgrace. Then, making his way down to the coast, Jourdain succeeded in getting on board Sir Henry Middleton's fleet, and accompanied it upon its punitive expedition to the Red Sea. Middleton, whose confidence he had completely won, next sent him in the *Darling* to the pepper ports of Sumatra, from whence he went on to Bantam. When it was resolved to despatch the *Darling* on a further voyage to the eastwards, Jourdain volunteered to take charge of her again, and this offer Middleton gladly accepted.

The vessel's first objective was Hitu, on the northern coast of the island of Amboina, and here she anchored on 21 March 1613. The Dutch Resident boarded the *Darling* and begged her commander not to attempt to buy any cloves from the natives, as he had written, he said, to his superior officer at Fort Victoria for permission to sell him any quantity he might require for his small vessel, hoping thus to avoid any disagreement. Jourdain agreed to wait two days for an answer to this letter; but when the period had expired, he made overtures to the native governor of the town for permission to trade and to settle a factory. The governor hesitated, and at length replied that he must consult the other chiefs. Before anything further could be done, the Dutch Resident appeared with the expected answer from Fort Victoria. This contained a peremptory refusal to allow the English to have any trade in the island, declaring that the natives had contracted to sell their cloves to the Dutch, who had been 'at an extreame charge in buildinge and mainetayneing castles to defend them against their enemyes'. Jourdain defiantly replied that the country was 'free for all men', that the natives, he understood, were not 'vassalls to the Hollanders', and that he saw 'noe cause butt that wee may buy and sell with them, if they are soe content (as they are)'. He soon found, however, that he was too sanguine as to

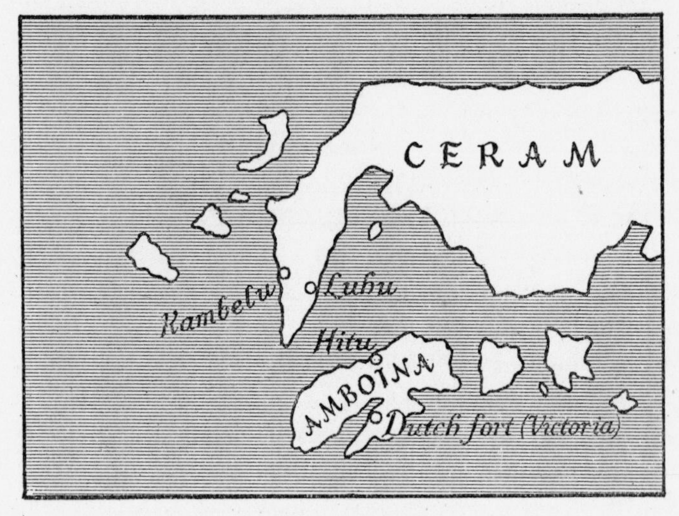


CERAM AND AMBOINA

this, and that the Hitu chiefs, while evidently desirous of dealing with him, were afraid to do so, in face of the Dutch threats; and so he resolved to take his vessel over to Luhu, on Ceram, from which place he had already received overtures for commerce.

In the western part of that island the Hollanders had already concluded the usual agreements with the chiefs of the districts that were the main sources of cloves, and had settled factories both at Luhu and at Kambelu. At the former place Jourdain got into touch with the natives, who assured him that they would gladly deal with him, were it not for the menaces of the Dutch, who had threatened 'to build a castle, if they did trade with us, and they durst not to displease them without order from the Kinge of Turnatto'. Thereupon he went boldly to the Dutch factory, where he was confronted by a young man who was destined to be the most striking figure in that quarter of the globe—the future Governor-General of the Dutch Indies, Jan Pieterzoon Coen. Coen was as downright as Jourdain himself, and at once 'in a chollericke manner' upbraided the Englishman for interfering 'in the countries that were under their proteccion, as itt were in dispight of them', declaring that, if he bought any cloves in those parts without the consent of the Dutch, 'it was soe much stolne from them, and therefore they would prevent itt, if by any meanes they might'. Jourdain answered that 'the countrye was as free for us as for them', and that he knew the people were anxious to trade with him. To prove this, he challenged Coen to summon the chiefs and put the question to them; if of their free will they declined to have anything to do with him, he would at once depart. To this course the Dutchman naturally declined to agree, and Jourdain thereupon proceeded to a neighbouring spot, where he knew that the natives had assembled. On learning what had passed, they insisted upon the attendance of the Dutch, and in their presence solemnly declared that it was their desire to trade with the English and that the threats of the Hollanders constituted the sole obstacle to this.

Next day the English were told by the natives that their chiefs had decided to appeal to the Sultan of Ternate for permission to deal with the English the next monsoon; and they were promised that meanwhile what cloves were available would be sold to them in secret. Accordingly a price (much higher than that given by the Dutch) was agreed upon; and for some days, with the connivance of one of the principal chiefs, the weighing and purchasing of cloves went on briskly at a spot 'out of sight of the Hollenders'. Before long, however, the latter discovered what was happening, and sent to Amboina for a couple of ships to frighten away the *Darling*; at the same time delivering to the English captain a written protest, which he declined to notice, on the pretext that he could not understand the Dutch language. The two ships failed to materialise, but threats to the country people, and particularly to the chief who had been prominent in dealing with the English, speedily produced an effect, and the supply of cloves dried up. On 12 April a fresh protest was sent to Jourdain—this time in Portuguese—warning him to depart or take the consequences. He returned a contemptuous answer; but, finding that he was not likely to get any more cloves, on the 20th he took his departure, after a farewell interview with the Luhu chiefs, in which he was begged to return the next year with a force adequate to defy the Dutch; in which case the natives would repay the latter any advances received, and then sell their cloves to the English.

A message had been received from Kambelu, on the western side of Ceram, that a quantity of cloves might there be had, if the *Darling* would fetch them; so thither the vessel now proceeded. On her way she tried to call again at Hitu, but was prevented by a sudden calm from actually reaching the roadstead. However, some of the chiefs came out in a boat, and made excuses for their failure to send cloves over to Luhu, as promised, 'sayinge that they had done as much as they durst doe, and . . . that the Hollanders would make them paye well for itt after our departure'. They urged Jourdain to come again the following year, with at least two ships 'to countenance the matter'; then they would break with their oppressors, and either obtain liberty to sell to all comers or give over the cultivation of cloves. According to the Dutch, the English captain assured them in reply that a further visit would be paid the next year. This done, he took his ship to Kambelu. There a small quantity of cloves was obtained, though the native chief was so terrified of the Dutch that he would not agree to an English factory being established in his territory. On 3 May the *Darling* sailed on her return voyage to Bantam.

On the way a call was made at Buton, the king of which pressed hard for the settlement of a factory in his town. But there seemed to be small prospect of profitable trade, and in any case none of the few merchants available could be spared for this purpose. Jourdain therefore made excuses and promised a visit the following year, when, if the king had succeeded in drawing to his country some trade in spices, his wishes should be met. The *Darling* next passed on to Macassar, which was reached on 11 July; and there, as already related, a factory was left. The voyage was then resumed. An attempt to call at Sukadana, in Borneo, was frustrated by the incompetence of the pilot; and Bantam was attained on 18 August 1613, nearly six months after the vessel had started from that port.

So far as the immediate object of the voyage was concerned—the obtaining of a cargo of cloves—it had been a success; while valuable information had been secured as to the strength of the Dutch position in

Amboina and Ceram. It is to be feared, however, that the prestige of the English in those parts was not enhanced in the long run by these sporadic attempts, undertaken without any settled policy behind them; and a heavy responsibility was incurred by encouraging the natives to break their contracts with the Dutch in the hope of English support. As a matter of fact, the year 1614 passed away without any attempt being made at Bantam to redeem the promises that had been given. It is true that, at the end of February, a junk was despatched in that direction from Macassar; but it got no farther than Buton, owing to an unexpectedly early change in the monsoon. Early in 1615 the *Concord*, accompanied by the pinnace *Speedwell*, sailed for the Bandas and Ceram, under the charge of George Ball and George Cokayne, the latter of whom had been with Jourdain in his voyage in 1613. Their experiences in the Banda Islands will be dealt with later; but we must here note that the *Concord*, on her return voyage, called in succession at Hitu, Luhu and Kambelu. At the second of these places she met the *Thomasine*, which had been sent from Bantam to assist her. The natives of Ceram were delighted at the arrival of the two vessels, and offered sites for factories at both Kambelu and Luhu. But the English were too weak to effect anything, and, although they actually exchanged shots with the Dutch at Kambelu, they were forced to give way and return to Bantam, leaving the unfortunate natives to settle accounts with the Hollanders as best they might.

## CHAPTER XXVI

## THE STRUGGLE IN THE BANDAS

THE perseverance of the English in the attempt to maintain a footing in the Moluccas was not merely the outcome of wounded pride or of unwillingness to submit to Dutch dictation; it was a deliberate policy, due to obvious commercial considerations. On all sides it was recognised that the traffic in spices was the most lucrative branch of Eastern commerce. As the English Company pointed out, in a letter to Bantam of 3 November 1614, even the best sort of pepper yielded in London only 1s. 11d. per lb., while cloves, in the roughest state, fetched nearly 7s.; and, in view of the heavy cost at which the trade was being carried on, it was imperative, they said, that the cargoes of the homeward-bound ships should include as large a proportion as possible of the finer spices. Moreover, the latter were in great demand all over the East, and any that could be spared for this purpose found everywhere a profitable market. The fact that the Dutch themselves were straining every nerve to obtain the command of the field was in itself a proof of its transcendent importance, and our countrymen can scarcely be blamed for struggling hard against the attempt to exclude them from all share in this commerce.

Allusion has already been made to the despatch of the *Concord* and *Speedwell* from Bantam to the Banda Islands in January 1615, under Ball and Cokayne.

They reached their destination in the middle of March, and anchored in the usual roadstead under the Dutch fort on the island of Neira. Somewhat to their dismay, they found there Gerard Reynst, the Dutch governor-general, with seven 'very tall' ships, intent upon completing the conquest of the group. Reynst was courteous, but displayed a firm determination to prevent the English from trading with the natives. After vainly endeavouring to get into touch with the chiefs of Lontor, with a view to leaving a factory there, Ball set sail in the pinnace for Wai, to which island the *Concord* had already gone. Two Dutch ships followed closely, but were evaded in the night. Next day the pinnace was beached at Wai, and there left under the charge of Sophonias (who had come in her from Bantam) to trade with the inhabitants, while the *Concord* went on to a roadstead on the south-eastern side of Ceram, to obtain provisions and await the change of the monsoon. At the end of April Ball took her back to Wai. He found a quantity of spices awaiting him, and, taking these on board, he departed for Amboina, leaving Sophonias at Wai with the pinnace to continue his trading. Before long a Dutch force landed upon the island, and proceeded to treat the little band of Englishmen very roughly. They were, however, soon rescued by the natives, who, mustering in great numbers, drove the invaders off the island, inflicting great losses upon them. Trading was then resumed, and in the middle of September, having filled his little vessel with mace and nutmegs, Sophonias departed for Bantam, leaving behind Richard Hunt and one other Englishman with a stock of goods, and carrying with him a representative of the chiefs to appeal to Jourdain for assistance against the Dutch. Active hostilities against the latter were, however, more than Jourdain and his colleagues had either the means or the authority to undertake, without express warrant from London; and, moreover, they must have been aware that negotiations were going on in Europe for a settlement of the dispute. So they temporised, promising a supply of provisions and a continuance of trading, and deferring a decision on other points until further conference had been held on the spot with the Banda chiefs.

To carry back the Bandanese envoy and to provide an opportunity for further negotiations, Jourdain in December 1615 prepared a fresh expedition, to consist of the *Concord* and *Speedwell*, as before, with the addition of the *Thomas*, with Ball and Sophonias in charge of the squadron. Just as they were ready to start, the *Clove* and *Defence* arrived from England, under the command of Samuel Castleton.[1] Thereupon it was arranged that all five ships should proceed to the Bandas, with Castleton in supreme command; and the fleet sailed accordingly in January 1616. Wai was duly reached, and the Bandanese envoy was landed. On the news of their arrival, a strong Dutch fleet was sent from Neira with orders to drive away the intruders at all costs. The two fleets met on 13 March, and both prepared for battle. But the conditions were too unequal for the English to hope for success. Their ships numbered only four (the pinnace being too small to count), and two of them were in bad condition, while all were undermanned. The Dutch, on the other hand, had nine good ships and a sloop, reinforced for the occasion by a

[1] In 1611–13 he had commanded an interloping vessel, the *Pearl*, in a voyage to Sumatra (see *Purchas His Pilgrimes*, vol. iii, p. 343). His employment on the present occasion seems to have been due to the Company's desire to keep him from doing further mischief, there being persistent rumours that he was about to engage in a fresh interloping venture.

strong force of soldiers from the castle. It seemed to Castleton that the only thing to be done was to make the best terms possible; and negotiations were facilitated by the fact that the Dutch commander, Jan Dirckszoon Lam, was already well known to him. On 16 March an agreement was concluded, practically on terms dictated by the Hollanders. Castleton gave an assurance that he had in no way assisted the people of Wai; while the Dutch undertook that, provided the English remained neutral in the coming struggle, their factors should not be interfered with, and, in the event of a Dutch success, should be allowed to quit the island with their goods. Should the Hollanders fail to conquer the island, the English were to be left at Wai undisturbed. In accordance with this compact, Castleton issued instructions to Hunt, who was to remain in charge of the factory, to maintain a neutral attitude in any fighting that might ensue, and, should the Dutch prove the victors, to put his goods aboard the pinnace and leave the island. Castleton himself departed immediately for Ceram with his four vessels.

In taking the course he did, Castleton shewed small concern, either for the honour of the British name or for the interests of his employers. Doubtless he was not in a position to repel force by force; but he might have withdrawn under protest with his fleet, leaving to the Dutch the embarrassment of dealing with the year-old factory on Wai. To that island they had as yet no valid claim, and to expel any English whom they might find settled there would have been to take a serious responsibility. Now, however, they had the English commander's undertaking that his subordinates should abandon the island in the event of its conquest by the Dutch, and of this they took full advantage.

However, Richard Hunt paid small attention to his instructions. His sympathy was entirely with the natives, and it was probably upon his advice that they, in the despairing hope that, if they took shelter under the British flag, the Dutch commander might yet stay his hand, made a formal surrender to Hunt of both Wai and the neighbouring island of Run, and hoisted English colours upon their hastily constructed fortifications. Naturally this availed them nothing. On 27 March the Dutch landed and quickly beat down all resistance. The greater part of the inhabitants fled to Run; the remainder submitted, on terms dictated by the conquerors, who thereupon erected a strong castle to secure their obedience. Hunt, whom the exasperated Dutch had threatened to hang if they caught him, managed to get in a boat to Macassar, and thence to Bantam, where he arrived, 'bringinge with him the earth of the countrye, sticks and stones, delivered him in signe of possession of the countrye'. The pinnace, which Castleton had left in Neira Road, was allowed to depart to Bantam with her cargo of spices.

Castleton's instructions had bidden him to proceed from the Bandas to Amboina and Ceram, and afterwards to Tidore and other islands in the Moluccas proper. He made in the first instance for Luhu; but finding a Dutch squadron on guard there, betook himself to Ternate and Tidore. The Hollanders succeeded in preventing the natives from selling him any cloves, though he managed to exchange rice for spices at the Spanish fortress on Tidore. Castleton's death put an end to the enterprise, and his ships straggled back to Bantam, with the exception of the *Thomas*, which, as previously arranged, went on to Japan.

Jourdain and his colleagues, acutely aware of the

need for speedy action, prepared a fresh expedition which should occupy the island of Run in the name of King James and lay claim to that of Wai, on the ground of the surrender made by the inhabitants. With the help of the latter and with the backing of the national flag, it was hoped to hold at least Run until diplomacy should have time to get to work in Europe. In any case, by taking this course, the factors would have done their duty to their employers, by making good a footing in the disputed territory and thus keeping open the door which the Dutch were so eager to close. Only two ships were available—the *Defence*, which had been one of Castleton's fleet, and the *Swan*, which had reached Bantam in the previous autumn. Nathaniel Courthope was placed in command, with Sophonias, Hunt and Thomas Spurway as his assistants. His instructions, drawn up by Jourdain, directed him to call at Macassar for a supply of rice and then make for Run. There he was to investigate the position, particularly as regarded the surrender made to Hunt. If he found the natives still desirous of becoming British subjects, they were to be induced to 'ratefie under thare hannds and seales the former surrender, yf lawfully made; yf not, then to make a new surrender of all or parte of such ilannds as are yet under thare owne commannds and att thare owne dispose, leaveinge out thease whare the Flemings are possessed and have command'. Nothing was to be attempted against Wai, though, if the surrender were found to be valid, the Dutch were to be notified of the English claim. Should the inhabitants of Lontor and Rosengijn be willing to put themselves under British protection, a formal agreement was to be made to that effect. If the natives of Run desired it, ordnance might be landed for their defence; and in the event of the

Hollanders offering violence 'to the countries of our soveraigne lord the Kinge, or to the shipes, goods, or persons of his subjects, you are, to the uttmoste of your power, even to the losse of lyves and goods, to make good the same'. Hunt was to be left at Run as chief factor.

Quitting Bantam at the end of October 1616, the two vessels reached Run two days before Christmas. The native chiefs assured Courthope that they had not concluded any agreement with their hated foes, and that the surrender to Hunt had been made before the Dutch attacked Wai. Nevertheless, the ceremony of ceding the two islands to the British sovereign was gone through afresh. Writings were 'drawne and confirmed by the principals of Polaroone and Polaway', who 'at the same instant delivered us a nutmeg-tree with the fruits thereon, in the earth, with other fruits and a living goat'. The English colours were then hoisted and saluted, and several guns were landed, with which a couple of batteries were constructed. The Dutch were not slow to take up the gauntlet thus flung down. On 3 January 1617 Cornelis Dedel came over from Neira with three vessels strongly manned. But the English ordnance looked formidable, and the natives swarmed down to the beach, eager for the fray. So Courthope had the satisfaction of ordering the Dutch commander to withdraw at once, or take the consequences; and Dedel thought it best to beat a retreat and send to Amboina for reinforcements. A week later a Dutch pinnace was observed to be taking soundings off a small island called Nailaka; and since the seizure of this would enable the Dutch to dominate the road in which the English ships were lying, some shots were fired at the pinnace, which thereupon fled. This incident was used by the Hollanders to justify their subsequent proceedings, they alleging that their opponents had thus been the first to commence hostilities.

In the middle of January, John Davis, the headstrong master of the *Swan*, insisted upon taking that vessel over to Lontor, in order to fill his water-casks. After remonstrating in vain against this division of forces, Courthope resolved to turn the expedition to account. He had already concluded an agreement with the inhabitants of the island of Rosengijn and of the town of Waier (on Lontor) for the surrender of their territory to the British Crown, and he now sent Sophonias and three other merchants in the *Swan* to take formal possession and establish a factory. When this had been effected, the vessel proceeded to the coast of Ceram to water. On 2 February, having filled his casks, Davis started on his return voyage to Run. His folly in quitting his consort and the shelter of the English batteries was soon apparent. The *Swan* was attacked by a Dutch ship, well filled with soldiers from Neira, and, after a brief engagement in which she lost more than half her scanty crew,[1] she was overpowered by boarding, and was towed in triumph into Neira Road; the Hollanders 'much glorying in their victorie and showing the Bandaneses their exploit, in the great disgrace of the English what they could, saying that the King of England might not compare with their great King of Holland, and that one Holland ship would take ten of the English ships, and that St. George is now turned child'.

More than three weeks elapsed before Courthope heard the heavy news of the capture of the *Swan*. He at once sent to Neira to demand her restitution, but was answered with taunts and threats. An early attack upon

[1] In the engagement Sophonias was 'beaten in pieces with a great shot', and thus ended an adventurous career.

the *Defence* was now to be expected; and fearing lest she should be burnt or boarded, it was resolved to empty her of her stores and guns, and with these to establish a fortified post upon the little island of Nailaka already mentioned, and then to draw up the ship on the beach under the shelter of the ordnance. Before this task was fully completed, on the night of 19 or 20 March the vessel drifted from her anchorage, either through carelessness or through her cable being purposely cut by some of the crew, sick of their detention at such an out-of-the-way spot. A few loyal men seized a boat and regained the island; the remainder ran the *Defence* into Neira Road and surrendered her to the Dutch.

A few days later Laurens Reael, the Dutch governor-general, arrived at Neira. He was a man of moderation, who saw the seriousness of what had been done by his subordinates and was anxious to reach an accommodation, if possible. At his invitation Courthope went over to Neira, and a long debate ensured. Reael offered to restore the captured ships and men, to make compensation for what had been taken out of them, and to assist the English to depart with the spices they had accumulated at Run. Courthope, however, was made of sterner stuff than his predecessor, Castleton. 'I answered', he says, 'I could not, unlesse I should turne traitor unto my king and countrey, in giving up that right which I am able to hold, and also betray the countrey people, who had surrendered up their land to our Kings Majestie.' After conferring, at his return, with his colleagues, he reaffirmed this decision, but made an alternative proposal, namely, that he would depart in the *Defence*, provided that Reael would leave the question of the right to the disputed territory to be settled by negotiation at Bantam or in Europe, and would give a written pledge to make no attack upon the Bandanese in the meantime. These terms were refused, and the negotiations were thereupon broken off. Reael debated with his council the advisability of making an immediate assault upon Run, but it was decided to await reinforcements before so doing. Courthope, on his side, despatched Spurway in a native vessel to Bantam to solicit speedy help. Before long the people of Rosengijn and Lontor were driven by hunger to make their submission to the Dutch, and thus Run was left the only island of the group as yet unsubdued.

Had Jourdain been still at the head of affairs at Bantam, we cannot doubt that he would have strained every nerve to send assistance to Courthope and his small garrison at Nailaka; but he had gone home at the close of 1616. It is true that his successor, George Berkeley, had (before the receipt of Courthope's letter) despatched a small vessel, named the *Attendant*, to the Bandas in February 1617. She, however, got no farther than Macassar, owing to the monsoon being too far spent. When Captain Pepwell arrived at Bantam, towards the end of July, the question of his proceeding in the same direction was mooted; yet nothing was done. Captain Newport, to whom a similar suggestion was made, was anxious to return to England as quickly as possible; and his death, shortly after his arrival, put an end to the design. In November 1617 Governor-General Reael addressed a letter to the President, requiring the evacuation of Run and declaring that any English ship found in the Moluccas would be attacked. In reply he was assured that the English would defend the island and people to the last, and was warned that he would be held responsible for any bloodshed that might result.

## CHAPTER XXVII

# THE TRIUMPH OF THE HOLLANDERS

BY the autumn of 1618 the relations between the Dutch and the English were strained to the breaking-point. The former had a settled policy and incomparably greater resources, as they were disdainfully aware. But their commitments were many and were spread over a vast area, and what they chiefly dreaded was that the natives in the Moluccas, encouraged by the English, and perhaps aided by them with munitions, would overpower their weak garrisons and bring to ruin the empire they had so laboriously built up. That the English must at all costs be prevented from interfering further in those regions was the universal opinion of the Dutch officials; and by none was this view more strongly held than by Jan Pieterszoon Coen, who in June 1618 took up the post of Governor-General of the Dutch Indies. A man of wide vision and ruthless determination, he at once bent his whole energies to the task of making his nation the dominant power in the Far East; and in so doing, the last thing he was willing to consider was the interests of his English competitors.

In the following November Coen's old opponent, John Jourdain, arrived at Bantam to take up once more his position as the head of the English Company's servants in those parts. While at home, he had had little difficulty in persuading his employers of the absolute necessity of asserting their rights to unrestrained traffic in the Moluccas and of offering an uncompromising resistance to the Dutch attempts to create a monopoly. The idea that this might lead to war he scouted, for he was confident that 'the Flemings either dare not, or will not, sett upon the English'. It was, however, necessary that he should be provided with a strong backing, and the Company accordingly furnished him with a fleet of six vessels, under the command of Sir Thomas Dale, who had won some credit as a military leader in the Netherlands and had recently been Governor of Virginia.

The fleet sailed in February 1618. The outward voyage was clouded by a sad disaster; for off the coast of Sumatra Dale's flagship, the *Sun*, was wrecked with great loss of life. The remaining vessels reached Bantam in bad condition and with scanty crews. There serious news awaited them. An attempt had been made in the preceding January to relieve Courthope, but the two ships sent on this errand had been attacked and captured when within sight of their goal. It was believed that the Dutch had treated their prisoners with savage cruelty; and to add to the provocation Englishmen had been assaulted in the streets of Bantam and an English pinnace had been fired upon in the harbour. To Jourdain's exasperated countrymen the time for vengeance seemed at last to have come. A fleet under Martin Pring was already in the roads when Dale arrived, and with this and his own squadron he was for the moment in a much stronger position than the Hollanders, the bulk of whose forces were far to the eastwards. At this juncture the Dutch *Zwarte Leeuw* came into Bantam harbour, with a cargo that had cost about £14,000. She was at once seized, with the intention of holding her as a hostage for the satisfaction of English losses and wrongs. As ill-luck would have it, ere long she was accidentally set on fire by some English sailors rummaging for liquor and was burnt with all her cargo, leaving a heavy liability instead of an asset. Coen, on hearing of the seizure, retaliated by burning the English factory at Jakatra, and the two nations were now actively at war in the Far East. Just before Christmas an engagement took place between the rival fleets, in which both claimed a victory. Then Coen, finding himself outnumbered and short of munitions, retired to Amboina to collect his forces. The English judged it unsafe to follow him and attempt the relief of Courthope at Run, and contented themselves with joining the King of Jakatra in besieging the Dutch fort at that place. This was soon reduced to such a state that the garrison made overtures for capitulation; but at the critical moment the Pangaran (Protector) of Bantam, who claimed suzerainty over all the country, intervened and demanded that the fort and the Dutch prisoners should be made over to him. Dale, unable to carry out the terms of the proposed capitulation, which included the release of the Hollanders, withdrew from the siege, and the garrison was thus enabled to hold out until Coen arrived to its rescue.

In the meanwhile the English at Bantam had quarrelled with the Pangaran and had decided to withdraw, at least for a time, from that place. Dale, whose ships badly needed refitting, determined to take them to the Coromandel Coast for that purpose and then arrange to meet the ships which would be coming on to Bantam from Surat. Thus reinforced, he might hope to be in a position to confront Coen and his forces on fairly equal terms. Accordingly Dale and Pring departed westwards with their respective fleets towards the end of May

1619; while Jourdain, whose relations with Dale were far from cordial, set out with two ships to visit the factories at Jambi, Patani and elsewhere. This proved a fatal step. The implacable Coen came sweeping back from the eastwards with a large fleet, relieved Jakatra (which he soon afterwards transformed into a strongly fortified station and renamed Batavia Nova), and then pressed on to Bantam. From thence he detached three vessels to the northwards in pursuit of Jourdain. They overtook him at Patani, and at once (17 July) attacked his two weak ships. After a short but stubborn resistance, he found himself compelled to negotiate for surrender; and while terms were being arranged, he was mortally wounded by a shot fired from one of the Dutch vessels—accidentally, according to the Dutch; intentionally, according to the English. Defeated and dismayed, he was at the least spared the humiliation of becoming a prisoner in the hands of the hated Hollanders.

Disaster now followed disaster. In August the *Star* was captured in the Straits of Sunda; and at the beginning of October four more English ships[1] were surprised and taken at Tiku, with valuable ladings. Meanwhile the main fleet was lingering on the Coromandel Coast. At last, however, Pring, who had succeeded to the command upon the death of Dale (9 August), left Masulipatam in December, and at Tiku effected a junction with three ships from Surat. In March 1620 the united squadrons set out for Bantam, to try conclusions with the Dutch. On 8 April, however, they

[1] One of these was the old *Dragon*, Lancaster's flagship in the First Voyage. She spent the next few months in carrying to and fro materials for the new Dutch fortress at Batavia, and got so worn in this service that at the conclusion of peace the English refused to accept her again, preferring to stand out for her supposed value at the time of her capture.

were met in the Straits of Sunda by a ship from England, bringing news that an agreement had been reached at home (July 1619), and that in future the two Companies were to share in certain fixed proportions the trade of the Eastern islands and the dependent factories (including those on the Coromandel Coast), and jointly to bear the cost of defending them against the Spaniards and Portuguese. Three days later the Dutch and English fleets met, not as enemies but as seeming friends; and on the following day they anchored at Bantam to arrange for future co-operation.

We must now look back to the gallant Courthope and his little garrison at Nailaka. Though in dire need of supplies and in constant danger of being attacked, they held on grimly to their post, conscious of the vital importance of keeping the British flag flying in the Bandas. As already mentioned, the *Solomon* and *Attendant* appeared in sight in March 1618, bringing the long-expected relief; but before they could reach the island they were attacked by four Dutch ships, captured, and taken into Neira Road. In June the Hollanders made a landing upon Run, only to be repulsed by the natives with considerable loss. Two months later Courthope despatched one of his small band to Bantam to represent the perilous position of the garrison and implore help. After a long wait, a small pinnace arrived, towards the end of January 1619, with a letter from Sir Thomas Dale encouraging them to hold out and promising speedy assistance; but the year wore away without any sign of an English ship. In like manner passed the first ten months of 1620. Then, towards the end of October, Courthope, returning in a boat from an excursion to Lontor, was intercepted near Wai by the Dutch and, in the fight that followed, was mortally wounded. Thus perished a brave and gallant Englishman; and it is pleasant to note that the Hollanders, admiring his courage and constancy, buried his corpse with all honour. His place at Nailaka was taken by Robert Hayes, who a month later learnt, from Dutch letters intercepted by the natives, that peace had been concluded. He sent the letters over to Neira, and thereupon hostilities ceased, though the English still remained on guard, isolated and ill-supplied, until it should please their superiors to take steps for their relief.

Before long the Hollanders, having recovered freedom of action, unhampered by British interference, determined to conquer the remaining islands once and for all. In March 1621 they subdued Lontor, seizing and imprisoning the English they found on the island; and thereupon the inhabitants of Run, finding their position hopeless, yielded to the inevitable. The Dutch occupied the island itself; but the English post on Nailaka they left contemptuously alone, confident that its defenders would soon quit it now that all advantage from its possession had ceased. A few days later Captain Humphrey Fitzherbert arrived in the *Royal Exchange*. He of course could do nothing; and the solemn proclamation of the agreement between the Dutch and the English, which took place at Neira on 19 March 1621, finally convinced the Bandanese that they had been delivered over to the mercy of their oppressors.

The so-called 'Treaty of Defence' of 1619 had pleased neither the Dutch nor the English Company, having in fact been concluded only under pressure from King James. Still less did it satisfy their servants in the East, where both parties were sore from past incidents, while the Dutch in particular held that the convention had actually snatched victory from their grasp. In these circumstances it is not surprising to find that the arrangements for co-operation broke down after a comparatively short trial. Disputes arose upon many points, especially as to the fairness of the financial charges which the Dutch put to joint account, and as to the amenability of Englishmen to the Dutch tribunals. Before long the English President and Council, who had settled at Batavia under the terms of the treaty, found themselves in a hopeless position. They were destitute of the means of meeting the expenses of their share of the trade or of furnishing their quota of ships for the warlike operations into which they were dragged by their allies, now that the Truce of Antwerp had expired (1621). They decided, therefore, to withdraw their factors from the various Dutch settlements and to leave Batavia for some fresh headquarters station. Before this could be effected, the members of their staff at Amboina were arrested by the Dutch on a charge of conspiring to seize the fortress, and ten of their number were tortured and put to death, after an irregular trial (February 1623). This was the famous 'Massacre of Amboina', which poisoned the relations between the two countries for half a century. Although a fresh agreement had been negotiated at home (January 1623), intended to remove the chief causes of friction, the Amboina outrage practically put an end to all hope of co-operation in the East. Quitting Batavia early in 1624, the English endeavoured to make a new centre upon an uninhabited island in the Straits of Sunda; but its unhealthiness drove them back, unwillingly, to their former station in the Dutch capital. At last, in 1628, a return was made to their old headquarters at Bantam, where they were safe under the protection of the

Sultan and free from the interference of their rivals, with whom that monarch was on bad terms.

From time to time it seemed as though Courthope's gallant resistance might yet bear fruit in giving his countrymen an independent share in the trade of the Bandas. By the convention of 1623 already mentioned the island of Run was recognised as English property; and though this agreement proved abortive and the Dutch remained in possession, the London Company held stubbornly to its claim and revived it upon every opportunity. On several occasions proposals for the occupation of the island were brought forward for consideration; but the Company's position in general was too weak for it to undertake the task of maintaining so distant a possession. The Treaty of Westminster, which in 1654 closed Cromwell's successful war against Holland, provided for the restitution of Run to the English Company and secured for it a sum of £85,000 as compensation for the losses it had suffered at the hands of its Dutch rival. Still nothing was done to take possession of the island, for the London Company was almost at its last gasp. The treaty concluded eight years later by Charles II again affirmed the right of the English to occupy Run; and in March 1665 the island was actually handed over, after the Dutch, it is alleged, had destroyed all the spice-bearing trees. The outbreak of the Second Anglo-Dutch War enabled the Hollanders to retake it in the following November, and by the Treaty of Breda (1667) it was finally ceded to them. A further blow to English trade in the Far East was dealt fifteen years later, when the Dutch, by interfering in a civil war at Bantam, were enabled to induce the new sultan to expel the English merchants from his territories. This put an end to the English connection with

Java, after a continuance of eighty years. Macassar, as we have seen, had already been closed to their trade; and thenceforth their headquarters were at Bencoolen, on the south-west coast of Sumatra, where they built a fortified settlement, known first as Fort York, and afterwards as Fort Marlborough.

## CHAPTER XXVIII

# THE MISSION OF ROE TO THE GREAT MOGUL

FROM the depressing story of defeat and failure contained in the last three chapters it is a relief to turn once more to the Indian peninsula and pick up the threads of the course of events there. And in so doing it may be remarked that the rebuff sustained in the Moluccas had at least one compensation; for it induced the English to concentrate more vigorously on the trade in India and its neighbouring countries, where they were at least on equal terms with the Dutch politically, and where they found full employment for their limited resources. In the long run, the trade in calicoes, indigo, saltpetre, coffee and pepper (of which there was an ample supply in south-western India) was to prove of greater value than that in cloves and nutmegs, although at the time, and for at least half a century longer, the latter seemed to be by far the more attractive branch of Asiatic commerce.

We left the East India Company's factors settled at Surat, enjoying a certain amount of prestige from Downton's repulse of the Portuguese armada, and hoping for successful results from the mission of William Edwards to the imperial court. In this last respect they were disappointed. Edwards was a man of weak character and of no experience in Eastern diplomacy; and although the lavish presents which he had brought procured him a good reception from the Emperor Jahangir (who was always avid of novelties, especially those from far countries), no progress was made as regards the object of his mission, which was to obtain the Emperor's sanction for the establishment of English trade in his dominions on a settled basis. Soon a real danger threatened from the Portuguese, who, weary of a war which was damaging their commerce, made overtures to Jahangir for peace, offering compensation for the junk they had seized, but requiring the expulsion of the English, and their permanent exclusion, as the price of agreement. Fortunately for our fellow-countrymen, this clause was unacceptable to the Emperor's advisers, who had taken to heart the lesson taught by Middleton's reprisals and were not prepared to hazard their Red Sea traffic. In the end, towards the close of 1615, the Portuguese waived their insistence on this point and were allowed to resume their trading operations in Gujarat without any formal treaty. This was, however, far from meaning any decision on the part of the Emperor regarding the continuance of English trade. The port of Surat had been handed over to the care of Prince Khurram, Jahangir's favourite son and ultimately his successor; and he, influenced no doubt by Mukarrab Khan, inclined to the view that Indian interests would be better served by a renewal of the long-standing commerce with the Portuguese than by encouraging the new-comers to whom they so strongly objected. In point of fact, on the arrival of the 1615 fleet, Khurram sent down an order that 'the English should dischardge one ship and have a monthes staye in trade, but no residences in the towne'.

At this juncture occurred a dramatic development. The Company at home, moved by the unanimous opinion of its agents in India that no settlement of their position could be obtained by negotiations conducted by one of themselves, since merchants were despised at court, had induced King James to despatch a special plenipotentiary for the purpose—of course at the Company's expense. Of the ability and qualifications of Sir Thomas Roe, who was chosen for the post, nothing need here be said, as they are now familiar. He reached Swally in the middle of September 1615, escorted by a fleet of four vessels (including our old friends the *Dragon* and the *Peppercorn*) under the command of Captain William Keeling; and a few days later he landed in state, amid the roar of salutes from the gaily decorated ships. After some stay in Surat and a sharp dispute with its arrogant governor, resulting in the utter discomfiture of that functionary, the ambassador proceeded by easy stages up-country, and reached the imperial headquarters at Ajmer (in Rajputana) two days before Christmas. His official reception, delayed by his ill state of health, took place on 10 January 1616. Despite the fact that the presents which he offered contrasted unfavourably with those brought by Edwards, he was received with every appearance of welcome; and he wrote home exultantly that the Emperor had 'never used any ambassadour with so much respect'.

Roe remained at the court for two years and nine months, and during that period followed the Emperor, first to Mandu (the ruined capital of Malwa, overlooking the Narbada valley) and then to Ahmadabad, the chief city of Gujarat. To give a detailed narrative of his negotiations would be out of place, but a broad outline of the main features may be attempted. He had come out with the idea of negotiating a formal treaty of commerce between his own sovereign and the Great

Mogul, which should place the position of the English in India on a firm and lasting basis and secure them against all oppression by the provincial officials; and such a treaty he had full power to sign as the representative of his royal master. A procedure of this nature, however, was entirely foreign to the ideas of the Emperor and his advisers, as indeed it would have been to the head of any other oriental state. According to their ideas, the Emperor was a personage far too exalted to enter into engagements with the monarch of a distant kingdom, especially on such despised topics as the trade of merchants; nor was it to be contemplated that he should limit his freedom of action in any such manner. His will was the sole law for everybody in his dominions; and he must remain at liberty to change his mind as often as he pleased. Moreover, the proposed agreement was obviously one-sided; for what had the English ambassador to offer in return for the advantages he was seeking? The trade of his countrymen was as yet very small—far inferior, indeed, to that of the Portuguese whom they were endeavouring to supplant. That Indian merchants should ever themselves visit Britain and need reciprocal treatment could not be seriously suggested. The only bait which Roe could hold out was an undertaking that the English would 'bring and furnish the said mighty king with all the rarietyes yearly that they can find, and with any other goods or furniture of warr which the said king shall reasonablie desire, at indifferent [*i.e.* fair] prices'. He added an offer that they would assist the Emperor and his subjects 'against any enemy to the common peace', obviously meaning the Portuguese; but this was contemptuously put aside as derogatory to Jahangir's power and foreign to his intentions.

There were, moreover, other reasons why Roe's

proposals were unacceptable. One was that he required permission for his fellow-countrymen to settle factories in any part of the Mughal empire, Bengal and Sind being especially named in this connection. The Portuguese had trading posts in both provinces, and it was argued by the opponents of the treaty that, were the English allowed to extend their operations in those directions, the result would be bickerings, if not actual hostilities, between the two nations which would be as detrimental to Indian interests as the quarrels in Gujarat had proved. A still stronger objection was that the ambassador was obviously endeavouring to use the Emperor's authority to exempt the English from control on the part of the local governors, even of Prince Khurram himself. This was contrary to the traditional system, which allowed such officials considerable freedom of action; and any limitation of their powers—with the resulting diminution of their personal profits—was sure to be distasteful, not only to those who were actually holding posts, but to all who hoped to do so in future. In particular, Khurram was firmly opposed to such a concession, both as damaging to his position and for special reasons. He was himself not indifferent to the curiosities that the Europeans were bringing—clocks, telescopes, jewels in novel settings—and in addition he found them particularly useful for securing his father's favour. Indeed, one of his objects in taking over the superintendence of Surat had been to make sure of the first chance of obtaining such novelties. Behind the scenes, therefore, he and his partisans used all their influence against the grant of the desired concessions.

For a time Roe, deceived by Jahangir's gracious attitude, hoped to carry his point, even against the manifest ill-will of the Prince and other interested parties. When he found, after considerable delay, that the objection to any form of treaty was insuperable, he changed his tactics and endeavoured to obtain his demands in the form of a *farman* from the Emperor; but this too was refused, and he was plainly told that his business must lie with the Prince, as the affairs of the English were a detail of the latter's administration. He was too well aware of Khurram's sentiments to be hopeful of effecting a satisfactory arrangement with him; and so he preferred to wait, on the chance that political developments would bring about a diminution of the Prince's power. For the time being Khurram's position was undoubtedly a strong one. He enjoyed the support of his father-in-law, Asaf Khan, who was virtually prime minister, and of the Emperor's favourite wife, Nur Mahal (Nur Jahan), who was Asaf Khan's sister. Yet it was by no means certain that even this powerful combination could maintain the Prince in favour. His eldest brother, Khusrau, who, since his rebellion in 1606, had been kept a prisoner, had many partisans at court, and was very popular among the common people. At one time Roe evidently hoped that this prince might regain his father's favour, and might then be disposed to smile upon English aspirations. However, as time went on, Jahangir's partiality for Khurram became more pronounced; and in February 1618 Roe was forced to admit that the latter was all-powerful ('his father growes dull and suffers him to write all commands and to governe all his kingdomes'), and that the only course open was to conciliate him as far as possible. Better relations had been established between them with the help of Asaf Khan, and the ambassador wrote that the Prince was now 'my effectuall mediator and will procure mee content'. By this time

Roe had persuaded himself that neither Sind nor Bengal offered any prospects for English trade, and that, since Khurram would not hear of any such extension of their sphere, it would be best to acquiesce and concentrate upon Gujarat, of which province the Prince had been named viceroy.

In the autumn of 1618 Roe, who had had several serious illnesses, decided to return to England by the next ship available. He had given up all hope of a general concession, as we have seen. 'Yow can never', he had written to the Company, 'expect to trade here upon capitulations that shalbe permanent. Wee must serve the time. . . . All the goverment depends upon the present will, where appetite only governs the lords of the kingdome.' So he resolved to content himself with what he could get. From Jahangir he procured a gracious letter to King James, containing assurances of good usage of the English; also a *farman* to the same effect. With Khurram (now known as Prince Shah Jahan) he negotiated an agreement—also in the form of a *farman*—for favourable conditions of trade at Surat. And having thus obtained (as he afterwards told the Company) 'priviledges which he thought as much in generall as he could expect or desire', he took leave of the Emperor (who was proceeding to Agra) and, after spending a few months at Surat, embarked for home in the middle of February 1619. Although the results of his mission had not come up to the sanguine expectations with which he had started, he had in reality effected a great deal. His arrival had stemmed the tide of reaction which was setting strongly against the English merchants, and had transferred the controversy regarding their continued stay to the cooler arena of the court, where local feeling was less powerful. It had also stayed the hands of the Portuguese, who could no longer pretend that their rivals were not countenanced by the British king, and who could hardly continue their attacks while an ambassador from that monarch was in the country. His presence at the imperial headquarters served to awe the Gujarat officials, who feared his influence with Jahangir; and thus time was given to his fellow-countrymen to develop their trade and accustom the Indians to their presence. Further, his high character, energy and skill had made a deep impression at court, and had much enhanced the prestige of his nation. As his chaplain (the Rev. Edward Terry) wrote afterwards: 'There can be no dealing with this king upon very sure terms, who will say and unsay, promise and deny. Yet we Englishmen did not at all suffer by that inconstancy of his, but there found a free trade, a peaceable residence and a very good esteem with that king and people; and much the better (as I conceive) by reason of the prudence of my Lord Ambassador, who was there (in some sense) like Joseph in the court of Pharaoh, for whose sake all his nation there seemed to fare the better.' Roe was in fact the first of the many great Englishmen who have served their country in India; and in point of ability, disinterestedness and devotion to duty he will bear comparison with even the best of his successors.

## CHAPTER XXIX

## COMMERCE WITH THE RED SEA PORTS

DURING the four years spent in India Sir Thomas Roe gave earnest attention to the commercial position of his fellow-countrymen, not only from the standpoint of the East India Company but also from the broader outlook of its effects upon the interests of the nation as a whole. As regards the profit accruing to the Company, there was no doubt that the newly established trade with Surat was advantageous; upon Roe's return to England, the Company itself declared that 'no place proveth so good, so sure, nor any trade so profitable; and by the abbundance and vent of callicoes [1] is in faire possibilitie to prove more and more profitable'. But whether this particular branch of commerce—and indeed the Company's trade in general—was of real benefit to his country was a question on which the ambassador felt serious misgivings. It was obvious that the products of England, such as cloth, lead and tin, were never likely to be in general demand in India, and that the purchase of return cargoes necessitated the yearly exportation of a large sum in

[1] Calicoes at once found a ready sale in England, as being much cheaper than the linens imported from the Continent. About 1624 the Company stated that, 'instead of paying £500,000 annually to Holland and France for linens, lawns and cambrics, half the consumption of those articles is now superseded by the use of India calicoes' (Macpherson's *European Commerce with India*, p. 109). On the other hand, the merchants engaged in the linen trade averred that English exports to the producing countries were suffering a proportionate diminution.

silver. This drain of treasure from the home country he, in common with many other economists of the time, regarded as a serious evil; and he set to work to devise a remedy. 'The surest way to rayse a stock without losse to our country', he wrote in September 1616, 'were from the sowth [Bantam, etc.], all China comodityes beeing as deare here as in England, and spices at good proffitt'; but the factors in the Far East were finding it increasingly difficult to procure spices and Chinese silk sufficient for home consumption, and there was little likelihood of their being able to spare any for Surat. Roe turned his attention, therefore, to another quarter, where the Dutch were developing a promising trade, namely, the port of Mokha, in the Red Sea, which the pilgrim traffic had made an important commercial centre. There merchants from Egypt bought eagerly all Eastern products, paying for them—and this was the important point—largely in gold and silver. The ambassador's suggestion was that one vessel of the yearly fleet from England should be sent from Surat to the Red Sea, with a lading partly of English goods and partly of calicoes and other Indian commodities, the produce of which would help materially towards the purchase of a cargo for England. Besides this commercial advantage, he thought that such a move would have a powerful political effect. The Red Sea trade was the main dependence of the Gujarat merchants; and Roe was sanguine enough to believe that they would be glad to freight their goods in the English vessels, and even to pay for the protection afforded to their own ships by the company of the English; while the opportunity that would be afforded of detaining the Indian junks on their return would be a guarantee against ill-treatment of the factors at Surat and elsewhere.

To this scheme Kerridge and his colleagues, who resented the ambassador's interference and were contemptuous of his ideas upon matters that lay outside his province, opposed many objections; and it was not until the Company put full authority into Roe's hands that he was able to carry his point, with the acquiescence, though not with the sympathy, of the Surat factors. The vessel chosen for the purpose was the *Royal Anne*,[1] commanded by Andrew Shilling; and Roe took care that one of the merchants employed in the venture should be Edward Heynes, who had come out with him as his secretary and upon whose fidelity he could rely. The choice of a cargo had perforce to be left to Kerridge, with the result that, as Roe indignantly declared, the goods put on board were 'the refuse of India'—a statement borne out by Heynes. The *Royal Anne* left Surat in the middle of March 1618, and reached Mokha a month later. After cautiously stipulating for the delivery of hostages, Joseph Salbank (the chief merchant) and Heynes landed and interviewed the Governor. They demanded *farmans*, alike from himself and from the Pasha of the Yemen, for their peaceable trade, 'both for present and future times, as intending to visit their ports yearely with plentie of English and Indian goods'. In reply he gave them profuse assurances of protection and furtherance, and ten days later he informed them that he had received instructions from the Pasha that they were to be well treated. Shortly afterwards he was superseded by the arrival of a new governor. This man, Rajab Agha, had been in charge of Aden at the time

[1] William Baffin was a master's mate aboard that vessel, and we may be sure that he welcomed this opportunity of adding to his knowledge of the Eastern seas. On his return to London he presented to the Company certain charts he had drawn of the coasts of Persia and of the Red Sea, and was given a gratuity for his pains.

of the *Ascension's* visit to that port and later Governor of Mokha when Sir Henry Middleton went there for the first time; and on both occasions he had behaved in a very treacherous manner towards the English. When Salbank and his companions discovered his identity, they were naturally nervous; but evidently he had learnt his lesson, for he now shewed them every consideration and gave them an ample *farman* for trade. It being deemed desirable to get this concession confirmed by the Pasha of the Yemen, Salbank on 23 June started for Sana for that purpose. He was well received and obtained all that he required; and by the end of July he was back again in Mokha. The *Royal Anne* departed for Surat on 20 August, carrying a complimentary letter from Rajab Agha to Roe, urging a further visit.

The ambassador was determined to persevere with the experiment; and on 17 February 1619, when he himself started for home in the *Royal Anne*, the *Lion* sailed for Mokha, carrying a reply from Roe to the Governor, pressing him to obtain, both from the Pasha of the Yemen and from the Turkish Emperor at Constantinople, such privileges as would encourage the English to continue their commercial operations regularly. In a letter to the East India Company, written upon his return, Roe assured that body that the trade was likely to absorb £100,000 worth of goods annually, and to yield 100 per cent. profit; while at one of his subsequent interviews with the Company he declared that 'this trade in tyme may be enlarged by the English, as other comodityes may be gotten from sundry other places of the Indies, and wilbe the life of the Surat and Persia trade, to supply both those places with monye; which trade being brought to good perfection, he hopeth they wilbe carefull to preserve and contynue it, notwithstanding any discouragment that may be objected by the factors at Surat, who are unwilling to have that trade prosper'. This ill-feeling, by the way, soon ceased to operate. The *Lion* returned to Surat in October 1619, having sold her cargo 'to contente' and made nearly 100 per cent. profit; whereupon Kerridge declared that the trade was too good to be lost, and resolved to prosecute it with energy.

The real trouble was with the local Indian merchants, who had never become entirely reconciled to English trade and had already found a grievance in the fact that the new-comers, instead of merely buying for England, were exporting calicoes and other Indian commodities to the eastwards in competition with themselves. That this rivalry should now be extended to the Red Sea ports was the last straw, and they were soon clamorous for protection. When, immediately after Roe's departure, Kerridge and his colleagues commenced their investments for the fleet expected in the autumn, a general boycott was organised, and they were plainly told that, if they persisted in the Red Sea traffic, they should not be allowed to buy a yard of calico for that purpose. Seeing no remedy, the factors unwillingly promised to make no investments for Mokha. An appeal by the English agent at court to Prince Shah Jahan, who was still Viceroy of Gujarat, produced no effect, for the principal men of Surat had already petitioned him 'not to graunt us that trade, for yf hee did, they were all undon and the cittye begered, haveinge noe other place to trade unto but the Red Sea'.

The arrival of a fresh fleet from England in October 1619, almost simultaneously with the return of the *Lion* from Mokha, renewed the dispute. Among the goods brought out by the fleet was a quantity of Mediterranean coral, an article in which there was an active trade, hitherto supplied by Indian importations from the Red Sea. The landing of this consignment was only effected in the teeth of strong opposition, and the clamour of the Surat merchants grew to such a height that the factors were forced to agree that none of the coral should be sold, pending a reference to the Prince Shah Jahan. After a long delay the English agent at court obtained an interview with the Prince on the subject, and took the opportunity to add a complaint of the refusal of the Surat authorities to allow his fellow-countrymen to continue their trade to the Red Sea. The Prince's reply was uncompromising. 'He absolutelye tould mee', wrote the agent, 'wee should not trade to the Red Sea . . . nor bringe anye corrall into these partes to sell; and yf [we] could not be contented to have free trade for all but Mocha, wee might goe out of the countrye yf wee would, for [he] must not begger his people for us.' A little later, upon the intercession of Asaf Khan, Shah Jahan agreed to allow the English to sell the coral that they had already brought; but, 'for the Mocha trade, hee would not here of itt'.

Deterred by this resolute refusal, the Surat Council made no attempt to send a ship to the Red Sea in 1620. In the spring of the following year, however, the two vessels intended for England missed the monsoon, and it was determined that, instead of waiting at Swally, they (together with a third vessel) should spend the interval in the Red Sea, though not for purposes of trade.[1] Before they left, fresh difficulties arose with the local officials, and the factors took the bold step of forcibly detaining the Indian junks about to sail for the

[1] As a matter of fact the squadron failed to reach its destination, and spent its time on the coast of Arabia before returning to Surat.

Red Sea until terms were come to, which included permission to land and sell their coral without molestation. Kerridge proposed to insist also upon the removal of all restrictions upon the trade with Mokha; but the majority of his colleagues thought it undesirable to revive so thorny a dispute.

In November 1621 the Surat Council wrote to the Company that they had decided to renew the traffic in the Red Sea, as the opposition to it had largely died down. Accordingly, in the following March three ships were despatched to Mokha, with Salbank and Heynes as the chief merchants. Their reception was favourable, and in 1623 three more vessels made an equally successful voyage. Since we are here concerned with the initiation, rather than the development, of commerce in any particular direction, we must refrain from any further detailed account of the varying fortunes of the Red Sea traffic. We may, however, note that the successful rebellion of the Arabs against the Turks in 1627, whereby the former regained control of the Yemen ports, temporarily disorganised the trade; but English ships soon resumed their visits and a more or less desultory traffic was carried on for many years. From about the middle of the seventeenth century the use of coffee spread rapidly in Europe, and in 1660 this commodity made its appearance in the sale lists at the East India House. The impetus thus given to the traffic between Surat and the Red Sea ports led to the establishment of a regular English factory at Mokha; and this was maintained until 1752, when different arrangements were made for the commerce. We have, however, already been led too far afield, and here we must leave the topic.

## CHAPTER XXX

# THE FOUNDATION OF THE PERSIAN TRADE

THE commencement of a regular trade with Mokha was not the only enterprise of the Surat Council at this period. A still more important development was the establishment of relations with southern Persia, in the hope of exchanging English woollens for raw silk, which was much in demand in London, owing to the efforts that were being made, under the patronage of King James, to promote the silk-weaving industry. In the case of the Persian venture Sir Thomas Roe and the Company's servants at Surat were again found on opposite sides; though in this instance it was the factors who urged and carried through the project, while the ambassador condemned and for a time opposed it.

Mention has already been made (p. 182) of the fact that in 1614 an English merchant, named Richard Steel, reached India after an overland journey through Persia. At Surat he received a warm welcome from the factors there, who listened favourably to his representations as to the great possibilities of trade in Persia, and were the more disposed to adopt them, because they were expecting to receive from England much more broadcloth than they had any hope of selling in India itself. So they resolved to send Steel back to Isfahan, accompanied by a factor named John Crowder, with the object of negotiating with the Shah for a trading concession, including permission to send a ship from Surat on a trial voyage to some Persian port, such as Jask. It was hoped that the pair would find at the Persian court an intermediary in the person of the celebrated Sir Robert Sherley, concerning whom something must now be said.

Even in that romantic age few careers were more remarkable than his. The youngest son of a Sussex squire, he was taken to Persia in 1599 by his elder brother, Sir Anthony.[1] The latter declared that his mission was undertaken by the order of his patron, Lord Essex, for the double purpose of inducing the Shah to join the princes of Europe in attacking the Turks, and of promoting commercial intercourse between England and Persia; but it can hardly be doubted that his real aim was to push his own fortunes by courting the favour of the Persian monarch. Proceeding by way of Aleppo and Baghdad, Sherley and his companions, after a hazardous journey, reached Kazvin in safety and were warmly welcomed by Shah Abbas. The idea of a general coalition against his troublesome western neighbour greatly attracted the Shah, who was easily persuaded to accredit Sir Anthony as his ambassador to the courts of Europe for the purpose of negotiating an arrangement for this purpose. Leaving his brother Robert behind as a hostage, Sherley set forth on his mission; but his efforts were attended by no success, and, fearing to return to Persia, he entered the service of the King of Spain. He died in poverty at Madrid at some date after

[1] Three years earlier, it may here be noted, Sir Anthony had been despatched by the Earl of Essex on a predatory excursion to the Cape Verde Islands and the West Indies, with some idea, it would seem, of afterwards going into the Pacific by Magellan's Strait and so home by the Indian Ocean; but, after raiding Jamaica, shortage of provisions forced him to return to England.

1635. Meanwhile the youthful Robert, despite the prejudice excited by his brother's defection, had won the Shah's favour by his military prowess; and, having married a Circassian lady, had apparently settled down to spend the rest of his life in his adopted country. Shah Abbas, however, was still eager for a European alliance which would relieve his kingdom from the Turkish menace, and was moreover desirous of opening up direct communication with the European markets for the raw silk of Persia, which was largely a royal monopoly. The passage of this product through the Turkish dominions yielded a valuable revenue to the Sultan, to deprive him of which would be a good stroke of policy. So in 1608 Robert Sherley was in his turn despatched on that errand with full credentials. Passing through Russia, he visited in succession the courts of Poland, Germany, Italy and Spain. Everywhere he was received with respect and curiosity, but nowhere did he find any disposition to entertain his overtures. The Emperor of Germany, Rudolph II, had just concluded a treaty of peace with the Turks, and was not anxious to renew a war which had inflicted such losses upon his subjects. At Madrid all Sherley's arguments in favour of an arrangement which would put the silk trade into the hands of the Portuguese at Hormuz found but a cold reception; and at last, in despair, he proceeded to England, where he presented himself to King James at Hampton Court in October 1611. It was a piquant situation—an Englishman being received by his own sovereign in the capacity of an ambassador from an oriental potentate; but he was treated with great distinction, and his negotiations with the merchants of London were facilitated as far as possible. The latter, however, could not be induced to respond favourably to his solicitations. The Shah's terms required the purchase of a very large quantity of silk, and the payment in ready money of at least half the price. The East India Company was finding great difficulty in raising sufficient funds to carry on its existing operations, and could not easily make a large addition to its cash resources; while the Levant merchants were resolutely opposed to any scheme for the diversion of the trade from its usual channels through Turkey. Moreover, Sherley himself seems to have inspired suspicion rather than confidence; for Roe, who was present at some of the interviews, declared afterwards that the envoy was as dishonest as he was subtle. King James obliged the East India Company to give the disappointed ambassador a passage back; and in September 1613 one of its ships landed him at Lahribandar (at the mouth of the Indus), whence, after a visit to Jahangir at Ajmer, he made his way to Persia overland.

Steel and Crowder started from Surat early in 1615, and after a long journey by way of Agra, Lahore, Kandahar and Farah, reached Isfahan in the middle of September. There they found Sir Robert Sherley preparing to set out for Hormuz, on his way to Goa and Lisbon. Apparently he had given the Shah a hopeful account of his negotiations with the Spanish monarch, and was thereupon commissioned to proceed afresh to Madrid, for the purpose of concluding a commercial treaty. The advent of the two Englishmen placed him in a difficulty, for he feared lest any aid extended to them might offend the Portuguese and be fatal to his mission; but an appeal to his patriotism induced him to procure for them, as secretly as possible, three *farmans*, ordering the governors of the Persian seaports to receive and assist any English vessels that might arrive.

One of these documents was sent to Jask; a second was carried by Steel overland to England; while the third was taken by Crowder back to India.

News of all this reached Roe at Ajmer in February 1616. He at once wrote home to the Company stating his views on the matter and deprecating any immediate action. He feared that Sherley's fresh overtures to King Philip would be successful, unless the English ambassador at Madrid could manage to defeat his schemes, or, as an alternative, could effect some amicable arrangement by which the Portuguese and English would share the trade. In Roe's opinion, until the issue were known, it would be a forlorn hope to send a ship to Persia, since little or no trade could be expected on the coast, and the Shah would certainly not send down his silk until he was sure of a purchaser. Meanwhile, in order to avoid any suspicion on the part of the Shah that the English had given over all thought of the trade, the ambassador addressed to him a letter of thanks in which he took the opportunity of pointing out the danger of allowing the Portuguese to become the masters of the Persian coast, and urged the establishment of a free port, open to all comers.

Kerridge and the other factors at Surat, however, were not at all disposed to accept Roe's views on the question. 'His Lordship', they said, 'is farr transported in errour of opynyon concerning merchandizeing and merchantes affaires in these partes'; and on the arrival in the autumn of a fresh fleet from England, bringing a supply of broadcloth for which there was no hope of sale in India, they decided to send a ship forthwith to Jask, and to entrust the management of the business to Edward Connock, who had just arrived in the fleet and became an enthusiastic advocate of the venture. The

*James* was accordingly despatched on 8 November 1616, and reached its destination early in the following month. The local authorities at Jask welcomed the newcomers, but referred them to the governor of the province, who was resident at Minab. Thither Connock repaired, with four of his assistants, and easily gained permission to land his goods, with promises of further-

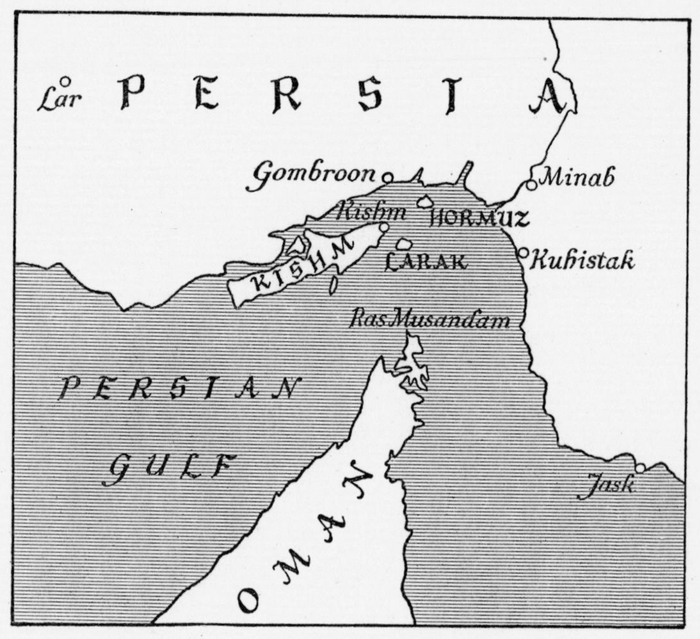


SOUTHERN PERSIA

ance in his business; whereupon the *James* was unladen and sent back to Surat. The next step was for the factors to proceed to Isfahan, where it was hoped to procure from the Shah a grant for regular trade. Connock, in his impatience, went on ahead, and arrived at the capital on 24 March 1617, only to find that Shah Abbas was far away, engaged in warfare against the Turks. Thomas Barker, the second in command, who was following with the goods, reached Shiraz on 2 April and there set up a factory, sending on to Isfahan a couple of merchants with the presents intended for the Shah and a portion of the stock of merchandise. Their arrival enabled Connock about the end of June to start for the Shah's head-quarters, carrying with him as interpreter William Robbins, an English jeweller who had settled at Isfahan. Connock was full of confidence in the prospects of a remunerative trade; indeed so sanguine that he had already written to the factors at Bantam requesting them to send a large supply of pepper and spices annually, and had assured the Company that a thousand broadcloths, with other goods in proportion, would sell yearly in Persia. At the same time he urged the Surat Council to send to Jask the whole of the next fleet from England, with English and Indian commodities, besides any freight goods that could be procured.

Connock's task was no light one, and it was made all the harder by the treacherous behaviour of Barker, his second in command, who, being next in rank to Kerridge at the time of Connock's arrival, had much resented the latter's appointment as head of the mission to Persia. He now did his best to discredit his rival in letters to Roe, which greatly disturbed the ambassador, already annoyed by the contemptuous way in which the Surat factors had treated his recommendations. One of the insinuations made by Barker against Connock was that he was representing himself as an ambassador; and Connock admitted that he was posing as a 'messenger' from King James, but pleaded that this was necessary, since he had in fact brought from Surat a royal letter,[1]

[1] It was the practice of the Company to obtain from the sovereign a number of commendatory letters to Eastern princes, in some cases with the name of the recipient left blank, to be filled in as occasion required. Connock seems to have used one of these.

and to let it be known that he was merely a merchant might be fatal to his success. That anyone should, without his authority, negotiate with the Shah seemed to Roe an infringement of his own rights, seeing that he was accredited not only to the Great Mogul but also to 'the bordering nations'. He accordingly wrote to the Surat Council urging the recall of the offender and his replacement by someone more trustworthy. Kerridge and his colleagues, however, refused to take this course, arguing that the reports on which Roe relied were false, and that in any case Connock would have reached the Persian court before fresh orders could overtake him. In these circumstances all that the ambassador could do was to warn the Surat factors that they alone were responsible for any ill effects that might ensue from their rejection of his advice.

Connock reached the royal headquarters on 11 July 1617; and ten days later he was received in audience by the Shah and with due ceremony presented the letter from his own king. Disregarding the protests of a friar who was representing Portuguese interests and who argued that the admission of the English would ruin the trade of Hormuz, Shah Abbas treated his visitor with marked cordiality, declared his earnest desire for friendship with the English nation, and promised to grant any facilities they might desire, including the use of the Persian ports. A *farman* for that purpose was given to Connock, together with some handsome presents in return for those he had brought; and, highly delighted at his success, the Englishman made his way back to Isfahan, and thence to Jask, where he hoped to meet the ships expected from Surat, with ample supplies of merchandise.

Meanwhile the Company at home, having digested Roe's representations and heard all that Steel could urge in favour of the Persia venture, had given a cautious approval to the negotiations, but had referred them to the management of the ambassador; while King James had written to the latter, giving him authority to conclude a treaty of commerce with the Shah. These documents, received in October 1617, completely vindicated Roe's claim to control the course of affairs, and gave him the opportunity to displace Connock, if he still wished to do so. Considering, however, that matters had gone too far for this, he contented himself with drawing up a commission to that individual and his associates, authorising them to negotiate further with the Shah, on the basis of the Company's instructions. Since no news had yet reached India of the outcome of the mission, it was deemed inadvisable to send a further supply of goods; but the commission was despatched to Jask in a small vessel called the *Bee*, which carried out two more factors, Edward Monnox and Francis Tipton.

The *Bee* reached its destination on 6 December 1617, and found Connock impatiently awaiting the arrival of shipping. His mortification was great on discovering that no merchandise had been brought; while the Company's stipulation that, before any trade was begun, a formal contract must be made with the Shah regarding the price of his silk, was a further aggravation, since this would entail a fresh journey to court. The news that the Governor of Minab had detained some of the silk that was coming down to Jask obliged Connock to set out for that town; but soon after starting he fell sick, and after a short illness he died on 24 December, worn out by his exertions and depressed by the apparent failure of his plans. Thus ended in gloom and misery the career of the man to whom was due in great part the initiation of a settled trade between England and Persia.

The task of carrying on the further negotiations with Shah Abbas now fell upon Barker. His efforts were unsuccessful. The Shah had found himself forced to conclude a disadvantageous peace with the Turks, and schemes for granting a monopoly of the silk trade, to either the Portuguese or the English, had perforce to be laid aside. He therefore refused to sign any formal contract, such as was desired by the Company, though he declared his readiness to exchange silk, at the market value, for any quantity of goods the English might bring. Fortunately for the factors, in November 1618 the *Expedition* reached Jask from Surat with a considerable cargo, and they were thus enabled to send her back with about seventy bales of raw silk, which arrived in time to be sent home with Roe in the *Royal Anne*, as the first-fruits of the Persian trade. This consignment fetched 26s. 10d. the 'great' pound of twenty-four ounces—about three times the cost price; and estimates then (November 1619) laid before the Company placed the profit to be made by the trade at from fifty to ninety per cent. per annum. Roe had for some time taken a more favourable view of the commerce and advised its continuance, though he saw many difficulties in the way. Writing from India in February 1618, he said: 'It is not now to bee given over, though begunn unperfectly. . . . The next consideration is how yow may securely use this trade, by want of a port, and compasse it without export of great quanteties of monies; for doubtles, if to bee done, it is the best trade of all India, and will yeild yow most certeyne profitt. For the safetye of your fleetes, I doubt the Sha will not fortefie for yow, except yow can satisfie his ends, to pass all his comoditie and to furnish him with silver. Ormus lies upon advantage. Yow must woorke your peace at home with them [*i.e.*

the Portuguese], and then yow cannot trade in these parts upon ill conditions.' In his opinion it was a great drawback that the sale of English goods in Persia would not provide one-tenth of the necessary capital. Indian wares would help, and still more, spices and the commodities of China, if available; yet a considerable balance must necessarily be provided in cash. Another factor of importance was the opposition of the Turkish sultan to any diversion of the silk trade, 'hee reaping as much by custome as the Sha by the prime comoditie'.

## CHAPTER XXXI

## THE CONSOLIDATION OF THE TRADE WITH PERSIA

THE clouds that hung over the nascent traffic with the dominions of the Shah lifted one by one. Sherley's mission to Europe was never a serious menace, in spite of Roe's forebodings, for his methods were too dilatory, and, as time went on, it became increasingly doubtful whether his capricious master would implement the promises made in his name.[1] The want of a secure port was certainly a drawback; yet Jask, though distant from any centre of trade, served the purpose well enough for the time being. The real difficulty lay

[1] After a long delay at Goa, Sherley reached Madrid in 1618, only to find that King Philip had in 1614 despatched to Persia an ambassador, named Garcia de Silva y Figueroa, the result of whose negotiations was still awaited. After lingering four years at the Spanish capital, Sherley paid a visit to the Pope, and then, in January 1624, made an unexpected appearance in England. As before, he was well received at court, but his proposals failed to elicit any support from the East India Company. Some progress was then made with a scheme for sending out shipping independently of the Company, to bring back silk on freight terms; but before this could materialise, a Persian arrived (February 1626) as envoy from Shah Abbas, bringing a letter in which no mention was made of Sherley, who was further denounced by the new-comer as an impostor. King Charles was at a loss to know what to do, but finally decided to send both of them back to Persia, accompanied by Sir Dodmore Cotton as English ambassador. The party sailed in the spring of 1627, and the Shah's headquarters were reached fifteen months later. The monarch refused to have anything more to do with Sherley; and, thus disgraced and thrown penniless on the world, he died at Kazvin on 13 July 1628. Ten days later Cotton followed him to the grave; and thereupon the members of his suite made their way back to India and so to England.

in the bellicose attitude of the Portuguese and their great advantage in the possession of Hormuz, which commanded the entrance to the Persian Gulf. Both in Goa and in Portugal alarm and concern were felt at the appearance of English vessels in those waters, and energetic steps were taken to drive them away.

Fortunately for the new-comers, Shah Abbas was as determined to free his coasts from Portuguese domination as the English were to persevere with their trade; and the high tone taken by King Philip's ambassador only widened the breach. Don Garcia's delays rivalled those of Sherley, for he did not reach the Persian court until the middle of 1618; and then, owing to the Shah's departure on a campaign, negotiations were not opened until the summer of the following year. Thereupon the ambassador arrogantly demanded not only the exclusive right to the seaborne trade, but also the restitution of the mainland territory conquered by the Persians from the titular king of Hormuz, who was a Portuguese pensioner. The refusal of the Shah to consider these demands was so emphatic that Don Garcia quitted Isfahan without delay. He died on his homeward voyage in 1624—ten years after he had started on his mission.

In the autumn of 1619, upon the arrival at Surat of the annual fleet from England, bringing a special supply of money for the factors in Persia, it was decided, in view of the danger from the Portuguese, to send to Jask the whole squadron, strengthened by the addition of the *Lion*. Sailing early in November, the fleet returned in the middle of the following January without having experienced any molestation. Barker had presented to Shah Abbas a fresh letter from King James, and this had been received with respect; while the factors had been assured that the promises previously made by the monarch would be faithfully kept. Secretly the Shah hinted to them an intention to take Hormuz at the first opportunity and to make it over to the English; and after the dismissal of the Spanish ambassador a *farman* was ordered to be drawn up, granting them the whole seaborne trade in silk. At the end of November 1619 Barker died, and the management of affairs fell into the hands of Edward Monnox. Prospects seemed so bright that in the following March that factor wrote to Surat, asking for a large supply of money and goods and holding out hopes of providing a thousand bales of silk for the next fleet.

The English were not long left in peace. A strong squadron of war vessels, under Ruy Freire de Andrade, had been despatched from Lisbon in 1619, and this reached Hormuz in the June of the following year. Ignorant of its presence in Persian waters, Captain Shilling, the commander of the fleet from England, had, in accordance with orders from the Company, detached two of his vessels with orders to proceed direct to Jask. On arriving at Swally, he learnt the danger to which he had exposed these ships, and at once sailed to their help. On his way he met them both. They had reached Jask, but, hearing of the neighbourhood of Ruy Freire's fleet, had prudently returned to seek assistance. Shilling, with his reunited fleet, now sailed for Jask, where he found the Portuguese waiting to intercept him. Having driven them off, he landed the money and goods which he had brought, and then (26 December 1620) put to sea again to try conclusions with the enemy. Two days later a stiff fight took place, in which the English were victorious, killing or wounding 360 of their adversaries. They had, however, to mourn the loss of their gallant commander, Shilling, who was badly wounded early in the engagement and died on 6 January 1621. Eight days later, having taken in at Jask about 520 bales of silk, the fleet departed for Surat.

Towards the end of September 1621 Captain John Weddell arrived at Swally from England with six ships, and found there some vessels of the previous year's fleet. It was known that Ruy Freire's squadron had been reinforced from Goa, and in view of this fact, the Surat Council resolved, after sending home two of the ships, to despatch all the rest to Jask, in order to convoy thither the goods and money designed for the factors' use. Accordingly, on 14 December Weddell anchored at Jask with five ships and four pinnaces. A message received there induced him to move to Kuhistak (a port much nearer to Gombroon), where he found Monnox and other factors awaiting him. The Portuguese and the Persians were now at open war. The former had burnt some of the coast towns; while the latter had retaliated by besieging the Portuguese fort on the island of Kishm, whence Hormuz drew many of its supplies. The real aim of the Persian commander was to gain possession of Hormuz itself; but there seemed little prospect of effecting this, for want of means to transport his army to the island, and meantime the operations against the fortress on Kishm made but slow progress. The approach of a strong English naval squadron was hailed, therefore, with joy. A demand was at once sent to its leader that he should assist in attacking both the Portuguese strongholds; and threats were added that, should this service be refused, all trading concessions would be cancelled. After anxious debate, and largely upon the insistence of

Monnox, it was resolved to join in the enterprise. A formal agreement regarding the terms of co-operation was concluded with the Persians, and then the English landed at Kishm and quickly obliged the castle to surrender, making prisoner the redoubtable Ruy Freire, who was conducting the defence in person.[1] The English casualties were few in number, but they included one notable name—that of William Baffin, the master of the *London*, who was killed by a musket shot while directing the battery that had been built on the shore.

From Kishm the triumphant allies passed over to Hormuz. The city was quickly taken, and the Portuguese withdrew into the strong castle which had been built by Albuquerque more than a century before and had ever since been the centre of Portuguese power in that region. Siege operations were commenced on 9 February 1622. The English battered the fortifications from the sea, and their steady fire gradually destroyed the vessels in the port. The Persians for their part attacked from the city, and after blowing up, by means of mines, part of the walls, made a determined attempt to carry the place by assault. This was repulsed; but the besiegers, no whit disheartened, prepared for a second attack. The Portuguese defended themselves desperately, though there was little hope of succour from Goa or elsewhere. At last, fearing that the next assault would be successful and would be followed by a general massacre at the hands of the victorious Persians, they opened negotiations with the English for surrender, on a guarantee that their lives should be spared. This was arranged, and on 23 April 1622 the

[1] He managed to make his escape at Swally from the vessel that conveyed him thither, and resumed his activities.

garrison hauled down its flag. A general pillage of the castle followed, the Persians getting by far the greater share of the plunder.

The news of the capture of so important a fortress created a great sensation, not only in Asia but in Europe. Diplomatic representations were of course made; but the Portuguese had no strong case, in view of the attacks they had made upon English merchantmen in Eastern waters, and the explanation offered at Madrid by the British ambassador—that the Company's servants had acted under compulsion from the Persians—was accepted without much demur. Nevertheless, the Company was far from escaping scot-free; for the Duke of Buckingham, King James's favourite, promptly claimed, as Lord High Admiral, a share in the spoils, which popular rumour had much exaggerated. He alleged that, at Hormuz and elsewhere in the East, captures had been made to the value of £100,000, and of this he demanded one-tenth as his lawful right. Against this the Company, who had already presented £2000 to Buckingham's wife in the hope of staving off further demands, protested that their ships had not been acting under letters of marque issued by the Duke and that therefore nothing was legally due. In reply they were confronted by the argument that either their servants had acted lawfully by way of reprisal, in which case the Lord High Admiral was entitled to his dues, or else they had committed piracy and must take the consequences. As they still resisted, Buckingham, early in 1624, detained their ships on the pretext that they might be needed for service against Spain, and further commenced an action against the Company in the Court of Admiralty. The only thing now to be done was to yield, and so the money was reluctantly paid.

The Duke's royal master then took advantage of their difficulties to extort from them a similar sum for himself, in return for which he gave them a formal grant of all booty taken by their servants in the Eastern seas, with a pardon to all concerned in the accompanying hostilities. The result of all this was that the Company was, for a time at least, pecuniarily a loser by the enterprise; but the removal of the menace of Hormuz, and the free access thus gained to the Persian Gulf, more than made up for the immediate loss.

The agreement concluded with the Persians before the commencement of operations had stipulated that, after the capture of Hormuz, the yield of the customs duties at that port should in future be divided between the two nations, and that in addition the English should for ever be free from such dues. But after the surrender and ruin of that stronghold, it was arranged that the trade should be transferred to Gombroon (Bandar Abbas), on the neighbouring mainland, and that the concessions in respect of the customs should hold good with regard to that port, where the English now established their headquarters. As a result, for many years the Company's representative received annually a sum supposed to be equivalent to a half-share of the customs revenue; though after a time the payment was withheld, the Persians alleging that it was intended to cover the defence of the Gulf and that the English had neglected to carry out this requirement. The privilege of passing their goods through the Gombroon custom-house duty-free proved valuable, especially to the Company's servants, who not only used it in their own private trade but were said to make money by passing off as their own the goods of Indian merchants who took freight in the English ships.

English commerce having been well established in southern Persia by this time, it is not our purpose to follow its vicissitudes further. We may, however, note that, as a natural corollary, some years later the trade was extended to Basra, at the head of the Persian Gulf. A small vessel, named the *Michael*, was despatched on this errand early in April 1636, but it was in so unseaworthy a state that it was forced to return after getting no farther than Daman. Four years later (March 1640) the same pinnace sailed again on the venture, and reached Basra safely at the end of May. The merchants it carried were received with favour by the Pasha, who was at that time practically independent; and the voyage proved sufficiently remunerative to encourage the President and Council at Surat to send two other ships thither in the following year. The hopes at first entertained of the resulting commerce proved to be too sanguine, partly because of the warfare that was being waged by the Pasha against his former masters the Turks, which had rendered all intercourse between Basra and Aleppo precarious; while from 1645 Dutch competition had to be reckoned with. However, the English held on to the trade until 1661, when the Company sent orders for the dissolution of the factory.

## CHAPTER XXXII

# DEVELOPMENTS IN INDIA

IN previous chapters we have narrated the commencement of trade at Surat, the chief port of the dominions of the Great Mogul, and at Masulipatam, on the other side of the Peninsula, in the territories of the King of Golconda. These two settlements proved to be permanent footholds for English commerce in India; yet it would hardly suffice for us to close our story at this point without giving at least a slight sketch of the subsequent spread of English commercial activity to other parts of that vast country.

The earliest extension of factories was naturally to Ahmadabad, Cambay, Baroda, Broach and other places in Gujarat itself. For the economical purchase of both calicoes and indigo it was necessary to make arrangements early in each season with the weavers of the one and the growers of the other, and to finance them by advances of money; and for such purposes, as also for the sale or barter of English commodities, permanent residences were advisable. Naturally the chief of these establishments was placed at Ahmadabad, the capital of the province and the seat of the Viceroy; and the importance of this factory was increased by the fact that Sarkhej, lying about five miles to the south-west, was the centre of the indigo district. Cambay, the chief port of the province (though it was fast being silted up), had an added value as the seat of the agate industry. Baroda and Broach provided large stocks of calicoes, the bleaching of which was mostly carried on at the latter place. It was upon this 'rich and fruitefull countrie', as Peter Mundy calls it, that the Surat factors chiefly relied for the provision of cargoes for England and for Persia; and great was their dismay when in 1630–31 a succession of bad seasons culminated in a frightful famine, which, followed by pestilence, left Gujarat ruined and desolate. Its inhabitants died in large numbers, while the survivors were mostly driven to emigrate to less afflicted provinces. Commerce of course practically ceased, and the English merchants, having nothing to do, were recalled to headquarters.

The factory at Agra, re-established in 1616, remained for about forty years an important centre of operations, both for the sale of goods from Europe and the purchase of commodities for export. In the neighbouring district of Biana was produced a variety of indigo much superior to that obtained at Sarkhej; calicoes from many parts of northern India were procurable in the Agra bazaars, as were also carpets of good quality; while sugar and (later) saltpetre from Bengal figured also in the lists of goods sent down regularly to Surat for shipment. In 1620 sub-factories were started at Lahore (in the Punjab), at Samana (in Patiala, where a particularly fine sort of cotton cloth was manufactured) and at Patna (in Bihar, for the purchase of the local calicoes and of Bengal silk); but all three were soon withdrawn and the trade was again concentrated at Agra itself. About 1647 a similar experiment was tried at Lucknow, the attraction being the calicoes produced in that district, which were of excellent quality; but six years later, when the Company at home found its trade seriously impaired, that factory was dissolved.

The troubles in England, due in part to the great Civil War, increased instead of diminishing, and in 1658, in obedience to orders from London, the factory at Agra itself was given up. Thenceforwards all purchases of the products of northern India were either carried out at Surat or were arranged by agents sent specially from that centre.

The disastrous famine in Gujarat provided the Surat Council with a serious problem. Although northern India had not been affected by the scarcity, and supplies of goods might therefore be counted upon from Agra, it was necessary to look for fresh sources of supply; and these were found in the province of Sind, where indigo and coarse calicoes were manufactured in large quantities at very reasonable prices. Towards the end of 1635, although by that time Gujarat was beginning to recover and the factories at Ahmadabad and Baroda had been reopened, a couple of ships were sent from Surat to Lahribandar, the port of Tatta, situated in the Indus delta. Hitherto that district had, so far as foreign trade was concerned, been largely a preserve of the Portuguese; but the Convention recently concluded at Goa between the Viceroy and President Methwold, providing for a cessation of hostilities and the admission of the English to the Portuguese harbours, had removed all fear of interruption from that quarter. The new-comers were cordially welcomed at Tatta, and were freely allowed to extend their operations throughout the province. The commerce thus inaugurated continued until 1662, when the factories in Sind were withdrawn, in pursuance of the Company's policy of contracting its trade in western and northern India to Surat—a policy that was partly the effect of the constant turmoil and insecurity that marked the close of the reign of Shah Jahan and the early years of that of Aurangzeb. About the same period the cession of Bombay to Charles II as part of the dowry of his Portuguese wife, and his subsequent transfer (1668) of the island to the East India Company, provided that body with a secure base of operations, albeit out of the way of regular trade, except by sea. The new possession rapidly developed, its rise being fostered by the increasing disorganisation of the Mughal empire and the constant warfare on the neighbouring mainland; until in 1687 it became the headquarters of the Company's administration on the western side of India.

We must now quit for a time the territories of the Great Mogul and look at those situated to the southwards. At the time when the English first established themselves in the dominions of that monarch, his southern boundary ran roughly in a line stretching from about Bombay on the western side of the Peninsula to the Chilka Lake, a little below Cuttack, on the eastern. South of this line lay a belt of territory occupied by three independent Muhammadan kingdoms—Golconda extending over the eastern half of the belt, while Ahmadnagar, and to the southwards of this Bijapur, constituted the western half. Below this belt we come to a number of Hindu states, occupying the rest of the Peninsula. With the kingdom of Ahmadnagar, which, after long wars, was finally absorbed in 1632 into the Mughal dominions, the English came little into contact. Chaul, which was practically its only port, was dominated by the Portuguese; and although the Company's ships visited it from time to time, no permanent trading relations were established. With the kingdom of Bijapur, which resisted the Mughal arms for a much longer period, the case was different. As early as 1612

Sir Henry Middleton's fleet called at its chief port, Dabhol, and he was invited to initiate a regular trade; but, although the advisability of establishing a factory there was considered from time to time, nothing resulted, as the perennial warfare with the Portuguese rendered ventures in that direction unsafe for any but a strong fleet. When, however, the conclusion of the Convention of 1635 led to an active trade between the English at Surat and the Portuguese at Goa, the vessels employed in this traffic began to call at Dabhol to sell and purchase goods. But it was at Rajapur, to the southwards of Dabhol, that the Company's servants got really into touch with the Bijapur kingdom. Although negotiations for a settlement at that place commenced as early as 1628, it was not until some nine years later that an English factory was actually installed there. Pushing inland, the merchants employed established themselves at various mart towns in Bijapur territory, despite the troubled conditions obtaining. The chief goods procurable were calicoes, cotton yarn, saltpetre and pepper; and a fairly active trade ensued until 1660, when the rebel Sivaji swooped down upon Rajapur and other Bijapur towns. A second raid in the following year resulted in the destruction of the English factory and the carrying off of some of the merchants to one of Sivaji's fortresses. The wars that led up to the annexation of Bijapur to the Mughal empire in 1686 made life and property insecure in those parts; and although trade at Rajapur was resumed, the factory was finally abandoned in 1679.

Pepper was extensively produced in all the countries bordering on the Malabar Coast, and it was the attraction of this commodity—more and more difficult to procure from Java and Sumatra as the Dutch hold upon those islands tightened—that led the English to make persistent efforts to establish themselves in that region and drew them ever farther down the western coast of the Peninsula. In these efforts the East India Company's servants found themselves much impeded for a time by the appearance of a rival body at home and its attempts to divide the trade. The Convention of Goa, to which allusion has already been made, had seemed, by removing the menace of Portuguese aggression and by opening their ports to the Company's vessels, to promise a considerable extension of commerce in all parts of the Indies; and the opportunity was at once seized by a number of London merchants to obtain permission from King Charles to invade the trade, on the pretext that the existing company was exploiting but a small portion of the wide sphere allotted to it by its charter and was incapable, with its old-fashioned methods, of attracting the funds necessary for the expansion of the commerce. The new body—known as Courteen's Association, from the name of its principal shareholder—proposed to trade with China, Japan, the Malabar Coast and other parts in which the East India Company had not yet settled factories; [1] and King Charles, in granting a charter (1637) to the Association, doubtless persuaded himself that, in favouring its formation, he was really helping to extend English commerce in the East without inflicting any serious injury upon the existing company. The new body, it

[1] The Association cast its nets very wide, for the royal commission for its first voyage (12 December 1635) included instructions that, on reaching China, Japan or any other suitable place, a ship or pinnace should be despatched 'to discover the north-east passage to the north part of the Californias on the backeside of America . . . and to meete with the north-west passage so farre discovered by Sir Thomas Button, Captain Luke Foxe, and others, so to enter into the straights of Hudson into the Westerne or Atlantique Sea'. No attempt was made, however, to carry out this design.

may be mentioned, had drawn away from its rival several of the latter's experienced servants, among them Captain John Weddell, to whose share in the capture of Hormuz allusion has already been made.

The meteoric career of Courteen's Association—for it only lasted about ten years—though at first causing much dismay and undoubtedly some loss to the older body, had little real influence upon the development of Eastern trade. On the Malabar Coast, with which alone we are here concerned, the Association established factories at Bhatkal, Karwar and Rajapur; but none of these had a long existence. Their speedy disappearance was followed by an extension of the East India Company's trade in that direction, in search, not only of pepper, but also of cardamoms, the seed-capsules of an aromatic plant, used as a spice, and cassia lignea, a coarse variety of cinnamon. The demand in England for both of these latter commodities had been much stimulated by the Dutch monopoly of the trade in spices from the Far East and the progress that they were making in the conquest of Ceylon, the main source of cinnamon. For a time the attempts at trade were limited to the despatch of ships to various Malabar ports; but in 1659 a factory was started at Calicut, and in the following year another at Karwar; while in 1662 Porakad, below Cochin, was added to the list.

Continuing our progress round the coast and turning up the eastern side of the Peninsula, we reach Kayal, near Tuticorin, where a trading settlement was established in 1659, under orders from Surat, only to be transferred to the Madras Agency four years later; this, however, was not of long continuance, as Dutch competition proved too strong. Passing northwards, we come to Karikal, in the dominions of the Raja of Tanjore. To this port, as early as 1624, an English ship was sent from Bantam to effect a settlement. The attempt proved a failure, for the Danes, fearing that their own factory at Tranquebar would suffer, bribed the Raja so heavily that he made impossible demands as a condition of the proposed concession, and the negotiations were thereupon broken off.

As regards the Coromandel Coast, it is convenient to begin our survey at Masulipatam, where, as we have seen, trading relations had been opened in 1611. The main object of these was to provide cotton piece-goods for the markets of the Far East, and although later a trade with Persia was developed, the Coromandel factories for many years remained under the direction of the Bantam president. At Masulipatam itself, and at the subordinate factories established in the neighbouring territory, a fairly flourishing trade was maintained, in spite of frequent quarrels with the governors, whose arbitrary exactions created difficulties; while in 1634 a grant from the King of Golconda of freedom from all customs duties gave the English a great advantage over their competitors. The factors, however, had at an early date discovered that the chintzes they desired were procurable at much cheaper rates in the Hindu territory lying to the southwards; with the result that in 1626 (imitating their Dutch rivals, who had already acquired a footing at Pulicat) they established a subordinate settlement at Armagon, in the dominions of the Raja of the Carnatic. Experience shewed that this place had many disadvantages; and when in 1639 an invitation was received from the ruler of the district round the village of Madraspatam, still farther to the southwards, his overtures were eagerly accepted. An agreement was concluded with him for the establishment there of a factory, with full permission to fortify it—a privilege which would never have been granted for any spot in Golconda territory—and early in 1640 the English removed from Armagon to Madraspatam, where they erected a castle ever since known as Fort St. George. In the following year the new settlement superseded Masulipatam as their headquarters on the Coromandel Coast, though the factory at the more northern port was still maintained. When in 1647 the district round Fort St. George was conquered by the forces of the King of Golconda, the special privileges of the English were not interfered with, and our countrymen thus acquired a secure base for their trading operations in those parts. Madras grew rapidly into a place of importance, and in 1652 the seat of the Eastern presidency was removed thither from Bantam.

We must now pass on to Bengal, where again we reach the dominions of the Great Mogul. We have already noted the attempts made from Agra to get into touch with this rich and extensive province. These had failed; but subsequent efforts to extend trade thither from Masulipatam were attended with more success. In 1633 some factors despatched from that port secured permission to settle at Hariharpur (in the Mahanadi delta) and at Balasore. Both these places were in Orissa, not in Bengal; but Hugli, the chief port of the latter province, was some distance up the main channel of the Ganges delta, and was difficult of access to sea-going vessels. Balasore thus proved a convenient half-way house. The Hariharpur factory was never of much importance and was given up in 1642. In 1651 English factors made their way up to Hugli and established a factory there, and after a time their sea-captains were induced to overcome their fears and take their ships thither. Before long the factors had pressed up the Ganges valley and settled at Kasimbazar and Patna, buying large quantities of raw silk, sugar, and especially saltpetre, the trade in which became an important feature, owing to the demand in Europe for this commodity for use in the manufacture of gunpowder. In 1657 the Bengal factories were constituted an agency, independent of Madras; and although this arrangement lasted but a brief period, it is a proof of the value attached by the East India Company to its trade in those parts. How that trade steadily developed, and led to the foundation of Calcutta at the end of the century, is another story, with which we are not here concerned.

## CHAPTER XXXIII

# THE ESTABLISHMENT OF TRADE WITH CHINA

LONG before tea was dreamt of as an article of consumption in Europe, the Western nations earnestly desired trading relations with China. Apart from its possibilities as a mart for their own products—and it was known to be both rich and populous—there was a good demand for its silks and porcelain, both in Asia and in Europe. But it was one thing to desire intercourse, and quite another to bring it about. China was an intensely conservative country, and so extensive as to be almost self-sufficing; while the arrogance of its rulers led them to despise and exclude all foreigners.[1] Chinese merchants were allowed to send ships and goods to Japan, Siam, Java and other oriental countries, but reciprocity was sternly denied. In consequence, for a long period all endeavours on the part of our fellow-countrymen to secure a footing proved futile; while even the pertinacious Hollanders were baffled again and again in the like attempt.

[1] Europeans in the East had their own way of accounting for this mortifying exclusiveness. A letter from Bantam of 19 January 1618 (I.O. Records: *O.C.* 595) says: 'yt was revealed by orackle unto the emperour [of China] that his countrey should be subdued by a gray-eyed people, and [they] doe therfore forbidd all Christians his countrey'. Similarly, in a representation from the city of Macao to Charles I on the subject of Weddell's voyage (*ibid., Lisbon Transcripts, Doc. Remett.* bk. 41, f. 220) it is stated that the Chinese objected to the coming of the English because the latter had blue eyes and would (it was feared) take the kingdom from its rightful possessors.

From an early date the servants of the East India Company cherished hopes of getting into touch with the Chinese authorities, either from Bantam or from Japan, and of thus obtaining permission to send shipping to Canton or some other port. Without such permission it was useless, and even dangerous, to venture, seeing that any European found in China was liable to the penalty of death. Disregarding this, the Dutch had sent ships to Canton in 1604, and again in 1607, but in each case they had been roughly rebuffed. On the other hand, the fact that the Portuguese were allowed to carry on a very restricted commerce with Canton from their settlement at Macao (which was actually on Chinese territory) seemed to shew that the Chinese were not entirely averse from trade with Europeans, if conducted under certain safeguards. The English Company's servants, therefore, continued to hope that by patient diplomacy and judicious bribery they might overcome the difficulty, and procure the necessary licence for their shipping. The diary of Richard Cocks, the Company's chief factor in Japan, shews how sanguine he was of effecting this, by the mediation of the Chinese merchants settled at Hirado; but it also shews how complete was the failure of all these attempts. Even a letter from James I to the Chinese Emperor, transmitted by the said merchants, evoked no answer; and when in 1623 the English quitted Japan, the prospect of obtaining a footing in China seemed as far off as ever. As a matter of fact, some Englishmen had already landed in that country, though their visit was involuntary.[1] The Company's ship *Unicorn*, while on a voyage from Bantam to

[1] Apparently the first Briton to tread Chinese soil was William Carmichael, a Scotsman, who came to England from Bantam in Best's ship in 1614. He stated that he had served the Portuguese for about thirty years, and had been in China (presumably at Macao).

Japan in 1620, was driven by a storm on to the Chinese coast near Macao. The crew got safely on shore, where they were allowed to purchase two small vessels in which to return. One of them succeeded in reaching Bantam, but the other was captured by the Portuguese and taken into Macao. This, however, was a mere incident, and did not contribute in any way towards furthering the desired intercourse with the Chinese empire.

For more than a decade the matter was left in abeyance. At Bantam and its subordinates the English merchants had difficulty in maintaining their existing trade and lacked the means of extending it; while Surat was too far distant for the English there to think of venturing a ship to China, especially as it would have to run the gauntlet of the Portuguese, who were intensely jealous of any further encroachment upon their sphere and nervous lest any attempt on the part of other Europeans should lead to their own expulsion from Macao. The situation was, however, changed by the Convention concluded at Goa in 1635. One of the motives of the Portuguese in seeking an accord with the English was a hope that the latter would assist them in maintaining communication with their Eastern settlements, which were in a precarious position owing to the hostilities with the Dutch. During the negotiations, the Viceroy of Goa suggested that the Surat factors should send a ship to Macao, to carry thither freight goods from Goa and bring away a quantity of Portuguese goods and ordnance which had long awaited transport, owing to the activity of the Dutch war vessels. Such an opportunity was not to be lost, and in April 1635 the *London* sailed from Surat on this errand. Macao was reached on 23 July, but the reception met with was far different from what was expected. The Portuguese authorities there were jealous of any interference on the part of the Goa Viceroy, and suspected, rightly enough, that the main object of the English was to get into touch with the Chinese and procure permission to trade. Only after much opposition, therefore, were the new-comers allowed to land; then they were closely watched and, although they contrived to make some overtures to the Chinese officials at Macao, nothing resulted. After shipping the freight goods which she had come to fetch, together with others bought in Macao, the *London* sailed again in October and reached Surat at the end of March 1636.

The merchants employed recommended a second venture, which should ignore Macao and endeavour to open up trade at some place nearer to Canton. But any such attempt was precluded by news from England that the newly founded Courteen's Association (see p. 319) had despatched a fleet for the same purpose, under Captain John Weddell. These ships went in the first instance to the Malabar Coast, and it was not until towards the end of June 1637 that Weddell, with four vessels under his command, anchored near Macao. The Portuguese, much annoyed at his coming, refused to allow him to enter the harbour and did their best to deter him from communicating with the Chinese, alleging that this would prove useless, owing to the hatred of that nation for all foreigners. After a month's delay Weddell lost patience and sailed boldly over to the Canton river, where he demanded leave to proceed up to the city itself. The Chinese temporised, pleading the necessity of consulting higher authority; but meanwhile they put into a better state of defence the fort commanding the passage, and on 12 August they fired upon one of the English boats, which was taking soundings. Thereupon Weddell turned all his ordnance upon the fort and quickly drove out its defenders. Cowed by this display of force, the Chinese permitted three of the English merchants to proceed to Canton, where they were allowed to arrange for the sale and purchase of goods. Having thus lulled the intruders into security, the Chinese suddenly (10 September) attempted to annihilate the fleet by means of fireships; but this failed, and Weddell retaliated by destroying a village and some shipping, afterwards retiring to Lintin Island, near the mouth of the river. With the assistance of the Macao authorities, some negotiations ensued, mainly in order to effect the release of the English merchants, who were prisoners in Canton. At last an agreement was reached, and towards the end of November the merchants rejoined the fleet, bringing with them a small quantity of goods purchased at Canton. Weddell had already agreed that, as soon as the prisoners were surrendered, 'hee would forthwith depart and never trouble these parts no more'; and at the close of the year he sailed away, with the conviction that the failure of the enterprise had been due as much to the intrigues of the Portuguese as to the unwillingness of the Chinese. His flagship, with all on board, was lost during its homeward voyage in 1639.

The Goa authorities, cut off from Malacca and Macao by the increasing pressure of the Dutch fleets, turned once more to the English at Surat for help. In 1639 a scheme for the despatch of shipping to those two places, carrying munitions of war under shelter of the English flag, was agreed to at Surat, but had to be abandoned owing to the fact that no vessel was available for the purpose. Two years later Malacca was stormed by the Dutch—a great blow to the power and prestige of the Portuguese. Soon, however, the situation was eased by the conclusion of peace between Holland and Portugal, which had now regained its independence of Spain. This enabled Goa to get once again into touch with Macao, without enlisting the aid of the English.

In 1644 the Surat Council again turned its attention to the possibility of trade with China, and sent to Macao a vessel named the *Hind*. She reached her destination in August, and found there the *William*, belonging to Courteen's Association. Neither ship, however, had much success, for the city was in a state of poverty and trade was stagnant; while the rapacity of the officials in the matter of port charges greatly reduced the chances of profit. No goods could be obtained from Canton, and the *Hind's* return lading consisted mostly of porcelain and gold. With this she got safely back to Surat in March 1645. Letters from home, brought by the fleet of that year, expressed grave disapproval of the venture, and vetoed any further experiment of the kind; while the Bantam factors also protested against such intrusions into what they deemed to be their exclusive sphere of action.

Three years later the Company wrote to Bantam suggesting that a voyage should be made to China from thence; but the President and Council replied (10 January 1649) that this could only result in 'the inevitable losse both of ship, men and goods'. The country, they said, had been overrun by the Tartars, and naval warfare between the invaders and the Chinese rendered the sea-coasts unsafe. In view of this discouraging report, the idea was abandoned. A few years later, however, it was revived by some merchants acting independently of the Company, whose hopes had probably been roused by the treaty of 1654 between England and Portugal, which formally sanctioned English commerce with the Eastern possessions of the latter country, including Macao. In May 1656 a private ship, the *King Fernandez*, set sail from England for China; while in the following year another, the *Richard and Martha*, left for the same destination. Little is known concerning these voyages, except that both vessels succeeded in penetrating to Canton, and returned in safety to England in 1659. In the meantime the East India Company itself, on three separate occasions, decided to send a vessel to China, but in each case reconsidered its determination. A similar venture was resolved upon at Surat in April 1660, only to be quickly abandoned. Four years later an attempt was actually made, this time from Bantam, from which port the *Surat Merchant* was despatched on 12 June 1664, and reached Macao a month later. Trade was found to be still in a bad state, and the Portuguese officials proved as exacting and obstructive as ever. No intercourse with the mainland was possible, and towards the close of the year the merchants in charge re-embarked their goods and sailed back to Bantam in despair.

Any further endeavour to obtain an entrance to Canton seemed hopeless, and the Company turned its attention to another possibility. As early as 1624 the Bantam factors had reported that some Chinese envoys visiting that place had invited both the Dutch and the English to establish themselves in the large and fertile island of Taiwan—better known by its Portuguese name of Formosa. The Hollanders promptly embraced the opportunity, and maintained themselves in the island until 1661, when they were driven out by Koxinga, the ruler of Amoy on the neighbouring mainland, who was holding that district for the Ming dynasty against the Manchu Tartars. The English now began to think that they might with advantage try to take the place of the Dutch; and when, at the beginning of 1671, five ships were despatched from England to Bantam, one of these, the *Advance Frigate*, was designated for a further voyage to Camboja and possibly to Taiwan and Japan. However, the Bantam factors had already moved in the matter by sending two vessels to Taiwan in August 1670. The merchants employed in this expedition secured a favourable concession from Kotsang, the son and successor of Koxinga; and, encouraged by this, two small ships were directed thither from Bantam in the following summer, only to be wrecked on the way. The Company at home were evidently determined to develop the new trade, for in the autumn of 1671 they sent out three vessels, by way of Bantam, for the express purpose of opening up relations with Tongking, Taiwan and Japan. Two of these—the *Experiment* and the *Return*—reached Taiwan in July 1672, only to find that its capricious ruler had spoilt the market by monopolising the principal articles of export. After a long delay, the *Experiment* transferred her cargo to her consort and departed for Bantam, while the *Return* proceeded to Japan. The failure of her attempt to reopen trade with that country has already been narrated (p. 225). She returned by way of Macao (September 1673) and Siam.

The *Flying Eagle*, sent from Bantam to Taiwan in 1675, found a ready welcome and a good market for her stock. What was even more important, her merchants obtained from Kotsang permission to trade at Amoy, which was still under his control. Accordingly, in 1676 a ship was sent to that port and a factory was established there. The English had now succeeded in securing a foothold on the mainland, and the rest of the story must be told as briefly as possible. In 1681 the Manchus conquered Amoy, and the English were obliged to withdraw their factory, though their ships were still permitted to enter the port. Two years later Taiwan

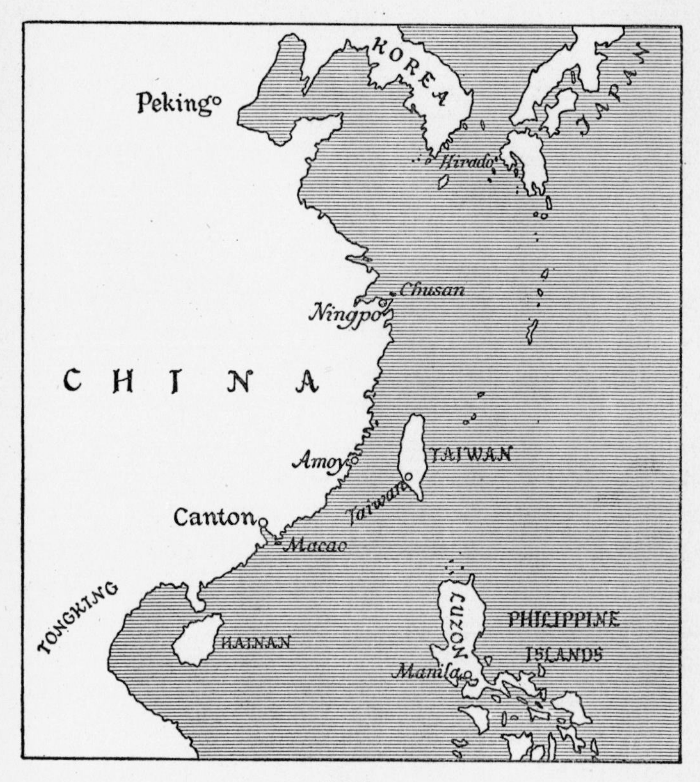


CHINA

was likewise subdued, but here the English factors were allowed to remain. These developments directed attention once more to Canton, where an attempt made in 1683 to reopen trade failed, as did also a similar experiment six years later. In 1699–1700 the *Macclesfield*, belonging to the New East India Company, was more successful and obtained a lading, though with much difficulty; and it also paid a visit to Chusan, the port of Ningpo. The barrier was now breaking down, and during the next few years several ships were permitted to trade at Canton, while tea began to figure regularly in the cargo lists. In 1700 a factory was settled at Chusan, but this was soon withdrawn, and the trade was carried on, alike there and at Amoy and Canton, by means of yearly voyages. By this time both the Chinese merchants and the Tartar officials had awakened to the fact that there was much profit to be drawn from the eagerness of the foreigner to be allowed to purchase cargoes of tea; while the distant court, although still, in its conservatism, disapproving of all such intercourse, remained loftily indifferent to the innovation. At last, however, it took notice of this ever-increasing commerce, and in 1757 an imperial edict prohibited Europeans from resorting to Chusan, Ningpo or Amoy, and confined all foreign trade to Canton. Their admission having thus been officially sanctioned, the English in 1762 obtained permission to establish a regular factory in that city; and thus the commerce was put upon a basis which lasted, with many vicissitudes, down to the abolition of the East India Company's monopoly.

One of the results was that China became to a considerable extent a mart for British woollens and metals. In the last decade of the eighteenth century the value of these imports averaged about £770,000 yearly, and later still these figures were much exceeded. It is true that such goods were to a large extent sold at a loss; but the manufacturers benefited, while the East India Company, which would otherwise have had to import larger quantities of silver in order to pay for its purchases of tea, found a certain convenience in this method, quite apart from the fact that, from 1693 to at least 1775, it was bound by charter or parliamentary enactment to export British products to a specified amount. Moreover, the loss on these imports was amply compensated by the profits derived from the purchase of Chinese tea, which proved to be easily the most lucrative branch of the East India Company's commerce, and still remains a very important feature of British trade.

Thus our narrative comes at last to a close. It began with a voyage for 'the discoverie of Cathay'; and it ends, appropriately enough, with the establishment, long years after, of a regular trade with that country—not as a preliminary to further extensions of commerce, but as the culmination of operations that had extended over the whole of the Orient. In the beginning, for half a century, indefatigable pioneers sought strenuously to find the best route for the purpose; trying in turn the icy regions of the Arctic, both eastwards and westwards, land routes through Russia and the countries of the Levant, and the long sea voyage by way of Magellan's Strait and the Pacific. At last they settled down to make the best of the Cape route, and slowly developed commerce with India and the Malay Archipelago before resuming the original purpose of opening communication with the Celestial Empire. It is a story of brave endeavour to place this country in line with Portugal, Spain and Holland in the matter of commerce with the East; and the British Empire—that unique feature of the world's history—is largely the outcome of the efforts thus made. And while recording the triumphant result, let us not forget to pay a tribute to the memory of those to whom this achievement was due. No one will deny that the directing minds in London deserve full credit for their vision and their perseverance in the face of many discouragements. But the place of honour must be given to the sailors who endured so manfully the dangers and difficulties of the sea voyage, and to the bold merchants who took without complaint the risks of residing or making long journeys in countries where life was unsafe and disease was rampant. As Froude has written, in his essay on 'England's Forgotten Worthies', 'they were cut off in the flower of their day, and few of them laid their bones in the sepulchres of their fathers. . . . Life with them was no summer holiday, but . . . a long battle, either with the elements or with men.' They were pioneers in the best sense of the word, working for the benefit of posterity as well as for their immediate livelihood; and, in closing this imperfect chronicle of their achievements, we salute their memory with respect and gratitude.

# BIBLIOGRAPHICAL NOTES

UNLESS otherwise stated, the references to Hakluyt's *Principall Navigations* and to *Purchas His Pilgrimes* are to the reprints issued by Messrs. Maclehose of Glasgow in 1903–7.

## CHAPTER I

Hakluyt's *Principall Navigations* forms the basis of the narrative of travels. For the career of Sebastian Cabot see Dr. J. A. Williamson's *Voyages of the Cabots* (1929).

## CHAPTERS II AND III

These are derived chiefly from the accounts given in Hakluyt, as collected, with other material, in *Early Voyages and Travels to Russia and Persia*, by E. Delmar Morgan and C. H. Coote (Hakluyt Society, 1886). For an interesting note on Centurione see the *Geographical Journal* for November 1932.

## CHAPTER IV

Sir Richard Collinson's *Three Voyages of Sir Martin Frobisher* (Hakluyt Society, 1867) gives Best's narrative, reprinted from Hakluyt, and adds a number of useful documents. The *Calendar of State Papers, East Indies, 1513–1616,* by W. N. Sainsbury, should also be consulted.

## CHAPTER V

The material for Drake's circumnavigatory voyage is too voluminous for detailed enumeration. For Fenton's expedition see Hakluyt and the *Calendar* just mentioned. For this, and also for the preceding chapters, Professor Eva Taylor's *Tudor Geography, 1485–1583* (1930), is very valuable.

## CHAPTER VI

Hakluyt is again the basis. Other works used are: *The Early History of the Levant Company*, by Dr. M. Epstein (1908), *The Travels of John*

*Sanderson, 1584–1602* (Hakluyt Society, 1931), *Early Voyages and Travels in the Levant*, edited by J. T. Bent (Hakluyt Society, 1893), and *The History of Joint Stock Companies to 1720,* by Dr. W. R. Scott (1910–12).

## CHAPTER VII

As stated in the text, narratives of Newbery's first and second expeditions will be found in *Purchas His Pilgrimes* (vol. viii, p. 449).

## CHAPTERS VIII AND IX

Hakluyt prints the narratives of Fitch and Eldred, the letters from Queen Elizabeth, six letters from Newbery and one from Fitch. Purchas supplements these by reproducing three letters from Eldred and two from Newbery. Translations of Linschoten's account are given by Hakluyt, and also in vols. 70, 71 of the first series of the Hakluyt Society's publications.

## CHAPTER X

The relevant documents regarding Davis's voyages are collected in a volume edited for the Hakluyt Society by Sir Albert Markham in 1878. Sir Clements Markham's biography of the navigator (1889) is a useful companion to this work.

## CHAPTER XI

Of Cavendish's circumnavigatory voyage Hakluyt in his first edition gave a narrative by 'N. H.'; but in his second edition (1598–1600) he substituted a longer one by Francis Pretty, followed by three supplementary documents. For Chudleigh's venture we are likewise dependent upon Hakluyt. The only account of Davis's voyage in 1590–91 is to be found in *The Travels of John Sanderson.* Cavendish's second expedition, as narrated by John Jane, is in Hakluyt's second edition; to this Purchas adds (vol. xvi, p. 177) an account by Anthony Knivet and Cavendish's farewell letter to his executor (*ibid.* p. 151). Mr. Coote's article on Cavendish in the *Dictionary of National Biography* is of great assistance.

## CHAPTER XII

Hakluyt gives two narratives of Lancaster's first voyage, and these were reprinted by Sir Clements Markham in *The Voyages of Sir James Lancaster* (Hakluyt Society, 1877). His raid on Pernambuco will also be found in both works. It is stated to be described in a very scarce pamphlet entitled *Lancaster his Allarums*, which I have not seen.

## CHAPTER XIII

The chief authorities are sufficiently indicated in the text. For the capture of the *Madre de Dios* see Monson's *Naval Tracts* (Navy Records Society), vol. i, p. 278.

## CHAPTER XIV

The first volume of the Court Minutes of the East India Company was published in full by Henry Stevens in 1886. Its contents had already been summarised in the *Calendar of State Papers, East Indies, 1513–1616*, which includes also other documents on the subject. Fulke Greville's memorandum is printed in Bruce's *Annals of the East India Company* (1810). References to the negotiations for peace with Spain will be found in Winwood's *State Papers*, vol. i, pp. 186, 209, 211. *The First Letter Book of the East India Company, 1600–19* (1893), contains several documents bearing upon the First Voyage and gives the text of the charter (for which see the Patent Rolls (43 Eliz. pt. vi) at the Public Record Office). The published volumes of *Acts of the Privy Council of England*, vols. xxx-xxxii, should also be consulted. Of the two accounts mentioned at the end of the chapter, the 1620 statement is in vol. xxxix of the 'Home Miscellaneous' Series of the India Office Records, while that of 1654 is in vol. xl of the same series. The former has been printed in the I.O. *List of Marine Records*, p. ix, and the latter in *Court Minutes of the East India Company, 1650–54*, p. 360.

## CHAPTER XV

A pamphlet, giving an account of the voyage of Lancaster's fleet as far as the Straits of Malacca, was published by William Apsley in 1603, but this I have not seen. The authority followed in the text is the narrative printed by Purchas and republished in *The Voyages of Sir James Lancaster*. A good modern account will be found in an article by Mr. H. B. Butcher, in the *Mariner's Mirror* for October 1932. For the events succeeding the return of the fleet see *The First Letter Book*. Lancaster's house in London is mentioned in Stow's *Survey* (ed. 1598, p. 165, and ed. 1633, p. 150). Some details of his charitable bequests will be found in *Victoria County Histories: Hampshire*, vol. iv.

## CHAPTER XVI

Most of the authorities mentioned under Chapter XIV have been also utilised here. For the Second Voyage itself see *The Voyage of Sir*

*Henry Middleton*, edited by Bolton Corney for the Hakluyt Society (1855); this also gives the licence granted to Michelborne. Weymouth's expedition is briefly narrated in *Purchas His Pilgrimes* (vol. xiv, p. 306). Edmund Scot's account of the experiences of the factors left at Bantam by Lancaster will be found in the same work (vol. ii, p. 438); also accounts of Michelborne's voyage (vol. ii, p. 347) and Knight's (vol. xiv, p. 353). Knight's expedition has further been described in *The Voyages of Sir James Lancaster* (p. 279), from a manuscript at the India Office.

## CHAPTER XVII

The primary authorities are indicated in the text. It may be added that Midnall's two notes have been reprinted in my *Early Travels in India* (p. 48), and that the *Calendar of State Papers, East Indies, 1513–1616*, will be found useful for his later history.

## CHAPTER XVIII

For the preliminaries of the Third Voyage see the *Calendar* mentioned above and *The First Letter Book*. Two narratives of the voyage, by William Keeling and William Finch, are printed in *Purchas His Pilgrimes* (vol. ii, p. 502; vol. iv, p. 1). Sir Clements Markham, in his *Voyages of Sir James Lancaster*, has summarised three MSS. in the India Office, one of which is an abstract of Keeling's journal; and in addition that office possesses two fragments, one being the first leaf of Keeling's journal and the other a portion of a journal kept on board the *Hector*. The British Museum has two MSS., viz. an incomplete diary of Anthony Marlow (*Titus B* vii, ff. 252-79) and a copy (possibly holograph) of Hawkins's own journal as far as Surat (*Egerton* 2100); the latter has been printed in *The Hawkins' Voyages* (Hakluyt Society, 1878). Hawkins's own account of his experiences in India, as given by Purchas (vol. iii, p. 1), had been republished in my *Early Travels in India* (p. 60). Accounts of the voyage of the *Ascension*, as well as some details of Hawkins's residence at Agra, are given in *The Journal of John Jourdain* (Hakluyt Society, 1905) and in *The True and Almost Incredible Report of Robert Covert* (1612). For the Sixth Voyage see the three journals abstracted in *The Voyages of Sir James Lancaster* and the two in *Purchas His Pilgrimes* (vol. iii, pp. 115, 194); also Jourdain's *Journal* (as above) and *Letters Received by the East India Company*, vol. i.

## CHAPTER XIX

For the voyage of the *Consent* see *Purchas His Pilgrimes* (vol. iii, p. 51), and for those of the *Dragon* and *Hector* the authorities cited under the last chapter. Extracts from a letter of David Middleton, describing the voyage of the *Expedition*, are given by Purchas (vol. iii, p. 90); while some valuable sidelights are thrown by the *Molukken Reise* of Johann Verken (The Hague, 1930). For the negotiations between the English and Dutch Companies see *The Journal of John Jourdain* (p. l) and *Letters Received* (vol. iii, p. xxxv).

## CHAPTER XX

Purchas gives two narratives of the Seventh Voyage, viz. one by Nathaniel Marten, master's mate of the *Globe* (vol. iii, p. 304), and another consisting of extracts from a translation of a journal kept by Floris (vol. iii, p. 319). That translation is still at the India Office, and will be printed in full by the Hakluyt Society in a volume now being prepared under the editorship of Mr. W. H. Moreland. The voyage of the *James* is described by Purchas (vol. iv, p. 77). For other information the reader should consult *The First Letter Book*, *Letters Received*, Dr. John Anderson's *English Intercourse with Siam* and Professor Hall's *Early English Intercourse with Burma*. The Dutch factories in eastern India are dealt with in Dr. H. Terpstra's *De Vestiging van de Nederlanders aan de Kust van Koromandel* (1911).

## CHAPTER XXI

Our chief authority is *The Voyage of Captain John Saris* to Japan (Hakluyt Society, 1900). The *First Letter Book* and *Letters Received* are also helpful. For the general history of the Hirado factory see *The Diary of Richard Cocks* (Hakluyt Society, 1883) and *A Glympse of the English House and English Life at Hirado, 1613–23*, by M. Paske-Smith, C.B.E. (1927).

## CHAPTER XXII

The original accounts of the voyages of Hudson and Baffin are collected in two volumes issued by the Hakluyt Society, edited by Dr. Asher and Sir Clements Markham respectively. Sir John Laughton's articles in the *Dictionary of National Biography* on those two explorers, and also on Button and Bylot, will be found useful. See also *The Voyages of Foxe and James* (Hakluyt Society, 1894), which gives a portrait of

Button and prints the charter of the Company of the North-West Passage; also *Henry Hudsons Reize*, ed. by S. P. L. Naber for the Linschoten Vereeniging (1921).

## CHAPTER XXIII

The India Office possesses contemporary copies of a log kept by Best and of another kept on board the *Hosiander*. The latter has been printed in part in *The Voyages of Sir James Lancaster*; while Purchas (*Pilgrimes*, vol. iv, pp. 119-74) gives extracts from the former and from other journals kept in the same voyage. For Downton's voyage see *ibid.* pp. 212-65. The *Letters Received* and the *Supplementary Calendar of India Office Records, 1600–40*, should also be consulted.

## CHAPTER XXIV

The materials for this section will be found in *Purchas His Pilgrimes*, *Letters Received*, *Calendars of State Papers, East Indies* and *The Journal of John Jourdain*.

## CHAPTER XXV

The English authorities are as enumerated for the last chapter. For the Dutch side see P. A. Tiele's *Bouwstoffen voor de Geschiedenis der Nederlanders in den Maleischen Archipel*, pt. i, p. 42.

## CHAPTERS XXVI AND XXVII

As in the last chapter, with the addition of *Purchas His Pilgrimes*, which contains (vols. iv and v) the narratives of Courthope and Spurway, etc. For a temperate account of the struggle from the Dutch point of view, J. A. Van der Chijs' *De Vestiging van het Nederlandsche Gezag over de Banda-Eilanden* (1886) should be consulted.

## CHAPTER XXVIII

The materials are assembled in my *Embassy of Sir Thomas Roe to India* (second edition, 1926).

## CHAPTER XXIX

Heynes' journal is given in *Purchas His Pilgrimes* (vol. iv, p. 549). For other details see *The Embassy of Sir Thomas Roe* and *The English Factories in India*.

## CHAPTER XXX

*The Embassy of Sir Thomas Roe*, the *Letters Received* (vols. ii-vi) and the first volume of *The English Factories in India* give the main facts. Purchas should be consulted for Steel's journey and the voyage of the *James*. The Sherley literature is voluminous; but see especially *The Three Brothers* (1825) and the notices in the *Dictionary of National Biography*.

## CHAPTER XXXI

The *English Factories* series continues to be our chief authority. For Cotton's embassy see my edition of the travels of Thomas Herbert, who was a member of the mission. The operations against Hormuz are dealt with by Purchas, and also in Luciano Cordeiro's *Como se perdue Ormuz* and C. R. Boxer's *Commentaries of Ruy Freyre de Andrada* (which prints in full an account by Monnox).

## CHAPTER XXXII

As before, the *English Factories* series is the main source of information. Col. H. D. Love's *Vestiges of Old Madras* and C. R. Wilson's *Early Annals of the English in Bengal* provide details; while W. H. Moreland's *From Akbar to Aurangzeb* gives a general view. For a full account of the famine in Gujarat see *The Travels of Peter Mundy*, vol. ii (Hakluyt Society, 1914).

## CHAPTER XXXIII

For the early period reliance has been placed chiefly upon the *English Factories* and *The Diary of Richard Cocks*. Weddell's visit to Canton is narrated in *The Travels of Peter Mundy*, vol. iii (1919). For the later period the best authority is Dr. H. B. Morse's *The East India Company Trading to China* (1926 and 1929).

# INDEX

THE END